THE ULTIMATE BUSINESS LIBRARY

THE
ULTIMATE
BUSINESS
LIBRARY

THE GREATEST BOOKS THAT MADE MANAGEMENT

STUART **CRAINER**

CAPSTONE

Copyright © Stuart Crainer and Des Dearlove, 2003

The right of Stuart Crainer and Des Dearlove to be identified as the authors of this book has been asserted in accordance with the copyright, Designs and Patents Act 1988

First Published 2003 by

Capstone Publishing Limited (a Wiley company)
8 Newtec Place
Magdalen Road
Oxford
OX4 1RE
United Kingdom
http://www.capstoneideas.com

All Rights Reserved. Except for the quotation of small passages for the purposes of criticism and review, no part of this publication may be reproduced, stored in a retrieval system or transmitted in any form or by any means, electronic, mechanical, photocopying, recording, scanning or otherwise, except under the terms of the Copyright, Designs and Patents Act 1988 or under the terms of a licence issued by the Copyright Licensing Agency Ltd, 90 Tottenham Court Road, London W1T 4LP, UK, without the permission in writing of the Publisher. Requests to the Publisher should be addressed to the Permissions Department, John Wiley & Sons Ltd, The Atrium, Southern Gate, Chichester, West Sussex PO19 8SQ, England, or emailed to permreq@wiley.co.uk, or faxed to (+44) 1243 770571.

CIP catalogue records for this book are available from the British Library and the US Library of Congress

ISBN 1-84112-059-6

Typeset in 10.5/13 pt Plantin
by Sparks Computer Solutions Ltd
http://www.sparks.co.uk
Printed and bound by
TJ International Ltd, Padstow, Cornwall

Substantial discounts on bulk quantities of Capstone Books are available to corporations, professional associations and other organizations. For details telephone Capstone Publishing on (+44-1865-798623), fax (+44-1865-240941) or email (info@wiley-capstone.co.uk).

CONTENTS

Acknowledgements   xi
Introduction   xiii

The Books which Made Management

Igor Ansoff, *Corporate Strategy* (1965)   3
Chris Argyris & Donald Schon, *Organizational Learning* (1978)   7
Charles Babbage,
    On the Economy of Machinery and Manufactures (1832)   12
Chester Barnard, *The Functions of the Executive* (1938)   15
Christopher Bartlett & Sumantra Ghoshal,
    Managing Across Borders (1989)   18
Meredith Belbin,
    Management Teams: Why They Succeed or Fail (1984)   24
Warren Bennis & Burt Nanus, *Leaders* (1985)   27
Robert Blake & Jane Mouton, *The Managerial Grid* (1964)   32
Marvin Bower, *The Will to Manage* (1966)   34
James MacGregor Burns, *Leadership* (1978)   38
Jan Carlzon, *Moments of Truth* (1987)   41
Dale Carnegie, *How to Win Friends and Influence People* (1937) 45
James Champy & Michael Hammer,
    Reengineering the Corporation (1993)   48
Alfred Chandler, *Strategy and Structure* (1962)   53
Karl von Clausewitz, *On War* (1831)   57
James Collins & Jerry Porras, *Built to Last* (1994)   61
Stephen Covey, *The Seven Habits of Highly Effective People* (1989) 65
Richard Cyert & James March,
    A Behavioral Theory of the Firm (1963)   69
Stan Davis & Christopher Meyer, *Blur* (1997)   72
W Edwards Deming, *Out of the Crisis* (1982)   75
Peter F Drucker, *The Practice of Management* (1954)   80

Peter F Drucker, *The Age of Discontinuity* (1969) — 86
Henri Fayol, *General and Industrial Management* (1916) — 90
Mary Parker Follett, *Dynamic Administration* (1941) — 93
Henry Ford, *My Life and Work* (1923) — 97
Harold Geneen, *Managing* (1984) — 101
Arie De Geus, *The Living Company* (1997) — 104
Frank Gilbreth, *Motion Study* (1911) — 107
Daniel Goleman, *Emotional Intelligence* (1995) — 109
Michael Goold, Marcus Alexander & Andrew Campbell,
    Corporate-Level Strategy (1994) — 113
Gary Hamel & C K Prahalad, *Competing for the Future* (1994) — 116
Charles Handy, *The Age of Unreason* (1989) — 121
Frederick Herzberg, *The Motivation to Work* (1959) — 125
Elliott Jaques, *The Changing Culture of a Factory* (1951) — 128
Joseph M Juran, *Planning for Quality* (1988) — 131
Rosabeth Moss Kanter, *The Change Masters* (1983) — 135
Robert S Kaplan & David P Norton,
    The Balanced Scorecard (1996) — 139
Philip Kotler, *Marketing Management* (1967) — 142
John Kotter, *Leading Change* (1996) — 147
Ted Levitt, *Innovation in Marketing* (1962) — 150
Rensis Likert, *New Patterns of Management* (1961) — 154
Nicoló Machiavelli, *The Prince* (1513) — 157
Douglas McGregor, *The Human Side of Enterprise* (1960) — 160
Abraham Maslow, *Motivation and Personality* (1954) — 165
Konosuke Matsushita, *Quest for Prosperity* (1988) — 167
Elton Mayo,
    The Human Problems of an Industrial Civilization (1933) — 170
Henry Mintzberg, *The Nature of Managerial Work* (1973) — 173
Henry Mintzberg, *The Rise of Fall of Strategic Planning* (1994) — 176
James Mooney & Alan Reiley, *Onward Industry* (1931) — 180
Akio Morita, *Made in Japan* (1986) — 182
John Naisbitt, *Megatrends* (1982) — 185
Kenichi Ohmae, *The Mind of the Strategist* (1982) — 189
Kenichi Ohmae, *The Borderless World* (1990) — 194
Taiichi Ohno, *Toyota Production System* (1978) — 197
David Packard, *The HP Way* (1995) — 200
C N Parkinson, *Parkinson's Law* (1958) — 203
Richard Pascale & Anthony Athos,
    The Art of Japanese Management (1981) — 206
Richard Pascale, *Managing on the Edge* (1990) — 210
Laurence Peter, *The Peter Principle* (1969) — 214

Tom Peters & Robert Waterman, *In Search of Excellence* (1982) 217
Tom Peters, *Liberation Management* (1992) 225
Michael Porter, *Competitive Strategy* (1980) 228
Michael Porter, *The Competitive Advantage of Nations* (1990) 232
Frederick Reichheld, *The Loyalty Effect* (1996) 235
Reg Revans, *Action Learning* (1979) 238
Edgar H Schein, *Organizational Culture and Leadership* (1985) 242
Ricardo Semler, *Maverick!* (1993) 246
Peter Senge, *The Fifth Discipline* (1990) 249
Patricia Seybold, *Customers.com* (1998) 253
Herbert Simon, *Administrative Behavior* (1947) 257
Alfred P Sloan, *My Years with General Motors* (1963) 260
Adam Smith, *The Wealth of Nations* (1776) 265
Thomas Stewart, *Intellectual Capital* (1997) 269
Don Tapscott, *Growing Up Digital* (1998) 272
Frederick W Taylor, *The Principles of Scientific Management* (1911) 275
Alvin Toffler, *The Third Wave* (1980) 279
Robert Townsend, *Up the Organization* (1970) 283
Fons Trompenaars, *Riding the Waves of Culture* (1993) 286
Sun Tzu, *The Art of War* (500 BC) 290
Thomas Watson Jr, *A Business and its Beliefs* (1963) 292
Max Weber, *The Theory of Social and Economic Organization* (1924) 295
William Whyte, *The Organization Man* (1956) 299

Bibliography 303
Index 319

'There are no answers. Just, at best, a few guesses that might be worth a try'

Tom Peters[1]

ACKNOWLEDGEMENTS

Mark Allin of Capstone Publishing came up with the idea of *The Ultimate Business Library*. It was so simple that we thought it must have been done before. But, as business people often discover, simple ideas are often the most elusive.

Grateful acknowledgement is made to the *Harvard Business Review* for permission to use the following extracts from:

- 'Teaching smart people how to learn' by Chris Argyris, *Harvard Business Review*, May–June 1991 © 1991 the President and Fellows of Harvard College; all rights reserved.
- 'Reengineering work: don't automate, obliterate' by Michael Hammer, *Harvard Business Review*, July-August 1990 © 1990 the President and Fellows of Harvard College; all rights reserved.
- 'Marketing myopia' by Ted Levitt, *Harvard Business Review*, July-August 1960 © 1960 the President and Fellows of Harvard College; all rights reserved.
- 'Musings on management' by Henry Mintzberg, *Harvard Business Review*, July-August 1996 © 1996 the President and Fellows of Harvard College; all rights reserved.
- 'Beyond Theory Y' by John Morse and Jay Lorsch, *Harvard Business Review*, May-June 1970 © 1970 the President and Fellows of Harvard College; all rights reserved.

INTRODUCTION

The Ultimate Business Library is a collection of the greatest books of management. Each book is summarized together with a biography of the author. The intention is to whet your appetite and encourage you to seek out the originals (though this is not easy in many cases). But, *The Ultimate Business Library* will also enable you to update your knowledge on an individual thinker's major ideas and areas of expertise.

To assemble such a list of the greatest books written on management 20 years ago would have been a straightforward task. The only problem might have been in finding a sufficient number. Times change. The last two decades have seen an explosion of interest in business and management books. They routinely feature in bestseller lists, arouse controversy and earn some of their authors large amounts of money. Along the way, usually through a process of osmosis rather than dramatic conversion, they also alter the ways in which managers manage.

In the instant, action-oriented, pressurized world of business, books change things. They change perceptions. They change behaviour. They alter expectations and aspirations. They inform. 'In no other profession [besides business], not excepting the ministry and the law, is the need for wide information, broad sympathies and directed imagination so great', reflected Owen D Young, then chairman of Radio Corporation and General Electric.[2] And never has the need been greater than the present.

In no other field do books now hold such a central role in the dissemination of best practice and new concepts. Helped by the fact that business is increasingly global and the skills of management often universal, books make their way round the world, shaping the management of the future.

Of course, books do not necessarily change things for the better. One author's interpretation of the future is not necessarily the right future for you or your organization. In spite of all the books, most executives are not great managers of their own time who hatch perfect corporate strategies in empowered teams. Nor do they work in virtual organizations harnessing the latest in technology. Ideas and our interpretations of ideas are rarely identical. And many of the ideas are best ignored.

Look at the wave of enthusiasm for reengineering which dominated the business book market at the beginning of the 1990s. Opinions differ on whether reengineering is the route to corporate nirvana or an overblown waste of corporate time and energy. But, whatever your opinion, there can be no doubting the effect reengineering has had. At the height of reengineering's popularity, a study of 624 companies by CSC Index found that 75 per cent of European companies had at least one reengineering project in progress and half of those which did not were planning to have one in the near future.[3]

James Champy who, with Michael Hammer, popularized the concept, estimated in 1993 that 50 per cent of large US companies were claiming to be in the process of reengineering.[4] Many found reengineering impractical, but that does not negate its influence and the changes of perception, behaviour and practice it instigated. Negative experiences are still experiences. (In the case of reengineering, James Champy estimated that over two-thirds of initiatives failed to meet expectations. One study showed only one company in ten achieving breakthroughs in performance and reported that most completed projects 'achieved only modest improvements'.[5])

This flurry of activity largely stems from Champy and Hammer's bestselling *Reengineering the Corporation* (1993), a book which seized managerial imaginations in a way that a succession of books have done over recent years. The book which ignited the business book market was undoubtedly *In Search of Excellence*, written by two McKinsey and Company consultants, Thomas J Peters and Robert H Waterman. Its publication in October 1982 marked a watershed in business book publishing and, some would say, in management.

In Search of Excellence has now sold around six million copies. Its success, however, took everyone by surprise – no one more so than its two authors. Prior to publication Peters and Waterman actually distributed 15,000 photocopies of the book to interested parties. Their publishers were appalled. It seemed as if the duo had given away many more copies than they were likely to sell. When the book appeared, to often lukewarm reviews, a groundswell began. The 15,000 free copies proved a piece of fortuitously brilliant marketing – the recipients were so impressed (or grateful) that they rushed out to buy their copy. The book took off in a way neither expected or previously experienced. Before long the Basking Ridge book store in New Jersey near AT&T headquarters was selling 2000 copies a week.

Thanks to the book's success, Thomas J Peters was transformed into the folksy and friendly Tom Peters, multi-millionaire, globe-trotting guru, the ultimate beneficiary of the business book boom – and, lest it be forgotten, its instigator. ('We should all be grateful to Tom', one business writer told me). After *In Search of Excellence* stormed into the bestseller lists, others quickly followed. Before long business books were everywhere. Airport book stalls confined the Harold Robbins blockbusters to a distant corner and filled their shelves with the latest outpourings from the array of consultants, academics, journalists, retired executives, charlatans and scribblers anxious to join the bandwagon.

The new knowledge imperative

Whether *In Search of Excellence* was a good book or not continues to be debated. But, its influence is undeniable. More broadly, the sudden and unexpected growth in management books can be attributed to a number of other factors. Since 1945 we have witnessed the inexorable 'professionalization' of management (indeed, some have argued that we have witnessed the professionalization of almost every occupation). Instead of being a slightly grubby and seedy profession, management has become accepted as an honourable and potentially lucrative means of earning a living. Managers were once mere supervisors, small-time dictators; now, they are executives, globe-trotting, intelligent, highly qualified, forging their own role.

Professionals they may be, but managers remain slightly reticent and ill-at-ease with the nobleness of their profession. They feel a need to explain themselves in a way in which lawyers or doctors do not. They are professionals, but where is the kudos? After all, young children do not express strong urges to become chief executives – and those who do are more likely to be taken to child psychologists than to witness their first production line in operation.

Managers frequently explain themselves with their business cards and their job titles. They explain themselves through their company cars and the stunning variety of executive perks. And they seek legitimacy through the acquisition of knowledge.

Managers crave a clear set of guidelines on the skills and knowledge required to become a manager. If theirs is a profession, they would like professional qualifications. There is a perennial and largely futile debate about the mythical 'chartered manager' – as if a single qualification could equip an executive to manage a steel producer in Illinois, a chain of shoe stores in Spain or a wine importing business in Auckland, New Zealand.

In the past, the quest for knowledge – new tools, techniques and ideas – was part of the process of professionalization. Now, it is the route to survival.

If knowledge means survival, managers cannot and should not be criticized for their relentless search for new skills and new approaches. But too often these resemble an indecent race to find the latest bright idea, the single-stop answer to all their business problems. Managers are addicted to the newest and brightest ideas. They buy the fashionable books of the moment and then within months, perhaps weeks, move on to the next fashion. This is good news for publishers.

For managers it means a relentless and largely impossible quest to keep up-to-date with the latest thinking. Books and articles are devoured and pored over. It is a losing battle, but one they must endeavour to fight – 'The only thing worse than slavishly following management theory is ignoring it completely', observes *The Economist.*[6]

Richard Pascale, author of *Managing on the Edge,* is a vehement critic of the managerial enthusiasm for fads and instant solutions. In *Managing on the Edge* he charts the rise and rise of fads since the 1950s. He calculates that over two dozen techniques have come and gone during this period – with a dozen arriving during the period 1985 to 1990 alone. Pascale believes that this trend is likely to continue. 'I think it is a packaged goods business. There is an unquenchable thirst', he says. 'If you take the premise, as I do, that corporations are the dominant social institutions of our age, you have to reckon with the fact that corporations are very influential. Certain trappings go with the party. It is part of the fanfare surrounding these institutions. With that comes a constant churn of material for corporate chieftains to feed on. Because of their prominence in society this is always going to be with us, though among the CEOs I speak to, there is a certain cynicism about the material.'[7]

The truth is that, despite the hype and the relentless stream of fads, the great ideas of management have been around for a while – indeed, some would say that the basics of management have existed since time immemorial. Ideas which purport to be bright and new are often colourful imitations of age old concepts or hackneyed re-workings. (Indeed, if you wanted to identify the first business blockbuster you would have to go back to the 1830s when Charles Babbage's *On the Economy of Machinery and Manufactures* reputedly sold 10,000 copies.)

And much of what is written is indigestible. Economist John Kay describes the formula for an article in the *Harvard Business Review*: 'One idea per article, although it will not be taken seriously if expressed in less than 3,000 words. Assume no prior knowledge of anything … definitely no jokes – our audience has no sense of humour – but frequent references to exchanges with senior executives such as John Harvey-Jones and Akio Morita.'[8]

Business and management writing is continually subject to such barbs. Better than anyone, managers know that quantity does not equate with quality. There are a lot of poor management books – laden with jargon, fashionable phrases and smart retrospective case studies. It is easy to forget that the same applies to the literature of any profession. Not all law books are authoritative. Many are unreadable, as bogged down in jargon as the worst managerial text.

Expectations of management books are extraordinarily high. A manager in Rutland, Vermont, reads a book by a French academic filled with case studies of Swiss-Swedish conglomerates and expects answers to his or her problems.

The sceptics are right to question the practical usefulness of much that is published. 'You can be very bold as a theoretician. Good theories are like good art. A practitioner has to compromise', says Warren Bennis.[9] Even so, the canon of management literature is full of ideas which have been implemented and which have affected the lives and performance of millions of managers. 'All the great business builders we know of – from the Medici of Renaissance Florence and the founders of the Bank of England in the late seventeenth century down to IBM's Thomas Watson in our day – had a clear theory of the business which informed all their actions and decisions', observes Peter Drucker in *Management*.[10] Cut through the dross and there is a broad swathe of carefully researched, well written, insightful books on what makes managers and their organizations tick.

The *Harvard Business Review* may be lacking in humour and brevity, but a great deal of the material it includes is perceptive and practically useful. There are business books which stand the tests of time and usefulness. They are not placebos, but vibrant cures.

And, lest it be forgotten, books, and the research behind them, do change things. Look at the part played by W Edwards Deming in the renaissance of Japan. Think of the impact of Michael Porter's work on the value chain, which has been taken up by companies throughout the world, as well as his work on national competitiveness, which has altered the economic perspectives of entire countries. Porter has been called in by countries as far apart as Portugal and Colombia to shed light on their competitiveness. Who thought customer service was a key competitive weapon before Peters and Waterman? In the business world, books are more than ornamental shelf-fillers.

And their domain is growing. The influence of best management practice and leading edge thinking is increasingly all pervasive. Ignore it at your peril.

The Books Which Made Management

Managerial prehistory

Sun Tzu, *The Art of War* (500 BC)
Nicoló Machiavelli, *The Prince* (1513)
Adam Smith, *The Wealth of Nations* (1776)
Karl von Clausewitz, *On War* (1831)
Charles Babbage, *On Machinery and Manufactures* (1832)

1900–1929

Frederick W Taylor, *The Principles of Scientific Management* (1911)
Frank Gilbreth, *Motion Study* (1911)
Henri Fayol, *General and Industrial Management* (1916)
Henry Ford, *My Life and Work* (1923)
Max Weber, *Theory of Social and Economic Organization* (1924)

The thirties

James Mooney & Alan Reiley, *Onward Industry* (1931)
Elton Mayo, *The Human Problems of an Industrial Civilization* (1933)
Dale Carnegie, *How to Win Friends and Influence People* (1937)
Chester Barnard, *The Functions of the Executive* (1938)

The forties

Mary Parker Follett, *Dynamic Administration* (1941)
Herbert Simon, *Administrative Behavior* (1947)

The fifties

Elliot Jaques, *The Changing Culture of a Factory* (1951)

Abraham Maslow, *Motivation and Personality* (1954)
Peter F Drucker, *The Practice of Management* (1954)
William Whyte, *The Organization Man* (1956)
C N Parkinson, *Parkinson's Law* (1958)
Frederick Herzberg, *The Motivation to Work* (1959)

The sixties

Douglas McGregor, *The Human Side of Enterprise* (1960)
Rensis Likert, *New Patterns of Management* (1961)
Ted Levitt, *Innovation in Marketing* (1962)
Alfred Chandler, *Strategy and Structure* (1962)
Thomas Watson Jr, *A Business and its Beliefs* (1963)
Richard Cyert & James March, *A Behavioral Theory of the Firm* (1963)
Alfred P Sloan, *My Years with General Motors* (1963)
Robert Blake & Jane Mouton, *The Managerial Grid* (1964)
Igor Ansoff, *Corporate Strategy* (1965)
Marvin Bower, *The Will to Manage* (1966)
Philip Kotler, *Marketing Management* (1967)
Peter F Drucker, *The Age of Discontinuity* (1969)
Laurence Peter, *The Peter Principle* (1969)

The seventies

Robert Townsend, *Up the Organization* (1970)
Henry Mintzberg, *The Nature of Managerial Work* (1973)
Chris Argyris & Donald Schon, *Organizational Learning* (1978)
James MacGregor Burns, *Leadership* (1978)
Taiichi Ohno, *Toyota Production System* (1978)
Reg Revans, *Action Learning* (1979)

The eighties

Michael Porter, *Competitive Strategy* (1980)
Alvin Toffler, *The Third Wave* (1980)
Richard Pascale & Anthony Athos, *The Art of Japanese Management* (1981)
Tom Peters & Robert Waterman, *In Search of Excellence* (1982)

John Naisbitt, *Megatrends* (1982)
Kenichi Ohmae, *The Mind of the Strategist* (1982)
W Edwards Deming, *Out of the Crisis* (1982)
Rosabeth Moss Kanter, *The Change Masters* (1983)
Meredith Belbin, *Management Teams* (1984)
Harold Geneen, *Managing* (1984)
Warren Bennis & Burt Nanus, *Leaders* (1985)
Edgar H Schein, *Organizational Culture and Leadership* (1985)
Akio Morita, *Made in Japan* (1986)
Jan Carlzon, *Moments of Truth* (1987)
Joseph M Juran, *Planning for Quality* (1988)
Konosuke Matsushita, *Quest for Prosperity* (1988)
Christopher Bartlett & Sumantra Ghoshal, *Managing Across Borders* (1989)
Stephen Covey, *The Seven Habits of Highly Effective People* (1989)
Charles Handy, *The Age of Unreason* (1989)

The nineties

Kenichi Ohmae, *The Borderless World* (1990)
Michael Porter, *The Competitive Advantage of Nations* (1990)
Richard Pascale, *Managing on the Edge* (1990)
Peter Senge, *The Fifth Discipline* (1990)
Tom Peters, *Liberation Management* (1992)
Ricardo Semler, *Maverick!* (1993)
James Champy & Michael Hammer, *Reengineering the Corporation* (1993)
Fons Trompenaars, *Riding the Waves of Culture* (1993)
Henry Mintzberg, *The Rise and Fall of Strategic Planning* (1994)
Michael Goold, Andrew Campbell & Marcus Alexander, *Corporate-Level Strategy*, (1994)
Gary Hamel & C K Prahalad, *Competing for the Future* (1994)
James Collins & Jerry Porras, *Built to Last* (1994)
David Packard, *The HP Way* (1995)
Robert Kaplan & David Norton, *The Balanced Scorecard* (1996)
John Kotter, *Leading Change* (1996)
Frederick Reichheld, *The Loyalty Effect* (1996)
Arie de Geus, *The Living Company* (1997)
Thomas Stewart, *Intellectual Capital* (1997)
Stan Davis & Chris Meyer, *Blur* (1997)
Don Tapscott, *Growing Up Digital* (1998)

Patricia Seybold, *Customers.com* (1998)

The Ultimate Business Library

This third edition of *The Ultimate Business Library* is, we hope, an objective selection of books. Views on the selection were canvassed on both sides of the Atlantic. Some contain the germ of a great idea; others are brimming with genius. Some were highly influential despite obvious deficiencies; others were commercial failures yet contain ideas which have proved enduringly important and practically useful.

Of course, even with this expanded volume, any selection excludes some books which could – sometimes should – have been included. The books selected in *The Ultimate Business Library* are, for ease of reference, arranged by author in alphabetical order.

Looking at the list of titles, it is notable that few of the books are written by practising managers or by women. Books by actual managers largely provide proof of why the individuals chose a career in business rather than in the media. They tend to be riddled with egotism and poor writing. Our selection includes a mere handful by practitioners (Chester Barnard, Alfred P Sloan, Thomas Watson, Henry Ford, Henri Fayol, Robert Townsend and Ricardo Semler). The vast majority are written by academics from the leading US business schools.

Critics of business books would suggest that therein lies the problem. Academics and consultants are routinely condemned as being out of touch with business reality. In some cases this is undoubtedly true. But the broad-ranging perspectives and research which goes into many of these works means that they are required reading. The individual experiences of a single executive in a particular organization are unlikely to provide a rich vein of inspiration for executives in wildly different situations.

The lack of women writers is a reflection of traditional prejudices. Even now, books on management and business are largely written by – and for – men. There are few exceptions. Rosabeth Moss Kanter ploughs a lonely furrow as the leading female managerial thinker of our time. Few other women have succeeded in shaping management – in the early part of the century, Harvard's Mary Parker Follett had a career of unsung brilliance which only now is gaining wider recognition.

There are drawbacks, prejudices and deficiencies in any selection. But the books celebrated in *The Ultimate Business Library* have unquestionably had profound effects on managers and organizations throughout the world. And, as is now being realized, what affects the business world affects us all.

Stuart Crainer and Des Dearlove
July 2002

Notes

1 Peters, Tom, 'A decade's worth of reflection', Syndicated column, 7 December 1991.
2 *Time*, January 6, 1930.
3 *The State of Reengineering*, CSC Index, 1994.
4 Lorenz, Christopher, 'Uphill struggle to become horizontal', *Financial Times*, 5 November 1993.
5 'Re-engineering: The Critical Success Factors', *Business Intelligence*, London, 1995.
6 *The Economist*, 26 February 1994.
7 Interview with the author.
8 Kay, John, 'Handy guide to corporate life', *Financial Times*, 17 August 1995.
9 Crainer, Stuart, 'Doing the right thing', *The Director*, October 1988.
10 Drucker, Peter F, *Management*, Harper & Row, New York, 1973.

The Books which
Made Management

IGOR ANSOFF

Corporate Strategy

1965

The author

Igor Ansoff was Distinguished Professor of Strategic Management at the US International University in San Diego, President of Ansoff Associates and a member of the board of Gemini Consulting.

Born in Vladivostock of an American father and Russian mother in 1918, Ansoff's early years were spent in Moscow. The Ansoff family arrived in New York in 1936. Ansoff trained as an engineer and mathematician. After leaving Brown University, he worked for the RAND Corporation and then the Lockheed Corporation where he became Vice-President of Planning and Programs at Lockheed Electronics. In 1963 he left industry for academia, joining Carnegie-Mellon's Graduate School of Business Administration. He was then founding Dean and Professor of Management at Vanderbilt University's Graduate School of Management before becoming a Professor at the European Institute for Advanced Studies in Management in Belgium. Ansoff has also taught at the Stockholm School of Economics. He joined the US International University in 1983.

Corporate Strategy was Ansoff's first book. He has followed it with a number of unstintingly serious academic studies including *Strategic Management* (1979) and *Implanting Strategic Management* (2nd edition 1990). A revised version of *Corporate Strategy*, entitled *New Corporate Strategy*, was published in 1988.

The classic

Igor Ansoff's *Corporate Strategy*[1] is not an easy book to read. Indeed, to the contemporary reader used to a stream of exhortations and personal

---

Gary Hamel on *Corporate Strategy*

'Truly the godfather of corporate strategy. Though Ansoff's approach may now appear overly-structured and deterministic, he created the language and processes that, for the first time, allowed modern industrial companies to explicitly address the deep questions of corporate strategy: how to grow, where to coordinate, which strengths to leverage, and so on.'

---

reminiscence, it frequently appears to be impenetrable and inaccessible. Yet, its influence was – and continues to be – significant.

Ansoff has explained its genesis: '*Corporate Strategy* integrated strategic planning concepts which were invented independently in a number of leading American firms, including Lockheed. It also presented several new theoretical concepts such as partial ignorance, business strategy, capability and competence profiles, and synergy. One particular concept, the product-mission matrix, became very popular, because it was simple and codified for the first time the differences between strategic expansion and diversification.'[2]

The book's starting point was a vacation during which Ansoff grew a beard, consumed half a case of Scotch and contemplated strategy. In writing *Corporate Strategy*, Ansoff's aim was 'to codify and generalize' his experiences working at Lockheed. The book intends 'to develop a practically useful series of concepts and procedures which managers can use to manage … a practical method for strategic decision-making within a business firm', says Ansoff in his preface.

Corporate Strategy was timely – 'It was published at a time of widespread enthusiasm for strategic planning and an increasing number of firms were joining the ranks of its users', recalls Ansoff.[3]

Until *Corporate Strategy*, strategic planning was a barely understood, *ad hoc* concept. It was practised, while the theory lay largely unexplored. Ansoff saw strategic management as a powerful applied theory, offering a degree of coherence and universality lacking in functionally-dominated management theorizing.

In *Corporate Strategy*, Ansoff provides a rational model by which strategic and planning decisions can be made. Ansoff looks at strategic, administrative and operating decisions. (The model concentrates on corporate expansion and diversification rather than strategic planning as a whole.) From this emerges the Ansoff Model of Strategic Planning, a complex sequence of decisions, or what Ansoff calls a 'cascade of decisions, starting with highly aggregated ones and proceeding toward the more specific'.

Central to this cascade is the concept of gap analysis: see where you are; identify where you wish to be; and identify tasks which will take you there. Ansoff explains: 'The procedure within each step of the cascade is similar.

1   A set of objectives is established.
2   The difference (the "gap") between the current position of the firm and the objectives is estimated.
3   One or more courses of action (strategy) is proposed.
4   These are tested for their 'gap-reducing properties'. A course is accepted if it substantially closes the gap; if it does not, new alternatives are tried.'

Corporate Strategy is also notable for its introduction of the word 'synergy' to the management vocabulary. This has become overused, though Ansoff's explanation ('2 + 2 = 5') remains memorably simple. And Ansoff also examines 'corporate advantage' long before Michael Porter's masterly dissection of the subject in the 1980s.

While *Corporate Strategy* was a remarkable book for its time, its flaws have been widely acknowledged – most honestly by Ansoff himself. *Corporate Strategy* is highly prescriptive and advocates heavy reliance on analysis. As a result, its adherents encountered what Ansoff labelled 'paralysis by analysis' – the more information they possessed, the more they thought they needed. This vicious circle dogged many organizations which embraced strategic planning with enthusiasm.

Strategic planning, as proposed in *Corporate Strategy*, provides more questions than answers. This was quickly acknowledged by Ansoff who regarded strategic planning as an 'incomplete invention' though 'on an intuitive level, I was convinced that strategic planning was an inherently useful management tool'.[4] He has spent the last 40 years attempting to prove that this is the case and that, rather than being prescriptive and unwieldy, strategic management can be a dynamic tool able to cope with the unexpected twists of turbulent markets as well as the more secure times described in *Corporate Strategy*.

Notes

1   Ansoff, H Igor, *Corporate Strategy*, McGraw Hill, New York, 1965.

2 Ansoff, H Igor, 'A profile of intellectual growth', in *Management Laureates*, JAI Press, London, 1994.

3 Ansoff, H Igor, 'A profile of intellectual growth', in *Management Laureates*, JAI Press, London, 1994.

4 Ansoff, H Igor, 'A profile of intellectual growth', in *Management Laureates*, JAI Press, London, 1994.

CHRIS ARGYRIS & DONALD SCHÖN

Organizational Learning

1978

The authors

C hris Argyris (born 1923) is the James B Conant Professor at the Harvard Graduate Schools of Business and Education. Argyris is a formidable intellectual even by Harvard's lofty standards. Prior to joining Harvard in 1971 he was at Yale and his qualifications embrace psychology, economics and organizational behaviour. His books include *Personality and Organization* (1957); *Overcoming Organizational Defenses* (1990); *On Organizational Learning* (1993); *Knowledge for Action* (1993); and *Flawed Advice and the Management Trap (2000)*.

Donald Schön (1930–97) was educated at Yale, the Sorbonne and Harvard University. After teaching philosophy at UCLA and the University of Kansas, he joined consultants Arthur D Little in 1957 and later worked for the US Department of Commerce. He was then President of the Organization for Social and Technological Innovation, a non-profit social research and development firm. In 1972, Schön became Ford Professor of Urban Studies and Education at MIT. Schön pioneered the concept of 'action science', an investigative and intimate approach to dealing with problems and errors. (*Organizational Learning's* sub-title is 'A theory of action perspective'.) Schön gave the 1970 Reith Lectures for the BBC, from which was born the book, *Beyond the Stable State* (1978).

Argyris and Schön also co-authored *Theory in Practice: Increasing Professional Efficiency* (1974).

The classic

Lean and ascetic of appearance, Chris Argyris' work is driven by a fundamental – some would say flawed – faith in human nature. His earlier work was well-received, but only as carefully argued academic studies;

Gary Hamel on *Organizational Learning*

'If your organization has not yet mastered double-loop learning it is already a dinosaur. No one can doubt that organizational learning is the ultimate competitive advantage. We owe much to Argyris and Schön for helping us learn about learning.'

thoughtful and profound, but not necessarily the stuff of commercial reality.

Argyris was part of the human relations school of the late 1950s and was involved in the work of the National Training Laboratories which had a mesmeric attraction for a host of other important thinkers. 'He was bespectacled, dark-complexioned, and slender, with a narrow face that tended, almost despite himself, to break into a delighted grin when arguments grew hot, as if he was overjoyed at the chance to test himself', says Art Kleiner in *The Age of Heretics*. 'His voice was distinctively mild-mannered and reedy with a slight European tinge. His style of debate was analytical – indeed, his approach to life was passionately devoted to inquiry, reasoning, and theory. But he was drawn to the kinds of problems that most analytical people eschew, the riddles of human nature. In particular, why did people fail to live up to their own professed ideals? Why was so much human behaviour so self-frustrating, particularly in organizations?'[1]

In the last decade, the tides of change have swept Argyris' way. Suddenly his ideas are fashionable. This is most apparent in the upsurge of interest in the concept of the learning organization. Argyris and Donald Schön's *Organizational Learning*[2] appeared in 1978, but it took the 1990 bestseller from MIT's Peter Senge, *The Fifth Discipline*, to propel the learning organization from academic concept to mainstream acceptance. (Not, of course, that the world has instantly been transformed. Managers may agree with the idea, but are usually loath to implement the learning organization's full ramifications.)

If you wished to trace the roots of the learning organization you would invariably find yourself reading Argyris and Schön's *Organizational Learning*.

Organizational Learning tackles the central paradoxes of business life. Such as, how can individual initiative and creativity work in an organizational environment where rules will always exist and how can teamworking and individual working co-exist fruitfully. Argyris and Schön's partnership produces interesting perspectives on such perennial problems, with Schön being more of a philosopher, Argyris a psychologist. *Organizational Learning* grew out of Argyris and Schön's 1974 book, *Theory in Practice*. 'Originally, we had planned in a chapter of that book to apply the theory of action perspective to the problem of organizational capacity for learning. But we could not write that chapter; it called for a conceptual bridge which we had not yet built – a bridge between the world of interpersonal behaviour and the world of the organization,' write Argyris and Schön. 'In the present work, we argue that organizations are not collections of individuals which can be understood solely in terms of the social psychology of group behaviour.'

Organizational Learning, therefore, acts as a theoretical bridge between a variety of disciplines. 'There is an urgent need for alternative visions of science, and Schön's work along with that of Argyris provides some of the best ideas and answers. Few have gone so far in reconciling the vigour of relevance and in building a bridge between the isolated academic fortresses of the sciences and the humanities', says Charles Hampden-Turner of the University of Cambridge's Judge Institute of Management.

Argyris and Schön investigate two basic organizational models.

Model 1 is based on the premise that we seek to manipulate and form the world in accordance with our individual aspirations and wishes. In Model 1 managers concentrate on establishing individual goals. They keep to themselves and don't voice concerns or disagreements. The onus is on creating a conspiracy of silence in which everyone dutifully keeps their head down. Defence is the prime activity in a Model 1 organization, though occasionally the best means of defence is attack. Model 1 managers are prepared to inflict change on others, but resist any attempt to change their own thinking and working practices. Model 1 organizations are characterized by what Argyris and Schön label 'single-loop learning' ('when the detection and correction of organizational error permits the organization to carry on its present policies and achieve its current objectives').

In contrast, Model 2 organizations emphasize 'double-loop learning' which Argyris and Schön describe as 'when organizational error is detected and corrected in ways that involve the modification of underlying norms, policies, and objectives'. In Model 2 organizations, managers act on information. They debate issues and respond to, and are prepared to, change. They learn from others. A virtuous circle emerges of learning and understanding. 'Most organizations do quite well in single-loop learning but have great difficulties in double-loop learning', conclude Argyris and Schön.

In addition, Argyris and Schön propose a final form of learning which offers even greater challenges. This is 'deutero-learning' which they describe as 'inquiring into the learning system by which an organization detects and corrects its errors'. It is here, in the examination of learning systems, where the roots of contemporary concepts of the learning organization can most easily be found. Learning, to Argyris, is powerfully practical. 'Increasingly, the art of management is managing knowledge. That means we do not manage people per se, but rather the knowledge that they carry. And leadership means creating the conditions that enable people to produce valid knowledge and to do so in ways that encourage personal responsibility,' Argyris has recently observed. 'I'm interested in action, and not simply knowledge for the purpose of understanding and exploring. I'd love that, but it has to be knowledge for understanding, exploring, in order to act.'[3]

Since *Organizational Learning*, Argyris has continued to chart the deficiencies of learning processes and the natural temptation for organizations and individuals to limit themselves to single-loop learning rather than its more demanding alternatives. The need to better understand learning in all its dimensions is now imperative, says Argyris: 'Any company that aspires to succeed ... must first resolve a basic dilemma: success in the marketplace increasingly depends on learning, yet most people don't know how to learn. What's more, those members of the organization that many assume to be the best at learning are, in fact, not very good at it.'[4] The challenge – and mystery – of learning remains profound.

Indeed, Argyris' more recent work suggests that most of the advice on organizational learning, transformational change and employee commitment does not work.

Argyris' *Flawed Advice and the Management Trap* is an indictment of the way advice is offered and applied in business. Organizations now have available to them, Argyris says, a broad array of advice from executives, change consultants and academics. 'Much of this advice is appealing; much of it compelling. Providing it has become big business in its own right. The only problem is, most of it doesn't work.'

In Argyris' view most of what passes for advice is 'too full of abstract claims, inconsistencies, and logical gaps to be useful as a concrete basis for concrete actions in concrete settings'. Most of what comes from gurus and consultants is simply not actionable. His core contention isn't that the advice doesn't work because its sellers are deliberately peddling snake oil (although there are plenty of those around, too). Rather, in Argyris' view it is because of the way in which organizations operate – including the consulting firms and academic institutions which generate advice.

His point is that the orthodox theory of action often makes advisers blind not just to the deficiencies of their advice, but also to the fact that they are blind. 'What they say is not the result of ignorance, but of "skilled unawareness and skilled incompetence".' These advisers, he suggests, are accomplished experts. 'Professionally, they are very good at being wrong.'

The same problems, and defensive reactions, exist in the organizations that consume the advice. At best, the outcome takes the form of a short-lived fad; which undermines the credibility of managers. Underpinning Argyris' argument remain the theories developed with Donald Schön.

Notes

1 Kleiner, Art, *The Age of Heretics*, Nicholas Brealey, London, 1996.
2 Argyris, Chris & Schön, Donald, *Organizational Learning*, Addison-Wesley, Reading, MA, 1978.
3 Kurtzman, Joel, 'An interview with Chris Argyris', *Strategy & Business*, First Quarter 1998.
4 Argyris, Chris, 'Teaching smart people how to learn', *Harvard Business Review*, May–June 1991.

CHARLES BABBAGE

On the Economy of Machinery and Manufactures

1832

The author

C harles Babbage (1791–1871) was one of the great minds of the first industrial revolution. Born in London, Babbage went to Cambridge University in 1810. He and others helped introduce the Leibnitz notation for the calculus. This had a major impact on the study of mathematics. Among many other activities, Babbage also championed signalling for lighthouses and investigated mathematical codebreaking.

Babbage's most substantial achievement was the plans he made for Calculating Engines – the Difference Engines and the Analytical Engines. Babbage's engines, though never actually built by him, were the precursors of the modern computer – recent years have seen increasing acceptance of Babbage as the 'pioneer of the computer'.[1]

The classic

In parallel to his career as an innovator, Babbage was also a political economist. In his book, *On the Economy of Machines & Manufactures,* his professed aim was to look at 'the mechanical principles which regulate the application of machinery to arts and manufactures'.

Babbage's fundamental approach was highly scientific. First, gather the evidence. Babbage did so through touring factories exhaustively in the UK and Europe. Indeed, in his book Babbage provides helpful hints and a checklist of questions on how to find the best information when touring a factory. 'Political economists have been reproached with too small a use of facts, and too large an employment of theory', he reflects.

'If facts are wanting, let it be remembered that the closet-philosopher is unfortunately too little acquainted with the admirable arrangements of the factory; and that no class of persons can supply so readily, and with so little sacrifice of time, the data on which all the reasoning of political economists are founded, as the merchants and manufacturer; and, unquestionably, to no class are the deductions to which they give rise so important. Nor let it be feared that erroneous deductions may be made from such recorded facts: the errors which arise from the absence of facts are far more numerous and more durable than those which result from unsound reasoning respecting true data.'

Babbage encourages managers to follow his example and gather their own data. 'The importance of collecting data, for the purpose of enabling the manufacturer to ascertain how many additional customers he will acquire by a given reduction in the price of the article he makes, cannot be too strongly pressed upon the attention of those who employ themselves in statistical "inquiries",' he writes.

To his data, Babbage adds masterly logic and the anticipatory instincts of the best futurist. Joseph Schumpeter called *On the Economy of Machinery and Manufactures* 'a remarkable performance of a remarkable man'.[2] *On the Economy of Machinery and Manufactures* is one of the first books to recognize the importance of factories, economically and socially. It is akin to the first book on the potential of the Internet. Contrasts can be made with Adam Smith whose economic viewpoint remained stuck in the agricultural era. Babbage beckons in the industrial era and, in doing so, lays the intellectual groundwork for Marx, Engels and John Stuart Mill.

Babbage notes: 'The arrangements which ought to regulate the interior economy of a manufactory, are founded on principles of deeper root than may have been supposed, and are capable of being usefully employed in preparing the road to some of the sublimest investigations of the human mind.'[3] Babbage recognized that the factory required an entire system of operation. It needed to be organized in a vastly different way to the conventional means of production.

Babbage provides insights in two central areas. First, economies of scale and, second, the division of labour. 'Perhaps the most important principle on which the economy of a manufacture depends, is the division of labor amongst the persons who perform the work', he writes. In the latter, Babbage's approach bears more than a passing resemblance to that later adopted by the American champion of scientific management, Frederick Taylor. While touring factories, Babbage closely observed the actions of workers. 'The number of operations performed in a given time may frequently be counted when the workman is quite unconscious that any person is observing him', he notes. 'Thus the sound made by the motion of a loom may enable the observer to count the number of strokes per minute, even though he is outside the building in which it is contained.'

Among the many other issues raised by Babbage is the life expectancy of capital equipment. 'Machinery for producing any commodity in great demand, seldom actually wears out; new improvements, by which the same operations can be executed either more quickly or better, generally superseding it long before that period arrives: indeed, to make such an improved machine profitable, it is usually reckoned that in five years it ought to have paid itself, and in ten to be superseded by a better,' he writes. *On the Economy of Machinery and Manufactures* was a bestseller of its times. Babbage was not only the pioneer of computing but also a true pioneer of modern management.

Notes

1 Hyman, Anthony, *Charles Babbage: Pioneer of the Computer*, Princeton University Press, Princeton, NJ, 1982. In the 1970s, a team at London's Science Museum successfully built Babbage's Second Difference Engine.
2 Schumpeter, Joseph, *History of Economic Analysis*, Oxford University Press, New York 1954, p 541.
3 Charles Babbage's *On the Economy of Machinery and Manufactures*, fourth edition, 1835 reprinted by Frank Cass & Co, London, 1963, p. 191. References are to the 1963 edition.

CHESTER BARNARD

The Functions of the Executive

1938

The author

Chester Barnard (1886–1961) was a rarity: a management theorist who was also a successful practitioner. After a spell at Harvard, Barnard joined American Telephone and Telegraph to begin work as a statistician. He spent his entire working life with the company, eventually becoming President of New Jersey Bell in 1927.

Barnard remained with the company until his retirement in 1952. His interests were varied. One Harvard professor compared Barnard's talents to those of Leonardo da Vinci and St Thomas. 'Chester I. Barnard possibly possesses the most capacious intellect of any business executive in the U.S.', observed *Fortune*.[1] During World War Two he worked as special assistant to the Secretary of the Treasury and co-wrote a report which formed the basis of US atomic energy policy.

Barnard's work has largely been ignored save for occasional bursts of interest when a contemporary guru uncovers a copy of *The Functions of the Executive*.

The classic

Chester Barnard's *The Functions of the Executive*[2] is a book of Barnard's lectures on the subject of management. The language is dated, the approach ornate, but comprehensive. 'It is doubtful if any other book since Taylor's *Scientific Management* has had a deeper influence on the thinking of serious business leaders about the nature of their work', observed Barnard's contemporary, Lyndall Urwick.

Indeed, there are many messages in *The Functions of the Executive* which resonate with contemporary management thinking. Barnard, for

Gary Hamel on *The Functions of the Executive*

'Each new generation suffers from the conceit that the problems it faces are unique. Anyone who re-reads Barnard's landmark tome, published nearly 60 years ago, will quickly realize that the context of management changes faster than the 'functions of the executive'. As we worship the cult of the new, it is sometimes helpful to harken back to the wisdom of the old.'

example, highlights the need for communication. He argues that everyone needs to know what and where the communications channels are so that every single person can be tied into the organization's objectives. He also advocates lines of communication which are short and direct. 'The essential functions are, first, to provide the system of communications; second, to promote the securing of essential efforts; and, third, to formulate and define purpose', he writes.

In a world yearning for simplistic solutions, Barnard recognized the organization as a complex riddle. 'I suppose it takes a certain and perhaps an unusual, course of experience, and a somewhat philosophic trend of mind to make sense out of the contradictions and confusions of life', he wrote. 'Most people most of the time seem to get along pretty well by disregarding the contradictions, and by assuming for the time being that many things are true which are not.'[3]

To Barnard the chief executive is not a dictatorial figure geared to simple short-term achievements. Instead, part of his responsibility is to nurture the values and goals of the organization. Barnard argues that values and goals need to be translated into action rather than meaningless motivational phraseology – 'strictly speaking, purpose is defined more nearly by the aggregate of action taken than by any formulation in words.'

This struck a chord with Peters and Waterman who, in *In Search of Excellence,* said that *The Functions of the Executive* 'probably deserves to be called a complete management theory'.[4] The broad scope of Barnard's work was also identified by Harvard's Kenneth Andrews in his introduction to an anniversary edition of the book: 'Barnard's aim is ambitious. As he tells us in his own preface, his purpose is first to provide a comprehensive theory of cooperative behaviour in formal organizations. Cooperation originates in the need of an individual to accomplish purposes to which he is by himself biologically unequal.'[5]

There is a hint of Taylor's Scientific Management in such observations, but Barnard also proposes a moral dimension to the world of work (one which Taylor certainly did not recognize). 'The distinguishing mark of the executive responsibility is that it requires not merely conformance to a complex code of morals but also the creation of moral codes for others', writes Barnard.

Barnard takes what would today be called a holistic approach arguing that 'in a community all acts of individuals and of organizations are directly or indirectly interconnected and interdependent'. Even so, for all his contemporary sounding ideas, Barnard was a man of his times – advocating corporate domination of the individual and regarding loyalty to the organization as paramount.

Notes

1 *Fortune*, June 1948.
2 Barnard, Chester I, *The Functions of the Executive*, Harvard University Press, Cambridge, MA, 1968.
3 Letter from Barnard to John Romanition, June 8, 1937.
4 Peters, Thomas J, and Waterman, Robert H, *In Search of Excellence*, Harper & Row, New York, 1982.
5 Andrews, Kenneth R, 'Introduction to the Anniversary Edition', *The Functions of the Executive*, Harvard University Press, Cambridge, MA, 1968.

CHRISTOPHER BARTLETT & SUMANTRA GHOSHAL

Managing Across Borders

1989

The authors

T he Australian-born academic Christopher Bartlett was born in 1943. Educated at the University of Queensland and Harvard University, he has worked as a marketing manager with Aloca, as a London-based McKinsey consultant, and as general manager of Baxter Laboratories' French operations. He joined the Harvard Business School faculty in 1979 and is now the MBA Class of 1966 Professor of Business Administration at Harvard Business School.

Sumantra Ghoshal (born 1948, in India) is the Founding Dean of the Indian School of Business in Hyderabad, a venture jointly sponsored by the Wharton School at the University of Philadelphia, the Kellogg School of Business at Northwestern University and the London Business School. Ghoshal also holds the Robert P. Bauman Chair in Strategic Leadership at the London Business School, where he is a member of the Strategy and International Management faculty; he has also previously taught at INSEAD and MIT's Sloan School of Management. Ghoshal's research focuses on strategic, organizational and managerial issues confronting large, global companies. He has published nine books, over 50 articles, and several award-winning case studies. *The Differentiated Network: Organizing the Multinational Corporation for Value Creation*, co-authored with Nitin Nohria, won the George Terry Book Award in 1997, and *The Individualized Corporation*, co-authored with Christopher Bartlett, won the Igor Ansoff Award in 1997, and has been translated into seven languages. *Managing Radical Change: What Indian Companies Must Do to Become World–class*, won the Management Book of the Year award in India in 2000.

The classic

In 1989, when *Managing Across Borders*[1] was published, understanding of globalization was in its infancy. It has since been listed by the *Financial Times* as one of the 50 most influential management books of this century and has been translated into nine languages. The international management model was simply to export your own way of doing things elsewhere. Colonization was the essence of managing internationally. Companies often believed that global operations were simply a means of achieving economies of scale. As a result, local nuances were overlooked in the quest for global standardization. Global and local were mutually exclusive. Companies either gave local operations autonomy or, more usually, loomed from afar, corporate despots laying down the law.

A great deal has happened in the intervening years – though despots still survive. Global presence with local responsiveness is one of the mantras of our time. Companies are slowly coming to terms with what it really means to operate globally. They are wrestling with the challenges of nurturing and enabling innovation in globally dispersed organizations and of how to disseminate knowledge and learning throughout such companies. The process might have been a great deal easier for a great many organizations if managers had read *Managing Across Borders* from cover to cover.

Managing Across Borders is one of the few business books of recent years which deserves recognition as a classic. Bartlett and Ghoshal map out the new business reality of globalization and the kinds of organizations a borderless business world requires.

Bartlett and Ghoshal identify a number of organizational forms prevalent among global companies. The first multinational form they identify is the multinational or multidomestic firm. Its strength lies in a high degree of local responsiveness. It is a decentralized federation of local firms (such as Unilever or Philips) linked together by a web of personal controls (expatriates from the home country firm who occupy key positions abroad).

The second is the global firm, typified by US corporations such as Ford earlier this century and Japanese enterprises such as Matsushita. Its strengths are scale efficiencies and cost advantages. With global scale facilities, the global firm seeks to produce standardized products, is often centralized in its home country, with overseas operations considered as delivery pipelines to tap into global market opportunities. There is tight control of strategic decisions, resources and information by the global hub.

Gary Hamel on *Managing Across Borders*

'Many of the companies that expanded internationally in the early decades of the twentieth century, woke up in the 1970s and 1980s and found themselves seriously behind the integration curve as trade barriers crumbled and customer needs converged. Bartlett and Ghoshal chronicle the quest of these companies to become "transnationals". In urging companies to develop dense networks of horizontal communication, transfer learning laterally, and embed a sense of reciprocity among far-flung organizational units, they give a tangible meaning to the concept of a borderless company.'

The third type of firm is the international one. Its competitive strength is its ability to transfer knowledge and expertise to overseas environments that are less advanced. It is a co-ordinated federation of local firms, controlled by sophisticated management systems and corporate staffs. The attitude of the parent company tends to be parochial, fostered by the superior know-how at the centre of the organization.

Bartlett and Ghoshal argue that global competition is forcing many of these firms to shift to a fourth model, which they call the transnational. This firm combines local responsiveness with global efficiency and the ability to transfer know-how, better, cheaper, and faster.

The transnational firm was the model many companies aspired to during the 1990s. (Inevitably, aspiration is one thing; making it a reality quite another.) The transnational firm is made up of a network of specialized or differentiated units, with attention paid to managing integrative linkages between local firms as well as with the centre. The subsidiary becomes a distinctive asset rather than simply an arm of the parent company. Manufacturing and technology development are located wherever it makes sense, but there is an explicit focus on leveraging local know-how in order to exploit worldwide opportunities.

Bartlett and Ghoshal effectively signal the demise of the divisional firm. First developed by Alfred P Sloan of General Motors, the divisional form gave divisions independence. Bartlett and Ghoshal argue that integration and the creation of 'a coherent system for value delivery' are the new drivers of organizational structure. The distant outposts of the transnational cannot be left to their own devices but have to be brought within the fold while also keeping in touch with their local business environment.

But what then is the glue binding the paradoxical global-local elements together? In *Managing Across Borders,* Bartlett and Ghoshal suggest that companies possess 'organizational psychology' – 'a set of explicit or implicit shared values and beliefs – that can be developed and managed just as effectively as the organizational anatomy and physiology. For companies operating in an international environment, this is a particularly important organizational attribute.'

In transnational organizations, Bartlett and Ghoshal say that there are three techniques crucial to forming an organization's psychology. First, there must be 'clear, shared understanding of the company's mission and objectives'. Second, the actions and behaviour of senior managers are vital as examples and statements of commitment – 'Particularly in a transnational organization, where other signals may be diluted or distorted by the sheer volume of information sent to foreign outposts, top management's actions have a powerful influence on the company's culture. When Sony's founder and chief executive, Akio Morita, relocated to New York to build the company's US operations, he sent the most convincing possible message about Sony's commitment to its overseas businesses.' Third, corporate personnel policies must be geared up to 'develop a multi-dimensional and flexible organization process'.

With its emphasis on networking across the global organization and transferring learning and knowledge, *Managing Across Borders* effectively set the organizational agenda for a decade. It created a new organizational model. Unfortunately, such is the complexity and cautiousness of the modern organization, many have chosen to remain one dimensional and inflexible rather than embrace Bartlett and Ghoshal's transnational alternative.

While *Managing Across Borders* was concerned with bridging the gap between strategies and organizations, Ghoshal and Bartlett's sequel, *The Individualized Corporation* (1997), moved from the elegance of strategy to the messiness of humanity.

One of the phenomena Bartlett and Ghoshal examine is the illusion of success which surrounds some organizations like a well burnished halo. 'Satisfactory under-performance is a far greater problem than a crisis', they say, pointing to the example of Westinghouse, which is now one seventh the size of GE in revenue terms. 'Over 20 years, three generations of top management have presided over the massive decline of a top US corporation', Ghoshal has said. 'Yet, 80 per cent of the time the company was thought to be doing well. Westinghouse CEOs were very competent and committed. They'd risen through the ranks and did the right things. Yet they presided over massive decline.'

The explanation he gives for this delusion of grandeur is that few companies have an ability for self-renewal. 'You cannot renew a company without revitalizing its people. Top management has always said this. After a decade of restructuring and downsizing, top management now believes it. Having come to believe it, what does it really mean?'

Bartlett and Ghoshal contend that revitalizing people is fundamentally about changing people. The trouble is that adults don't change their basic attitudes unless they encounter personal tragedy. Things that happen at work rarely make such an impact. If organizations are to revitalize people, they must change the context of what they create around people.

'The oppressive atmosphere in most large companies resembles downtown Calcutta in summer', says Ghoshal. 'We intellectualize a lot in management. But if you walk into a factory or a unit, within the first 15 minutes you get a smell of the place.'

Vague and elusive though smell sounds, Ghoshal – no touchy, feely idealist - believes that it can be nurtured. 'Smell can be created and maintained – look at 3M. Ultimately the job of the manager is to get ordinary people to create extraordinary results.'

To do so requires a paradoxical combination of what Bartlett and Ghoshal label stretch and discipline. As an example of this in practice they cite Intel: 'At Intel there is constructive confrontation. It is demanded that you express your point of view. The flip side is that at the end of a meeting a decision is made and you have to commit to it. Stretch and discipline are the yin and yang of business.'

These factors do not render attention to strategy, structure and systems obsolete. Businesses can still be run by strict attention to this blessed corporate trinity. These are, in Bartlett and Ghoshal's eyes, the legacy of the corporate engineer, Alfred Sloan, and the meat and drink of business school programs. They are necessary, but Ghoshal adds a warning: 'Sloan created a new management doctrine. Sloan's doctrine has been wonderful but the problem is that it inevitably ends up creating downtown Calcutta in summer.'

The way out of the smog is through purpose ('the company is also a social institution'); process ('the organization as a set of roles and relationships'); and people ('helping individuals to become the best they can be'). Undoubtedly these factors are less hard and robust than the three S's, but Ghoshal believes they are the way forward.

Over time, Bartlett and Ghoshal's work has become more human-centred. Human capital appears their guiding light. 'Companies must address human capital at a more profound level. Often we make the mistake of thinking of human capital as just knowledge. A second important aspect is social capital – networks and relationships. The third dimension is emotional capital – the ability and willingness to act,' explains Ghoshal. 'The new source of competitive advantage is dreams and ambitions. Today we are in the world of the volunteer employee. People choose to invest their human capital in companies to get the best returns. They are mobile investors.'

Clearly, this focus on the individual, and the uniquely human components of the organization, calls organization structure and strategy into question. 'William Whyte's *Organization Man* of the 1950s is still the model organizational citizen for too many companies. But the philosophy of that day suggested that if strategy, structure, and related organizational systems were well defined, the rest – namely the individuals – were not important. That model is obsolete. It is necessary to change the focus from the organization to the individual. That is a fundamental and necessary shift,' Ghoshal explains.

Note

1 Bartlett, Christoper & Ghoshal, Sumantra, *Managing Across Borders*, Harvard Business School Press, Boston, 1989.

MEREDITH BELBIN

Management Teams: Why They Succeed or Fail

1984

The author

The British academic Meredith Belbin is the doyen of the theory of teamworking. He read Classics and Psychology at Cambridge University before becoming a researcher at the Cranfield College of Aeronautics. He worked in Paris for the Organization for Economic Co-operation and Development, with the Industrial Training Research Unit at University College, London, and in a number of manufacturing companies.

Belbin's other books include *Team Roles at Work* (1993) and *The Coming Shape of Organization* (1996).

The classic

In his foreword to *Management Teams*[1] Antony Jay writes: 'Corporations have been preoccupied with the qualifications, experience and achievement of individuals; they have applied themselves to the selection, development, training, motivation, and promotion of individuals; they have discussed and debated the strengths and weaknesses of individuals; and yet all of us know in our hearts that the ideal individual for a given job cannot be found. He cannot be found because he cannot exist.' Jay goes on to conclude that 'it is not the individual but the team that is the instrument of sustained and enduring success in management'.

In 1967 the UK's Henley Management College introduced a computer-based business game onto one of its courses. In this game, known as the Executive Management Exercise, 'company' teams of members competed to achieve the best score, according to the criteria laid down

Gary Hamel on *Management Teams*

'High-performing companies increasingly believe that teams, rather than business units or individuals, are the basic building blocks of a successful organization. Belbin deserves much credit for helping us understand the basic building blocks of successful teams.'

in the exercise. Henley arranged to collaborate with Meredith Belbin, then with the Industrial Training Research Unit at University College, London.

Belbin was interested in group performance and how it might be influenced by the kinds of people making up a group. Members engaging in the exercise were asked, voluntarily and confidentially, to undertake a personality and critical-thinking test. From his observations, based on the test results, Belbin discovered that certain combinations of personality-types performed more successfully than others. Belbin began to be able to predict the winner of the game and realized that, given adequate knowledge of the personal characteristics and abilities of team members through psychometric testing, he could forecast the likely success or failure of particular teams. As a result, unsuccessful teams can be improved by analysing their team design shortcomings and making appropriate changes.

Belbin's first practical application of this work involved a questionnaire which managers filled out for themselves. The questionnaire was then analysed to show the function roles the managers thought they performed in a team. This had one drawback: what *you* think you do is not of much value if the people with whom you work think differently. Belbin refined his methods and worked with others to design a computer program to do the job. (His work is now available on CD-ROM.)

From his first-hand observation at Henley's unique 'laboratory', Belbin identified nine archetypal functions which go to make up an ideal team. These are:

- **plant** – creative, imaginative, unorthodox; solves difficult problems. Allowable weakness: bad at dealing with ordinary people.
- **coordinator** – mature, confident, trusting; a good chairman; clarifies goals, promotes decision-making. Not necessarily the cleverest.
- **shaper** – dynamic, outgoing, highly strung; challenges, pressurizes, finds ways round obstacles. Prone to bursts of temper.

- **teamworker** – social, mild, perceptive, accommodating; listens, builds, averts friction. Indecisive in crunch situations.
- **completer** – painstaking, conscientious, anxious; searches out errors; delivers on time. May worry unduly; reluctant to delegate.
- **implementer** – disciplined, reliable, conservative, efficient; turns ideas into actions. Somewhat inflexible.
- **resource investigator** – extrovert, enthusiastic, communicative; explores opportunities. Loses interest after initial enthusiasm.
- **specialist** – single-minded, self-starting, dedicated; brings knowledge or skills in rare supply. Contributes only on narrow front.
- **monitor evaluator** – sober, strategic, discerning. Sees all options, makes judgments. Lacks drive and ability to inspire others.

These categories have proved robust and are still used in a variety of organizations. The explosion of interest in teamworking during the last decade has prompted greater interest in Belbin's work. He has since continued to refine and expand his theories in a series of books.

Note

1 Belbin, Meredith, *Management Teams*, Butterworth-Heinemann, Oxford, 1984.

WARREN BENNIS & BURT NANUS

Leaders

1985

The authors

W arren Bennis' lengthy career has involved him in education, writing, consulting and administration. Born in 1925, he was the youngest infantry officer in the European theatre of operations during World War II; an early student of group dynamics in the 1950s; a futurologist in the 1960s and the world's premier leadership theorist in the 1970s and 1980s.

Bennis received his PhD in economics and social science at the Massachusetts Institute of Technology (MIT) and later served on the school's faculty and was chairman of the Organization Studies Department. Bennis studied under Douglas McGregor at Antioch College and later became an academic administrator – he was Provost at SUNY, Buffalo (1967–1971) and President of the University of Cincinnati between 1971 and 1978. He is now Distinguished Professor of Business Administration at the University of Southern California and is founder and chairman of the school's Leadership Institute.

Psychologist Abraham Maslow described Bennis as 'one of the Olympian minds of our time'. In his book *Future Shock*, Alvin Toffler claimed: 'If it was Max Weber who first defined bureaucracy, and predicted its triumph, Warren Bennis may go down as the man who first convincingly predicted its demise and sketched the outlines of the organizations that are springing up to replace it.'

His books include *Co-Leaders* (1999); *The Temporary Society* (1968); and *Organizing Genius* (1997).

Burt Nanus was Bennis' co-author and founder and director of the Centre of Futures Research at the University of Southern California.

The classic

Warren Bennis and Burt Nanus' *Leaders: The Strategies for Taking Charge*[1] is a thoroughly populist book following the conventional formula of seeking out lessons on how to become successful from successful people. It is based on Bennis' research with 90 of America's leaders. While the book's formula is hackneyed, it is given an extra dimension by the eclectic selection of leaders. They include Neil Armstrong, the coach of the LA Rams, orchestral conductors, and businessmen such as Ray Kroc of McDonald's. 'They were right brained and left-brained, tall and short, fat and thin, articulate and inarticulate, assertive and retiring, dressed for success and dressed for failure, participative and autocratic', says Bennis.[2] The link between them is that they have all shown 'mastery over present confusion'. The message is that leadership is all-encompassing and open to all.

From the 90 leaders, four common abilities are identified: management of attention; of meaning; of trust; and of self.

Management of attention is, says Bennis, a question of vision. Indeed, he uses a definition of leadership as: 'The capacity to create a compelling vision and translate it into action and sustain it'. Successful leaders have a vision that other people believe in and treat as their own.

Having a vision is one thing; converting it into successful action is another. The second skill shared by Bennis' selection of leaders is management of meaning – communications. A vision is of limited practical use if it is encased in 400 pages of wordy text or mumbled from behind a paper-packed desk.

Bennis believes effective communication relies on use of analogy, metaphor and vivid illustration as well as emotion, trust, optimism and hope.

The third aspect of leadership identified by Bennis is trust, which he describes as 'the emotional glue that binds followers and leaders together'. Leaders have to be seen to be consistent.

The final common bond between the 90 leaders studied by Bennis is 'deployment of self'. The leaders do not glibly present charisma or time management as the essence of their success. Instead, the emphasis is on persistence and self-knowledge, taking risks, commitment and challenge but, above all, learning. 'The learning person looks forward to failure or mistakes', says Bennis. 'The worst problem in leadership is basically early success. There's no opportunity to learn from adversity and problems.'

The leaders have a positive self-regard, what Bennis labels 'emotional wisdom'. This is characterized by an ability to accept people as

Gary Hamel on *Leaders*

'Here we find the antithesis of a technocratic view of management. This truly is a book about leaders, not about managers. And while Bennis and Nanus succeeded in isolating the deep attributes of leadership, I remain unconvinced that leadership can be taught. Nevertheless, I am absolutely convinced that we must all aspire to be leaders. A heartfelt thanks to Warren and Burt for helping us raise our sights.'

they are; a capacity to approach things in terms of only the present; an ability to treat everyone, even close contacts, with courteous attention; an ability to trust others even when this seems risky; and an ability to do without constant approval and recognition.

Leadership, Bennis believes, can be learned. He is an optimist and this lies at the heart of his work, and *Leaders* in particular: 'Every person has to make a genuine contribution in their lives. The institution of work is one of the main vehicles to achieving this. I'm more and more convinced that individual leaders can create a human community that will, in the long run, lead to the best organizations.'[3]

If this is to be achieved, five myths of leadership need to be overcome. First, it needs to be understood that leadership is not a rare skill. Second, that leaders are made rather than born. Third, leaders are mostly ordinary people – or apparently ordinary – rather than charismatic. Fourth, leadership is not solely the preserve of those at the top of the organization – it is relevant at all levels. And, finally, leadership is not about control, direction and manipulation. Instead, leaders align the energies of others behind an attractive goal.

Leaders was a bestseller and cemented Warren Bennis' reputation as one of the world's premier leadership theorists. Its importance lies not in the common characteristics of leaders identified in the book, but in its exploding of the myth of the leader as hero. In the hands of Bennis and Nanus, leadership is fundamentally humane, human and achievable.

Bennis has continued to explore the subject in his subsequent books, which include *On Becoming a Leader* (1989); *Why Leaders Can't Lead* (1989); *Organizing Genius: The Secrets of Creative Collaboration* (1997) and *Geeks and Geezers* (2002).

In these books, Bennis has switched his attention to the dynamics of group-working. He prefers the terminology of groups rather than the more fashionable teams – 'Teams has a Dilbertian smell to it. Everyone is talking about teams and there is a lot of bullshit written. I'm not sure how useful it is to business people. I think you can learn more from extraordinary groups than the run of the mill. None of us is as smart as all of us. These are exceptional groups with great intensity who had belief in their collective aspiration. The groups are a series of vivid utopias whether they are Xerox's Palo Alto Research Centre, the group behind the 1992 Clinton campaign, Lockheed's Skunk Works or the Manhattan Project which invented the atomic bomb.'[4]

The relationship between groups and their leaders is clearly of fundamental interest to Bennis. 'Greatness starts with superb people. Great Groups don't exist without great leaders, but they give the lie to the persistent notion that successful institutions are the lengthened shadow of a great woman or man. It's not clear that life was ever so simple that individuals, acting alone, solved most significant problems.'

Indeed, the heroic view of the leader as the indomitable individual is now outdated and inappropriate. 'The Lone Ranger is dead. Instead of the individual problem solver we have a new model for creative achievement. People like Steve Jobs or Walt Disney headed groups and found their own greatness in them,' says Bennis. 'He or she is a pragmatic dreamer, a person with an original but attainable vision. Ironically, the leader is able to realize his or her dream only if the others are free to do exceptional work. Typically, the leader is the one who recruits the others, by making the vision so palpable and seductive that they see it too, and eagerly sign up. Inevitably, the leader has to invent a leadership style that suits the group. The standard models, especially command and control, simply don't work. The heads of groups have to act decisively, but never arbitrarily. They have to make decisions without limiting the perceived autonomy of the other participants. Devising and maintaining an atmosphere in which others can put a dent in the universe is the leader's creative act.'

There is a rich strand of idealism which runs through Bennis' work. He is a humanist with high hopes for humanity. 'Most organizations are dull and working life is mundane. There is no getting away from that. So, these groups could be an inspiration. A Great Group is more than a collection of first-rate minds. It's a miracle. I have unwarranted optimism. By looking at the possibilities we can all improve. With T-Groups in the fifties, people said it is not real life. But it shows you the possibilities.' To accusations of romanticism, Bennis puts up a resolute and spirited defence: 'If a romantic is someone who believes in possibilities and who is optimistic then that is probably an accurate description. I think that every person has to make a genuine contribution in their lives and the institution of work is one of the main vehicles to achieving this. I'm more and more convinced that individual leaders can create a human community that will, in the long run, lead to the best organizations.'

Bennis continues to study and shape the reinvention of leadership. He explains:

> 'The post-bureaucratic organization requires a new kind of alliance between leaders and the led. Today's organizations are evolving into federations, networks, clusters, cross-functional teams, temporary systems, ad hoc task forces, lattices, modules, matrices – almost anything but pyramids with their obsolete top-down leadership. The new leader will encourage healthy dissent and values those followers courageous enough to say no.
>
> 'This does not mark the end of leadership – rather the need for a new, far more subtle and indirect form of influence for leaders to be effective. The new reality is that intellectual capital (brain power, know-how, and human imagination) has supplanted capital as the critical success factor; and leaders will have to learn an entirely new set of skills that are not understood, not taught in our business schools, and, for all of those reasons, rarely practiced.'

Notes

1 Bennis, Warren, & Nanus, Burt, *Leaders: Strategies for Taking Charge,* Harper & Row, New York, 1985.
2 Crainer, Stuart, 'Doing the right thing', *The Director,* October 1988.
3 Crainer, Stuart, 'Doing the right thing', *The Director,* October 1988.
4 Interview with author.

ROBERT BLAKE & JANE MOUTON

The Managerial Grid

1964

The authors

R obert Blake (born 1918) co-founded Scientific Methods, Inc. with Jane Mouton (1930–87) in 1961. He has a psychology degree from Berea College (1940), an MA from the University of Virginia (1941), and a Ph.D. in psychology from the University of Texas at Austin (1947), where he later worked as a professor.

Jane Mouton was a mathematician and a student of Blake's at the University of Texas. She led T-Groups at the National Training Laboratories in the 1960s.

The classic

In the 1950s, the American oil company Exxon employed Robert Blake and Jane Mouton as consultants. To the dirty and macho oil business, Blake and Mouton brought refined sensitivities. As they examined the behaviour of the people at Exxon, Blake and Mouton concluded that there was a sizeable gap in management theorizing, especially in terms of leadership and motivation.

Popular among theories of the time was that of Douglas McGregor and his motivational extremes of x and y. The trouble found by Blake and Mouton was that many behaviours and motivations fell in the middle of these extremes. They saw with their own eyes that theories x and y were only a part of the overall picture of organizational behaviour.

Blake and Mouton's conclusion was that a model with three axes was a more accurate representation of reality. The three crucial axes they determined were concern for productivity, concern for people and motivation. Concern for production and people were both measured on a scale of one to nine with nine being high. Blake explains: 'The reason you have to have a people axis is that managers achieve things indirectly. They don't produce nuts and bolts themselves, they organize others so that the production line can be productive.'[1] Motivation was measured on a scale from negative (driven by fear) to positive (driven by desire).

Work by Blake and Mouton's Scientific Methods company found that, when left to rank themselves, some 80 percent of people give themselves a 9,9 rating. Once this is discussed and considered, this figure is routinely reduced to 20 percent. Given such capacity for self-deception (and the figures are drawn from experience in over 40 countries), Blake has reflected that it is little wonder that change programs often hit the buffers.

From the grid emerge five key manager styles:

- 1 (production); 1 (people): Do nothing manager. The leader exerts a minimum of effort to get the work done with very little concern for people or production.
- 1 (production); 9 (people): Labelled the Country Club Manager. This manager pays a lot of attention to people, but little to production. Can be seen in small firms that have cornered the market and some public sector organizations.
- 9 (production); 1 (people): This manager emphasizes production and minimizes the influence of human factors.
- 5 (production); 5 (people): Organization man who diligently fosters mundanity.
- 9 (production); 9 (people): Managerial nirvana. The ultimate with an emphasis on team working and team building. Personal and organizational goals are in alignment; motivation high.

Note

1 Flower, Joe, 'Human Change by Design: Excerpts from a conversation with Robert R. Blake', *Healthcare Forum Journal*, July–August 1992, Vol. 35, No. 4.

MARVIN BOWER

The Will to Manage

1966

The author

Marvin Bower (born 1903) is the man who did more than any other to create the modern management consulting industry – perhaps only Bruce Henderson of the Boston Consulting Group can come close to Bower's long lasting impact at McKinsey & Company. While few claims can be made for Bower as an outstandingly innovative thinker, he was a rigorous setter of standards and extraordinarily successful practitioner. Under Bower's astute direction McKinsey became the world's premier consulting firm. Interestingly, recent years have also seen the structure and managerial style of the company receiving plaudits.

Marvin Bower joined the fledgling firm of James O McKinsey (1889–1937) in 1933 at a time when management consulting was still called 'management engineering'. Bower was a Harvard-trained lawyer, originally from Cleveland. Soon after Bower's arrival, McKinsey left to run Marshall Field & Company. He died in 1937 and this left Bower in the company's New York office and AT Kearney in the Chicago office. In 1939 the two split with Kearney setting up a new company in his own name.

Throughout the 1940s and 1950s, McKinsey expanded in North America. It opened its first overseas office in 1959, followed by Melbourne, Amsterdam, Dusseldorf, Paris, Zurich and Milan. By the late 1990s, McKinsey had 74 offices in 38 countries.

The classic

On James McKinsey's death and his succession to control the company's New York office, Marvin Bower could have changed the name of what was now his firm. He did not, shrewdly deciding that clients would demand his involvement in projects if his name was up in lights. 'My vision was to provide advice on managing to top executives and to do it with the professional standards of a leading law firm', said Bower. 'In all successful professional groups, regard for the individual is based not on title but on competence, stature and leadership.'[1]

The McKinsey-Bower story and philosophy is partly explained in *The Will to Manage: Corporate success through programmed management*[2] and in Bower's other much later book *The Will to Lead* (1997). Both, however, are inadequate summations of the McKinsey story and the McKinsey way.

Turning Bower's vision into reality meant that McKinsey consultants were 'associates' who had 'engagements', rather than mere jobs, and the firm was a 'practice' rather than a business. 'The entire ethos of McKinsey was to be very respectable, the kind of people CEOs naturally relate to. That's the enduring legacy of Marvin Bower', says former McKinsey consultant George Binney.[3]

Bower's gospel was that the interests of the client should precede increasing the company's revenues. 'Unless the client could trust McKinsey, we could not work with them', said Bower. If you looked after the client, the profits would look after themselves. (High charges were not a means to greater profits, according to McKinsey, but a simple and effective means of ensuring that clients took McKinsey seriously.)

Bower's other rules were that consultants should keep quiet about the affairs of clients; should tell the truth and be prepared to challenge the client's opinion; and should only agree to do work which is both necessary and which they could do well. To this he added a few idiosyncratic twists such as insisting that all McKinsey consultants wore hats – except, for some reason, in the San Francisco office – and long socks.

Bower's view was that values maketh the man and the business. American Express chief Harvey Golub, an ex-McKinsey consultant, labels Bower as 'one of the finest leaders in American business ever' and says that 'he led that firm according to a set of values, and it was the principle of using values to help shape and guide an organization that was probably the most important thing I took away'.[4]

Bower also changed the company's recruitment policy. Instead of hiring experienced executives with in-depth knowledge of a particular industry, he began recruiting graduates students who could learn how to be good problem solvers and consultants. This was novel at the time but set a precedent and changed the emphasis of consulting from passing on a narrow range of experience to utilizing a wide range of analytical and problem solving techniques.

Another element of Bower's approach was the use of teams. He thought of McKinsey as a 'network of leaders'. Teams were assembled for specific projects. The best people in the organization were brought to bear on a particular problem no matter where they were based in the world. 'McKinsey had a culture that fostered rigorous debate over the right answer without that debate resulting in personal criticism', recalls IBM chief Lou Gerstner, another McKinsey alumni.[5]

Though the management consulting world developed a high charging, opportunistic reputation, Bower managed to stand apart. True or not, he created an impression of hard working, clean living, decency. Even now, once recruited, McKinsey consultants know where they stand. The firm's policy remains one of the most simple. 'Seniority in McKinsey correlates directly with achievement', it says. The weak are shown the door. 'If a consultant ceases to progress with the Firm or is ultimately unable to demonstrate the skills and qualities required of a principal, he or she is asked to leave McKinsey', says the company's recruitment brochure.

Bower himself set an impressive example – in 1963, on reaching the age of sixty, he sold his shares back to the firm at their book value. McKinsey laid its cards on the table. It played it hard, but straight. If Big Blue was the company to trust, McKinsey was the consulting firm to trust. This is something which McKinsey has largely managed to sustain.

Bower's approach was commonsensical and free of fashionable baggage. 'Business has not changed in the past sixty years. The basic way of running it is the same. There have been thousands of changes in methods but not in command and control. Many companies say they want to change but they need to empower people below. More cohesion is needed rather than hierarchy', he said in 1995.[6]

The culture Bower created continues. The mystique of McKinsey – The Firm – is untouched. It has become more than a mere consultancy. It is an ethos. Staid suits and professional standards. Clean-cut and conservative. It is obsessively professional and hugely successful; a slick, well-oiled financial machine not given to false modesty – 'We do not learn from clients. Their standards aren't high enough. We learn from other McKinsey partners,' a McKinsey consultant once confided to *Forbes* magazine.

And yet, McKinsey is not the oldest consultancy company. Arthur D Little can trace its lineage back to the 1880s. Nor is McKinsey the biggest consultancy company in the world – Accenture dwarfs it in terms of revenues and numbers of consultants (but not, significantly, in revenue per consultant). McKinsey is special because it likes to think of itself as the best and has developed a self-perpetuating aura that it is unquestionably the best. Marvin Bower was the creator of this organizational magic.

Notes

1 Huey, John, 'How McKinsey does it', *Fortune*, 1 November 1993.
2 Bower, Marvin, *The Will to Manage*, McGraw Hill, New York, 1966.
3 Interview with author.
4 Byrne, John, 'The McKinsey mystique', *Business Week*, 20 September 1993.
5 Byrne, John, 'The McKinsey mystique', *Business Week*, 20 September 1993.
6 Hecht, Françoise, 'The firm walks tall', *Eurobusiness*, February 1995.

JAMES MACGREGOR BURNS

Leadership

1978

The author

James MacGregor Burns is a political scientist. Not simply a theorist, he has stood, unsuccessfully, for Congress as a Democrat and worked in John F Kennedy's presidential campaign.

His books include *Congress on Trial* (1949); *Government by the People* (with Jack Peltason, 1950); *Roosevelt: The Lion and the Fox* (1956); *John Kennedy: A Political Profile* (1960); *The Deadlock of Democracy* (1963); *Presidential Government: The Crucible of Leadership* (1965); *Roosevelt: The Soldier of Freedom* (1970); *Uncommon Sense* (1972) and *Edward Kennedy and the Camelot Legacy* (1976).

The classic

'The crisis of leadership today is the mediocrity or irresponsibility of so many of the men and women in power, but leadership rarely rises to the full need for it. The fundamental crisis underlying mediocrity is intellectual. If we know all too much about our leaders, we know far too little about leadership,' observes James MacGregor Burns in the prologue to *Leadership*.[1]

There are literally hundreds of definitions of leadership. Burns suggests that, as a result, 'leadership as a concept has dissolved into small and discrete meanings. A superabundance of facts about leaders far outruns theories of leadership.' Undaunted, in *Leadership*, Burns provides yet another – but one which has proved more enduring: 'Leadership over human beings is exercised when persons with certain motives and purposes mobilize, in competition or conflict with others, institutional, political, psychological and other resources so as to arouse, engage and satisfy the motives of followers.'

To Burns, leadership is not the preserve of the few or the tyranny of the masses. 'The leadership approach tends often unconsciously to be elitist; it projects heroic figures against the shadowy background of drab, powerless masses', he writes. 'The followership approach tends to be populistic or anti-elitist in ideology; it perceives the masses, even in democratic societies, as linked with small, overlapping circles of conservative politicians, military officers, hierocrats, and businessmen. I describe leadership here as no mere game among elitists and no mere populist response but as a structure of action that engages persons, to varying degrees, throughout the levels and among the interstices of society. Only the inert, the alienated, and the powerless are unengaged.' To Burns, leadership is intrinsically linked to morality and 'moral leadership emerges from, and always returns to, the fundamental wants and needs, aspirations, and values of the followers'.

Aside from his thoughtful definition, in *Leadership* Burns identifies two vital strands of leadership – transformational and transactional leadership.

Transformational leadership 'occurs when one or more persons engage with others in such a way that leaders and followers raise one another to higher levels of motivation and morality. Their purposes, which might have started out separate but related ... become fused. Power bases are linked not as counterweights but as mutual support for common purpose,' writes Burns. 'Various names are used for such leadership: elevating, mobilizing, inspiring, exalting, uplifting, exhorting, evangelizing. The relationship can be moralistic, of course. But transforming leadership ultimately becomes moral in that it raises the level of human conduct and ethical aspiration of both the leader and the led, and thus has a transforming effect on both ... Transforming leadership is dynamic leadership in the sense that the leaders throw themselves into a relationship with followers who will feel "elevated" by it and often become more active themselves, thereby creating new cadres of leaders.'

Transformational leadership is concerned with engaging the hearts and minds of others. It works to help all parties achieve greater motivation, satisfaction and a greater sense of achievement. It is driven by trust and concern and facilitation rather than direct control. The skills required are concerned with establishing a long-term vision, empowering people to control themselves, coaching and developing others and challenging the culture to change. In transformational leadership, the power of the leader comes from creating understanding and trust.

Alternatively, transactional leadership is built on reciprocity, the idea that the relationship between the leader and their followers develops from the exchange of some reward, such as performance ratings,

Gary Hamel on *Leadership*

'There is no theme in management literature which is more enduring than leadership. Among the many contributions which Burns makes to our understanding of leadership, two seem central: leadership must have a moral foundation; and the responsibility for leadership must be widely distributed. Self-interested autocrats, whether political or corporate, ignore these truths at their peril.'

pay, recognition and praise. It involves leaders in clarifying goals and objectives, communicating to organize tasks and activities with the co-operation of their employees to ensure that wider organizational goals are met. Such a relationship depends on hierarchy and the ability to work through the mode of exchange. It requires leadership skills, such as the ability to obtain results, to control through structures and processes, to solve problems, to plan and organize and work within the structures and boundaries of the organization.

In their apparent mutual exclusiveness, transformational and trans-actional leadership are akin to Douglas McGregor's Theories X and Y. The secret of effective leadership appears to lie in combining the two elements so that targets, results and procedures are developed and shared.

Burns' book provides an important link between leadership in the political and business worlds. For all the books on leadership, the two have usually been regarded as mutually exclusive. His examination of transformational and transactional leadership also stimulated further debate on leadership at a time when it was somewhat neglected. In the 1980s it returned to prominence in management literature as a subject worthy of study.

Note

1 Burns, James MacGregor, *Leadership*, Harper & Row, New York, 1978.

JAN CARLZON

Moments of Truth

1987

The author

Jan Carlzon is a Swedish businessman. He shot to international prominence by leading a turnaround at the Scandinavian airline, SAS. He is now an investor in various high-tech related businesses.

The classic

In Spring 1977 a young McKinsey consultant called Thomas J Peters was given an intriguing assignment. He was told to seek out organizational best practice. Where were the best organizations in the world and what were they doing that made them different?

Japan was the emerging industrial powerhouse, but Peters went elsewhere for his initial inspiration. He called his long-time Swedish friend, Lennart Arvedson, and asked who he should talk to in Scandinavia. Arvedson set up meetings in Norway and Sweden to introduce Peters to Scandinavian best practice. The American met with Einar Thorsrud, a former war-time resistance leader and champion of industrial democracy; visited Volvo's factory floor, where technicians were taking over the flow of work; and the Scania factory outside Stockholm which was following a new socio-technical design. His eyes were opened.

Peters was not alone. For students and practitioners of management, the lure of Scandinavian-style business leadership and management has always been a surprisingly strong one. In the wake of Peters came the emergence of Jan Carlzon, chief executive of the airline SAS during the 1980s. Carlzon proclaimed, 'All business is show business', and actually made customer service work. He used it as a vehicle for turning the airline around (in a similar way to Gordon Bethune at Continental). Indeed,

Carlzon was Bethune and Southwestern's Herb Kelleher rolled into one, long before Kelleher and Bethune hit the front pages.

SAS was an indifferent performer until Carlzon introduced it to customer service. Most notably, Carlzon came up with the phrase 'moments of truth' – the sequence of critical transactions across each stage of the ownership or use cycle. 'Anytime a customer comes into contact with any aspect of a business, however remote, is an opportunity to form an impression', writes Carlzon.

These were broken down into:

- Initial contact
- First use
- Problem solving
- On-going support
- Further purchases
- Recommendations to others

Evaluating the degree to which satisfaction and value are affected at these different points in the cycle, and how they vary by customer type, can be the key to understanding customer behaviour.

Carlzon truly understood the process and decided to dramatically prove the company's dedication to moments of truth by sending tens of thousands of SAS managers on training programs. It was a dramatic but meaningful statement. (There are parallels elsewhere – Larry Bossidy, CEO of AlliedSignal put all the company's 86,000 employees through a development program and managed to speak to 15,000 of them during his first year in the job.[1] Along the way, Bossidy also increased the market value of the company by 400 percent in six years.)

In doing so, Carlzon set in train SAS's revival and became a benchmark for international best practice in customer service, celebrated, by among many others, Tom Peters in *A Passion for Excellence*. For a time, with a neat line in phrase-making and a great story to tell, Carlzon was hardly out of the business magazines. Carlzon's *Moments of Truth* (*Riv Pyramiderna!* – 'flatten the pyramids' in Swedish) was an international bestseller selling three million copies.[2]

After Carlzon left SAS and the company's halo slipped a little, Scandinavian role models were thin on the ground for a number of years. During the 1990s, however, there were a steady stream of corporate benchmarks. Carlzon has not been left behind – he has successfully reinvented himself as a high-tech venture capitalist and consultant.

Scandinavian companies hold a continuing fascination. The new Scandinavian role models – IKEA, Skandia, Oticon and ABB – remain indebted to Carlzon's example. One reason for the attraction is that English is virtually universally spoken throughout Scandinavia. Beneath the surface, the Scandinavian attraction becomes clearer. Carlzon's *Moments of Truth* epitomizes this. First, there is the management style. This, by popular renown, is humane and people-centred. This may explain why there was little interest in Scandinavian role models during the early 1990s when downsizing and reengineering held sway – corporations didn't want their consciences pricked by touchy-feely Danes who treated employees like drinking buddies.

Like most stereotypes, the image of highly motivated, well rewarded, hard working and contented Scandinavians is only partly true. Scandinavian companies have a track record in managing their human resources in innovative ways – they were champions of teamworking and employee participation long before they became the height of managerial fashion. Even so, it is easy to overstate this. 'There is a belief that we are better at caring for people, that we have a more humanitarian view of business. I think it is vastly exaggerated', says Jan Lapidoth, an SAS vice-president under Carlzon, who now runs the Customer Focus Institute in Stockholm. 'More significant is the fact that we are a very stable political society and a fairly homogeneous society. We have solved our problems through negotiation. Historically, there has been little unrest but the counter to this is that often without a crisis you don't achieve advancement.'

Indeed, the Scandinavian business culture shares some characteristics with that of the Japanese. Saving face is important and, rather than direct frontal attack, Scandinavians prefer a more abstruse and subtle approach.

Old-fashioned virtues are in. Typically, in one survey, American executives rated honesty as the prime business virtue; Swedish executives did not include honesty at all – it was assumed. 'Our business is built on trust. A handshake is a handshake', says Jan Lapidoth. 'This means that we keep legalities to a minimum. We talk to each other, settle it and get on with it.'

Even so, Nike's call 'Just do it' does not quite work in Scandinavia. It is recounted that the typical Swedish edict is 'See what you can do about it'. Forget command and control. The Scandinavian leader à la Carlzon is decidedly anti-authoritarian. Highly personal and practical theories, such as coaching and mentoring, find fertile ground. Being up-front and communicating openly is expected.

Percy Barnevik (formerly of ABB and now imparting Swedish wisdom as a non-executive director at GM) and Carlzon remain the best known of Swedish business leaders – though they are not fêted quite as much within Sweden as without. Jan Lapidoth believes their approaches share important characteristics: 'With Carlzon and Barnevik, there is a certain amount of showmanship. They play their roles to perfection. They stand in the middle of their strategy. They don't preach the strategy; they are the strategy. They communicate consistently and continually. They repeat the same messages again and again. It is like advertising. But they never grow tired of saying it – there is no sign of boredom, no cynicism, no sarcasm. They give words real meaning.' This appetite for communication is clearly linked to a more humane style of management. The people deserve to be told.

Notes

1 Bossidy was helpful to GE in introducing its Six Sigma quality initiative - AlliedSignal had already done so.
2 Carlzon, Jan, *Moments of Truth*, Harper, New York, 1987.

DALE CARNEGIE

How to Win Friends and Influence People

1937

The author

orn on a Missouri farm in 1888, Dale Carnegie (originally Carnegey) began his working life selling bacon, soap and lard for Armour & Company in south Omaha. He turned his sales territory into the company's national leader, but then went to New York to study at the American Academy of Dramatic Arts – he toured the country as Dr. Harley in *Polly of the Circus*. Realizing the limits of his acting potential, Carnegie returned to salesmanship – selling Packard automobiles. It was then that Carnegie persuaded the YMCA schools in New York to allow him to conduct courses in public speaking.

Carnegie's talks became highly successful. He wrote *Public Speaking and Influencing Men in Business* and a variety of other variations on his theme – *How to Stop Worrying and Start Living*; *How to Enjoy Your Life and Your Job*; and *How to Develop Self-Confidence and Influence People by Public Speaking*. He is best known, however, for *How to Win Friends and Influence People*, which has sold over 15 million copies (its first edition had a print run of a mere 5,000). Dale Carnegie died in 1955.

The classic

Dale Carnegie's *How to Win Friends and Influence People*[1] is the original self-improvement book. 'If by the time you have finished reading the first three chapters of this book – if you aren't then a little better equipped to meet life's situations, then I shall consider this book to be a total failure', Carnegie writes in its opening. It was written by Carnegie as a textbook for his courses in 'Effective speaking and human relations.' Carnegie's aim was to write 'a practical, working handbook on human relations'.

To do so, Carnegie eagerly explains that no stone was left unturned. He read extensively and hired a researcher to spend 18 months reading the books he had missed – 'I recall that we read over one hundred biographies of Theodore Roosevelt alone.' Carnegie then interviewed some famous names – from Clark Gable to Marconi, Franklin D Roosevelt to Mary Pickford.

Carnegie was a salesman extraordinaire. Names are dropped, promises made. Upbeat and laden with sentiment, *How to Win Friends and Influence People* is a simple selling document – 'The rules we have set down here are not mere theories or guesswork. They work like magic. Incredible as it sounds, I have seen the application of these principles literally revolutionize the lives of many people.'

The result is a number of principles from which friends and influence should, Carnegie anticipates, surely emerge. First, there are the 'fundamental techniques in handling people' – 'don't criticize, condemn or complain; give honest and sincere appreciation; and arouse in the other person an eager want'. Then Carnegie presents six ways to make people like you – 'become genuinely interested in other people; smile; remember that a person's name is to that person the sweetest and most important sound in any language; be a good listener. Encourage others to talk about themselves; talk in terms of the other person's interests; make the other person feel important – and do it sincerely.'

Carnegie's advice comes adorned with a host of anecdotes from the famous to the not so famous – characters such as George Dyke of North Warren, Pennsylvania, who 'was forced to retire from his service station business after thirty years when a new highway was constructed over the site of the station'. Undeterred, Dyke became a travelling fiddler in demand throughout the country.

It is easy to be critical and cynical of much of what is written in *How to Win Friends and Influence People*. In one interview, Peter Drucker dismissed the self-help genre as based on the hope that 'you can make a million and still go to heaven'. However, there is a perennial demand – and, presumably, a need – for such books. Indeed, there are echoes of Carnegie in many books published even now. Peters and Waterman's celebration of customer service owes something to Carnegie's advice on 'the big secret of dealing with people' and books by the like of Mark McCormack are often simply contemporary versions of the truisms espoused by Carnegie over half a century earlier.

Carnegie's message remains relevant: people matter and, in the world of business, how you manage and relate to people is the key to

Gary Hamel on *How to Win Friends and Influence People*

'I recently attended a conference with the title "Implementing strategy through people". I asked the sponsor whether there was an alternative – perhaps one could implement strategy through dogs? When the focus is on technology, structure and process it is easy to lose sight of the deeply personal nature of management. Though Dale Carnegie's advice sometimes borders on the manipulative, it is a warm and fuzzy, eager salesman kind of manipulation. What a contrast to the hard-edged, got-you-by-your-paycheck manipulation familiar to thousands of anxiety-ridden survivors of corporate restructuring.'

success. Proof of its continuing relevance is evidenced by the fact that Dale Carnegie Training lives on and has over 4.5 million graduates.

Note

1 Carnegie, Dale, *How to Win Friends and Influence People*, Simon & Schuster, New York, 1937.

JAMES CHAMPY &
MICHAEL HAMMER

Reengineering the Corporation

1993

The authors

J ames Champy (born 1942) was co-founder of the consultancy company CSC Index. CSC became one of the largest consultancy companies in the world with revenues in excess of $500 million and over 2,000 consultants worldwide. In 1996, Champy left CSC to join Perot Systems. Champy is also the author of *Reengineering Management: The Mandate for New Leadership* (1995); co-author of *The Arc of Ambition (1999)* and of *X-engineering* (2002*)*.

Michael Hammer (born 1948) is a former computer science professor at MIT and President of Hammer and Company, a management education and consulting firm. He is widely credited with being the founding father of reengineering. Its roots lie in the research carried out by MIT from 1984 to 1989 on 'Management in the 1990s'. Hammer's sequel was *The Reengineering Revolution* (with Steven Stanton, 1995).

The classic

Reengineering was unquestionably *the* business idea of the first half of the 1990s. James Champy and Michael Hammer's *Reengineering the Corporation*[1] was the manifesto for a promised revolution, one that – except in a few instances – largely failed to materialize. The claims made for reengineering and for Champy and Hammer's book, were large. 'When people ask me what I do for a living, I tell them that what I really do is I'm reversing the Industrial Revolution', proclaimed Hammer with apparent sincerity. Indeed, the opening of the book positions it as the

Gary Hamel on *Reengineering the Corporation*

'Scientific management, industrial engineering, business process improvement, and now, new and improved, reengineering. The idea might be old, but the language was new and the time was right. A brutally tough competitive environment and the explosion of information technology compelled companies to take a fresh look at inefficient and sclerotic processes. Too bad reengineering usually exacted the same human toll as restructuring – fewer, more cynical employees.'

ready replacement for Adam Smith's *the Wealth of Nations*. It has now sold over two million copies.

Cutting away the hype and hyperbole, the basic idea behind reengineering is that organizations need to identify their key processes and make them as lean and efficient as possible. Peripheral processes (and, therefore, peripheral people) need to be discarded. Champy and Hammer define reengineering as 'the fundamental rethinking and radical redesign of business processes to achieve dramatic improvements in critical measures of performance such as cost, quality, service and speed'.

To Champy and Hammer, reengineering is more than dealing with mere processes. They eschew the popular phrase 'business process reengineering', regarding it as too limiting. In their view the scope and scale of reengineering goes far beyond simply altering and refining processes. True reengineering is all-embracing.

In *Reengineering the Corporation*, Champy and Hammer advocate that companies equip themselves with a blank piece of paper and map out their processes. 'It is time to stop paving the cow paths. Instead of imbedding outdated processes in silicon and software, we should obliterate them and start over', pronounced Hammer with characteristic fervour and idiosyncratic imagery in his *Harvard Business Review* article which set the reengineering bandwagon rolling.[2] Having come up with a neatly engineered map of how their business should operate, companies can then attempt to translate the paper theory into concrete reality.

The concept is simple. (Indeed, critics of reengineering regard it as a contemporary version of Taylor's Scientific Management with its belief in measurement and optimal ways of completing particular tasks.) Making it happen has proved immensely more difficult. The first problem is that the blank piece of paper ignores the years, often decades, of cultural evolution which have led to an organization doing something in a certain way. Such preconceptions are not easily discarded. Indeed, discarding them may well amount to corporate suicide.

Champy and Hammer say that reengineering is concerned with 'rejecting conventional wisdom and received assumptions of the past … it is about reversing the industrial revolution … tradition counts for nothing. Reengineering is a new beginning.' In *Leaning into the Future*, British academics Colin Williams and George Binney are dismissive of such talk: 'The last time someone used language like this was Chairman Mao in the Cultural Revolution. Under the motto "Destroy to build", he too insisted on sweeping away the past. Instead of such wanton destruction, successful organizations do not deny or attempt to destroy the inheritance of the past. They seek to build on it. They try to understand in depth why they have been successful and they try to do more of it. They are respectful of the learning accumulated from experience and recognize that much of this learning is not made explicit at the top of the organization.'[3]

Henry Mintzberg has also expressed his concern about reengineering. 'There is no reengineering in the idea of reengineering', he says. 'Just reification, just the same old notion that the new system will do the job. But because of the hype that goes with any new management fad, everyone has to run around reengineering everything. We are supposed to get superinnovation on demand just because it is deemed necessary by a manager in some distant office who has read a book. Why don't we just stop reengineering and delayering and restructuring and decentralizing and instead start thinking?'[4]

The second problem is that reengineering has become a synonym for redundancy. For this Champy and Hammer cannot be entirely blamed. Often, companies which claim to be reengineering are simply engaging in cost-cutting under the convenient guise of the fashionable theory. Downsizing appears more publicly palatable if it is presented as implementing a leading edge concept. In 1994 research covering 624 companies, CSC Index found that on average 336 jobs were lost per reengineering project in the US and 760 in Europe.[5]

The third obstacle which has emerged is that corporations are not natural or even willing revolutionaries. Instead of casting the reengineering net widely they tend to reengineer the most readily accessible process and then leave it at that. Related to this, and the subject of Champy's sequel, *Reengineering Management*, reengineering usually fails to impinge on management. Managers are all too willing to impose the rigours of a process-based view of the business on others, but often unwilling to inflict it upon themselves.

Champy has now concluded that it is 'time to reengineer the manager': 'Senior managers have been reengineering business processes with a passion, tearing down corporate structures that no longer can support the organization. Yet the practice of management has largely escaped demolition. If their jobs and styles are left largely intact, managers will eventually undermine the very structure of their rebuilt enterprises.'[6] Champy suggests that reengineering management should tackle three key areas: managerial roles, managerial styles and managerial systems.

'Many people don't understand the subtleties of managing', laments Champy. 'They believe that a manager must be decisive, that the world is black and white. In fact, a good bit of the business world today is gray; you may not know immediately what to do. It's okay to think for a while. There is a lot of intellectual work to management – but that counters the macho approach that managers often adopt to maintain power. Operating only through control diminishes your power to lead people. It suggests that you really don't know what's going on.'

It is the human side of reengineering which has proved the greatest stumbling block – 'Most reengineering efforts will fail or fall short of the mark because of the absence of trust – meaning respect for the individual, his or her goodwill, intelligence and native, but long shackled, curiosity', observed Tom Peters.[7]

In his review of the book in the *Financial Times*, the late Christopher Lorenz noted: 'They [Champy and Hammer] are ... inconsistent about whether they think behavioural and cultural change ... are an automatic result of the reengineering of business processes or whether such soft change needs to be launched in parallel or even beforehand. Controversially, much of the book suggests that soft follows hard automatically.'[8]

Champy and Hammer would counter that true reengineering is actually built on trust, respect and people. 'It is astonishing to see the extent to which the term reengineering has been hijacked, misappropriated and misunderstood', Hammer lamented. By cutting away peripheral activities, companies provide an environment which places a premium on the skills and potential of those it employs. This, as yet, has not been supported by corporate experience.

James Champy's verdict on the impact of reengineering is more positive than negative. 'I think that the balance is very positive. In global terms, I think that we have only reached 10 or 20 per cent of what we intended, so there is still a lot to be done. In this moment there is a very real reaction to reengineering that comes from people who do not understand the concept. Many consider it very similar to the downsizing trend. Others have not yet understood the need for a fundamental change in the way in which corporations work. Reengineering is exactly that – it is a radical change in the way people perform their work in corporations.

The basic idea of reengineering is now a global phenomenon. More than a management fad and a buzzword, it is really a genuine need.'

Indeed, Champy suggests that a number of industries need to reengineer themselves as soon as possible – these include industries linked with technologies, the telecommunications, and media enterprises, financial services, health services, and transport industries.

Notes

1 Champy, James & Hammer, Michael, *Reengineering the Corporation*, HarperBusiness, New York, 1993.
2 Hammer, Michael, 'Reengineering work: don't automate, obliterate', *Harvard Business Review*, July–August 1990.
3 Binney, George & Williams, Colin, *Leaning into the Future*, Nicholas Brealey, London, 1995.
4 Mintzberg, Henry, 'Musings on management', *Harvard Business Review*, July–August 1996.
5 The State of Reengineering, CSC Index, 1994.
6 Champy, James, 'Time to reengineer the manager', *Financial Times*, 14 January 1994.
7 Peters, Tom, 'Out of the ordinary', Syndicated column, 23 July 1993.
8 Lorenz, Christopher, 'The very nuts and bolts of change', *Financial Times*, 22 June 1993.

ALFRED CHANDLER

Strategy and Structure

1962

The author

Alfred D Chandler (born 1918) is a Pulitzer Prize-winning business historian. After graduating from Harvard, he served in the US Navy before becoming, somewhat unusually, a historian at MIT in 1950. Later he became Professor of History at Johns Hopkins University. He has been Straus Professor of Business History at Harvard since 1971. His hugely detailed research into US companies between 1850 and 1920 has formed the cornerstone of much of his work.

The classic

Alfred Chandler's *Strategy and Structure*[1] is a theoretical masterpiece which has had profound influence on both practitioners and thinkers. Its sub-title is 'Chapters in the history of the American industrial enterprise', but its impact went far beyond that of a brilliantly researched historical text.

'The decision to write *Strategy and Structure* came in 1954 when I was invited to create and teach a course at the Naval War College in Newport, Rhode Island on "the basis of national strategy"', Chandler later recalled in an interview marking the book's fortieth anniversary. 'William Rietzal, who was at the College in another capacity, had become interested in the post World War II changes in military organizational structures, particularly those that came with the creation of the post-war Department of Defense. I was then developing my interest in the evolution of modern business structures. So we agreed that each of us would write a book on our respective intellectual concerns. Rietzal never completed his book. Mine came out in 1962.'[2]

Gary Hamel on *Strategy and Structure*

'Those who dispute Chandler's thesis that structure follows strategy miss the point. Of course strategy and structure are inextricably intertwined. Chandler's point was that new challenges give rise to new structures. The challenges of size and complexity, coupled with advances in communications and techniques of management control produced divisionalization and decentralization. These same forces, several generations on, are now driving us towards new structural solutions – the 'federated organization', the multi-company coalition, and the virtual company. Few historians are prescient. Chandler was.'

From his research into major US corporations between 1850 and 1920, Chandler argues that a firm's structure is dictated by its chosen strategy – 'Unless structure follows strategy, inefficiency results.' First, a company should establish a strategy and then seek to create the structure appropriate to achieving it. Chandler defines strategy as 'the determination of the long-term goals and objectives of an enterprise, and the adoption of courses of action and the allocation of resources necessary for carrying out these goals'.

Chandler observes that organizational structures in companies such as Du Pont, Sears Roebuck, General Motors and Standard Oil were driven by the changing demands and pressures of the marketplace. He traces the market-driven proliferation of product lines in Du Pont and General Motors and concludes that this proliferation led to a shift from a functional, monolithic organizational form to a more loosely-coupled divisional structure. (Interestingly, Chandler's family has historical connections with DuPont – and DuPont is, in fact, Chandler's middle name. At the time DuPont also controlled General Motors.)

'The management structures whose evolution are described in *Strategy and Structure* were primarily adopted by enterprises in increasingly capital and knowledge intensive industries, as pointed in its concluding chapter', says Chandler. 'This is because the new multidivisional structure permitted the commercialising of new technologies producing products for different markets. For example, chemical companies were from the 1920s on producing a variety of chemicals, fibres, film, finishes, plastics, explosives and other things. The structure thus permitted them to lower their unit costs through the economies of scope as well as scale.'[3]

Until recent times, Chandler's conclusion that structure follows strategy has largely been accepted as a fact of corporate life. Now, the debate has been rekindled. 'I think he got it exactly wrong', says Tom Peters with typical forthrightness. 'For it is the structure of the organization that determines, over time, the choices that it make about the markets in attacks.'[4]

Another contrary view comes from Kathleen M Eisenhardt of Stanford: 'The Chandler idea that strategy is set and then structure follows makes sense in clear, static markets. In ambiguous, dynamic markets, the two are much more intertwined. In my view, in the overall approach, structure and, more important, the processes by which structure changes are the constants while strategy changes.'[5]

In *Managing on the Edge*, Richard Pascale observes: 'The underlying assumption is that organizations act in a rational, sequential manner. Yet most executives will readily agree that it is often the other way around. The way a company is organized, whether functional focused or driven by independent divisions, often plays a major role in shaping its strategy. Indeed, this accounts for the tendency of organizations to do what they best know how to do – regardless of deteriorating success against the competitive realities.'[6]

While this debate rumbles on, Chandler's place in the canon of management literature remains secure. In particular, he was highly influential in the trend among large organizations for decentralization in the 1960s and 1970s. While in 1950 around 20 percent of *Fortune 500* corporations were decentralized; this had increased to 80 percent by 1970. In *Strategy and Structure*, Chandler praises Alfred Sloan's decentralization of General Motors in the 1920s. He was later influential in the transformation of AT&T in the 1980s from what was in effect a production-based bureaucracy to a marketing organization.

In *Strategy and Structure* Chandler gives a historical context to the multi-divisional organization. Its chief advantage, he writes, is that 'it clearly removed the executives responsible for the destiny of the entire enterprise from the more routine operational responsibilities and so gave them the time, information and even psychological commitment for long-term planning and appraisal'.

The book also ignited the strategy-based consulting industry. 'Chandler's work took place just as the first strategy consulting firms were emerging', says the historian Christopher McKenna of Oxford University's Said Business School. 'Prior to the 1960s, McKinsey was not a *strategy* firm, since strategy as a discipline did not exist, but instead concentrated on restructuring organizations. Similarly, BCG, which was founded in the early 1960s after Bruce Henderson left Arthur D Little, also benefited from this new interest in strategy as a subject. The key addition that Chandler made was to connect strategy and structure. Thus restructuring was an outgrowth of strategy and this meant that a company should first review its strategy before pursuing a different structure. Since corporations are always reviewing new strategies, the growth of strategy consulting gave a tremendous boost to consulting as a field and the consultancies that were able to profit from this growth did very well.[7]

Strategy and Structure also contributed to the 'professionalization of management'. Chandler traces the historical development of what he labels 'the managerial revolution' fuelled by the rise of oil-based energy, the development of the steel, chemical and engineering industries and a dramatic rise in the scale of production and the size of companies. Increases in scale, Chandler observes, led to business owners having to recruit a new breed of professional manager.

Chandler believes that the roles of the salaried manager and technician are vital, and talks of the 'visible hand' of management coordinating the flow of product to customers more efficiently than Adam Smith's 'invisible hand' of the market (see Chandler's 1977 book, *The Visible Hand*). The logical progression from this is that organizations and their managements require a planned economy rather than a capitalist free-for-all dominated by the unpredictable whims of market forces. In the more sedate times in which *Strategy and Structure* was written, the lure of the visible hand proved highly persuasive.

Notes

1 Chandler, Alfred D, *Strategy and Structure*, Doubleday, New York, 1962.
2 Interview with Alfred Chandler by Jorge Nascimento Rodrigues, 2002.
3 Interview with Alfred Chandler by Jorge Nascimento Rodrigues, 2002.
4 Peters, Tom, *Liberation Management*, Alfred P Knopf, New York, 1992.
5 Interview with Jorge Nascimento Rodrigues 2002.
6 Pascale, Richard, *Managing on the Edge*, Simon & Schuster, New York, 1990.
7 Interview with Jorge Nascimento Rodrigues 2002.

KARL VON CLAUSEWITZ

On War

1831

The author

arl von Clausewitz (1780–1831) was a Prussian general and military strategist. Von Clausewitz fought in the Napoleonic wars and in the Rhine campaigns (1793–94). Working on behalf of Russia from 1812 until 1814, von Clausewitz helped negotiate the convention of Tauroggen (1812). This laid the ground for an alliance of Prussia, Russia, and Great Britain in opposition to Napoleon. In his later career, von Clausewitz rejoined the Prussian army, fought at the Battle of Waterloo, and became director of the Prussian war college in 1818. *On War* was unfinished and published posthumously.

The classic

Soldiers have a surprisingly lengthy heritage as managerial exemplars – both in terms of practice and theory. Look back to Hadrian, the enigmatic wall-building Roman Emperor from 117 to 138. He was a champion of people power long before the advent of such niceties as human resource departments. Pomp and circumstance were not for him. His military reputation was forged on his willingness to share the same conditions as his troops. One anecdote describes his refusal to wear his cloak or cap no matter what the weather. Similarly, Hadrian was reputed to join his troops on lengthy marches in full armour.

A series of other humanitarian decisions cemented his reputation. He prohibited castration, and was concerned about slaves. Hadrian was also a globe-trotter. He didn't seek to control his empire from Rome but travelled throughout it. In modern parlance, he accepted the diversity of his Empire – coins issued during his reign celebrated the numerous provinces he had visited. Hadrian also brought to an end the inexorable

Roman expansionism. He sought to draw a line around the Empire rather than engaging in endless foreign wars.

Hadrian was also reputed to have had an eye for financial management – though he started his reign by announcing an amnesty of all debts owed to the government. While his predecessor frittered away the money in the treasury, Hadrian was more frugal and built up reserves to fund building projects and social welfare programmes. At the same time, he didn't raise taxes. (Modern politicians would no doubt like to know exactly how he managed to achieve the political equivalent of squaring the circle.)

Claiming similar credence as a path-breaking managerial practitioner was the Duke of Wellington (1769–1851). Wellington can lay claim to managing by wandering around during the Napoleonic Wars. Historian John Keegan has noted: '[Wellington's methods] required a particularly intense "managerial" style – "taking trouble" with the battle, as Wellington himself would later put it. The general must make himself the eyes of his own army … must constantly change position to deal with crises as they occur along the front of his sheltered line, must remain at the point of crisis until it is resolved and must still keep alert to anticipate the development of crises elsewhere.'[1]

Given these interpretations of history, it is less surprising to see Karl von Clausewitz's On War included in this selection. Indeed, von Clausewitz was firmly of the mind that comparisons between the military and commercial worlds were both valid and useful. 'Rather than comparing it [war] to art we could more accurately compare it to commerce, which is also a conflict of interests and activities; and it is still closer to politics, which in turn may be considered as a kind of commerce on a larger scale', he writes in On War.[2]

As one would expect of a military theorist, von Clausewitz possesses a strong strain of pragmatism. 'To be practical, any plan must take account of the enemy's power to frustrate it; the best chance of overcoming such obstruction is to have a plan that can be easily varied to fit the circumstances met; to keep such adaptability, while still keeping the initiative, the best way is to operate along a line which offers alternative objectives', he advises. Mere theory will get you nowhere. (In this, and other areas, von Clausewitz was heavily influenced by the wily power politics so potently mapped out by Machiavelli.) 'Knowing is different from doing and therefore theory must never be used as norms for a standard, but merely as aids to judgement', von Clausewitz writes. Pragmatism is combined with a desire to achieve results through minimal effort – 'A prince or general can best demonstrate his genius by managing a campaign exactly to suit his objectives and his resources, doing neither too much nor too little.'

Most famously, von Clausewitz observes that war 'is merely the continuation of policy by other means'. Instead of being catastrophic, he views war as a normal and acceptable part of politics. Little wonder, perhaps, that Mao and Lenin were fans of von Clausewitz's work.

Von Clausewitz differentiates between strategy – the overall plan – and mere tactics – planning of a discrete part of the overall plan (i.e. the battle). Above this, von Clausewitz placed what he labelled 'grand strategy', the overall political aims. Arguments over the difference between strategy and tactics have raged inconclusively ever since.

Von Clausewitz's view was that success came through concentrating on one battle at a time. This is the distant precursor of the managerial theory of Management By Objectives. 'By looking on each engagement as part of a series, at least insofar as events are predictable, the commander is always on the high road to his goal', he writes.

More recently, management thinkers have sought inspiration from leading military thinker Basil Liddell Hart (1895–1970) – in particular from his 1967 book, *Strategy*. And, today's management gurus – including Richard Pascale – have examined military approaches to such issues as leadership, training, motivation and strategy.

Indeed, von Clausewitz is undergoing something of a renaissance. A 2001 book, *Clausewitz on Strategy: Inspiration and Insight from a Master Strategist,* gathered a selection of his *bons mots.*[3] The selection was made by consultants from the Boston Consulting Group and an academic from the US's National War College.

While von Clausewitz's insights are interesting – especially for nineteenth century Prussian military enthusiasts – their usefulness is debatable. Traditional military role models look increasingly tired and out of kilter with business reality.

'Across the world there is a move away from military role models which essentially exercise control on not only team-members' behaviours but also on their thinking', says motivation expert David Freemantle. 'For companies to survive in this increasingly competitive global world it is essential to have front-line people who can think for themselves and exercise a high degree of creativity. The traditional military model of command and control militates against this.

'Today, it is essential to have people who can think for themselves and do what they believe is right for their customers and their company – as opposed to acting as robots and following a pre-programmed set of procedures (as detailed in the training manual). What I teach and preach is "Be yourself, not what someone else wants you to be". Traditional military models force you to be what someone else – your general or commander – wants you to be. It is dangerous to force people to do what their bosses want of them. The freedom of choice is of paramount importance. I'm not convinced a military role model provides this. Exceptional industrial leaders give employees this freedom.'

'Obviously there will be some aspects of military leadership that are applicable to the leadership of today – trust and precision for example', says Fons Trompenaars, co-author of *21 Leaders for the 21st Century*. 'However, in the military I have seen lot of extravagances go unpunished because of the simplicity of the goal or the enemy. In the modern business world things are more complex than having just one adversary.'

Notes

1 Keegan, John, *The Mask of Command*, Penguin Books, New York, 1987.
2 von Clausewitz, Karl, *On War*, transl. and ed. Howard, Michael & Paret, Peter, Princeton University Press, Princeton, NJ, 1984.
3 von Ghyczy, Tiha, von Oetinger, Bolko & Bassford, Christopher (eds), *Clausewitz on Strategy*, John Wiley, 2001.

JAMES COLLINS & JERRY PORRAS

Built to Last

1994

The authors

Jerry Porras is Lane Professor of Organizational Behaviour and Change and director of the Leading and Managing Change programme at Stanford Business School. He has been based at Stanford since 1972. Prior to that he was in the US Army and worked at the Lockheed Missiles and Space Corporation, General Electric and in Argentina.

James Collins (born 1958) runs a management learning laboratory in Boulder, Colorado and is a visiting professor at the University of Virginia. He has also taught at Stanford and worked at McKinsey & Company and Hewlett-Packard.

The classic

Aristotle observed: 'Values are qualities, human excellence, reflected through our habits, skills and behaviours.' Honesty, integrity wealth, fairness are all values that we may be able to relate to on an individual personal basis. But what about values in the context of business and corporations?

While the term 'corporate values' is a relative newcomer to the business lexicon, the concept of values as an important aspect of corporate life is not. Although not always described as such, many companies have long recognized the importance of possessing a set of guiding principles. The evolution of the concept can be traced through some of the most influential business books over the last fifty years.

In his 1963 book *A Business and Its Beliefs*, Thomas Watson Jr, CEO of IBM, observed: 'Consider any great organization – one that has lasted over the years – I think you will find it owes its resiliency not to its form of organization or administrative skills, but to the power of what we call beliefs and the appeal these beliefs have for its people.' When Watson talks about beliefs, he is talking about fundamental principles or standards, about what is valuable or important to IBM, the organization. He is talking about values.

Similarly, Tom Peters and Robert Waterman thought corporate values important enough to warrant an entire chapter in their 1982 book *In Search Of Excellence*. For them the terms beliefs and values were interchangeable. Other writers touched on the subject with varying degrees of interest.

But the debate took a leap forward in 1994 with *Built to Last* by James. C. Collins and Jerry I. Porras.[1] The two business academics from Stanford University set out to identify the qualities essential to building a great and enduring organization; what the authors called 'successful habits of visionary companies'. The 18 companies they wrote about had outperformed the general stock market by a factor of 12 since 1925.

Core values, they say, are: 'The organization's essential and enduring tenets – a small set of guiding principles; not to be confused with specific cultural or operating practices; not to be compromised for financial gain or short term expediency'. For Collins and Porras, values are timeless guiding principles that drive the way the company operates – everything it does – at a level that transcends strategic objectives. For Hewlett-Packard, for example, values include a strong sense of responsibility to the community. For Disney, they include 'creativity, dreams and imagination' and the promulgation of 'wholesome American values'.

'Companies that enjoy enduring success have core values and a core purpose that remain fixed while their business strategies and practices endlessly adapt to a changing world', write Collins and Porras. This, they say, is a key factor in the success of companies such as Hewlett-Packard, Johnson & Johnson, Proctor & Gamble, Merck, and Sony. Collins and Porras recommend a conceptual framework to cut through some of the confusion swirling around the issues. In their model, vision has two components – core ideology and envisioned future.

Core ideology, the Yin in their scheme, defines what the company stands for and why it exists. Yin is unchanging and complements Yang, the envisioned future. The envisioned future is what the company aspires to become, to achieve, to create – something that will require considerable change and progress to attain.

Core ideology provides the glue that holds an organization together through time. Any effective vision must embody the core ideology of the organization, which in turn has two components – core values (a system of guiding principles and tenets) and core purpose (the organization's most fundamental reason for existence).

The success of *Built to Last* was a refreshing surprise – not least to the authors. Says Collins: 'I'm continuously surprised to see that the book keeps selling and selling. I think we're pushing 1 million copies in print after some 64 months on the best-seller lists. Why does it continue to fascinate readers? My guess is that there are three reasons. First, Jerry and I talked about *the* corporate icons of the 20th Century; we focused on companies like IBM and Sony and Walt Disney. That draws a lot of people. Second, the quality of our research has obviously stood the test of time; the book uniquely looked at companies historically (to their roots) and comparatively (against their major competitors). Lastly, a lot of what's in that book are revelations about humans at work; we weren't afraid to have business findings mixed in with non-business, human findings.'[2]

Collins has followed *Built to Last* with *Good to Great* (2001). He suggests that this should be read before *Built to Last* – 'We didn't know it at the time, but the two books, combined, tell the story about how a new company can become a good company, then a great one, then one that is an enduring, visionary company.'

Central to this book is the distinction between being good and being great. Collins explains: 'Good is the enemy of great. Society doesn't have great schools because we have good schools; we don't have great government because we have good government; and we don't have that many great companies because too many are simply good. Ultimately, it's sad but true that many people don't have great lives because they're willing to settle for good lives. To be a great company, you have to adhere to relentlessly stiff standards. You have to stop accepting good-enough behaviors and performance. One of the major findings in the new book is that what companies and managers STOP doing is infinitely more important than what's on their "To Do" list.'

The good news is that the 'greatness gene' is embedded in all companies, managers, and employees. Says Collins: 'Any company – *any* company – and I mean ANY organization can become a great one. That is truly one of my own epiphanies in the last decade. I feel that we learned exactly how good companies become great ones. But the people inside a good company, starting with the leaders, have to commit – and stay committed.'[3]

Notes

1 Collins, James & Porras, Jerry, *Built to Last*, HarperBusiness, New York, 1994.
2 Interview with Tom Brown, 2001.
3 Interview with Tom Brown, 2001.

STEPHEN COVEY

The Seven Habits of Highly Effective People

1989

The author

S tephen Covey (born 1932) is the founder, chairman and president of the Covey Leadership Center at Provo, Utah. A devout Mormon, Covey has an MBA from Harvard Business School and spent the bulk of his career at Brigham Young University where he was first an administrator and then professor of organizational behaviour.

The classic

Self-improvement is one of the cornerstones of the publishing industry. Look at the booming market in feng shui, Pilates and similar titles. You can change yourself; change where you live and how you live; change how and where you work.

But away from the alternative health market, business self-improvement books also fill bookshop shelves. Look through the current bestseller lists and you find *Who Moved My Cheese?*, Spencer Johnson's mousy-take on coping with change; *Get Everything Done and Still Have Time to Play* by Mark Forster; and Marcus Buckingham and Donald Clifton's *Now, Discover Your Strengths*. There are many more. The secrets of career success, decision-making dynamite, entrepreneurial excellence, and much, much more, are only £5.99 away and usually concealed in an uncompromisingly hard-selling cover.

Mock not. The genre has a lengthy bestselling pedigree. The book generally acknowledged as the starting point was Dale Carnegie's *How to Win Friends and Influence People*.

The book that re-ignited the sector was *The One Minute Manager* by Ken Blanchard & Spencer Johnson, published in 1982. Simple idea. Small book. Big sales. *The One Minute Manager* is light on pages – a reasonably quick reader can polish it off comfortably in sixty minutes – and big on ideas.

The book discusses three main techniques: one minute goal setting; one minute praising; and one minute reprimands. Goals look to ensure that employees have a good understanding of their roles within an organization. Praising is about giving immediate positive feedback when deserved. Reprimands is of course about dealing with what went wrong and why.

A minute may be a little too brief a period to do justice to the needs of 'the managed' and some less empathetic managers may be tempted to take the sixty second period literally. However the authors do strike a chord. 'People are not pigeons', they say. 'People are more complicated. They are aware, they think for themselves, and they certainly don't want to be manipulated by another person. Remember that and respect that. It is a key to good management.' It is a sentiment that resonates with employees everywhere (enough to sell 10 million copies worldwide at least).

The Carnegie-style remains the stock-in-trade of self-improvement authors. They are gushingly positive. Sceptics – and there a few – blanch at the saccharine salesmanship, the relentless optimism and the Machiavellian appetite for manipulation.

If the tone is off-putting, there is also the content to contend with. Self-improvement books are chock-full with neat aphorisms to help you make it through the day. They assault the senses. Some stick. You eventually begin to believe that 'There is no "i" in team' is a life-changing profundity.

'The bridge to success is never crossed alone', suggests the irresistibly named Zig Ziglar. 'Success is a process – not an event' is another one of Ziglar's wise phrases. In America, Ziglar is a big name. He fills auditoriums and has created a corporate empire around his particular brand of self-improvement. His books include *Something to Smile About* and *Raising Positive Kids in a Negative World*.

Stating the blindingly obvious is par for this particular course. So you are advised that talking to people face-to-face is good. Meet their eyes. Shake hands firmly. Ask about their children. Enquire about their golf handicap. Then, when they are weak at the knees with gratitude, clinch the deal (and make sure you remember their name afterwards). Being nice is only useful if it makes you money.

The business self-improvement master of our times is undoubtedly Stephen Covey. Covey is a shaven-headed Mormon who has created a business empire on the back of his bestseller *The Seven Habits of Highly Effective People.*

Covey's doctoral research looked at 'success literature'. His research interest led him to found his Leadership Center in 1984 and then to write *The Seven Habits of Highly Effective People.* As befits the genre, Covey's message tends to be of the commonsense variety – 'be proactive; begin with the end in mind; put first things first; think win/win; seek first to understand then to be understood; synergize; sharpen the saw'. Yet, it is its very simplicity and accessibility which partly explains Covey's astonishing success. *Seven Habits* has sold over six million copies.

An interesting take on the book comes from the unlikely source of Chris Argyris of Harvard. In *The Seven Habits of Effective People* Covey advises that the first step to effectiveness is to start with one's self. The advice is to develop trust; generate positive energy; and avoid negative energy. These principles are illustrated with a story of how he managed his son, after setting him the task of clearing up the yard. In his book, *Flawed Advice and the Management Trap,* Argyris exposes how Covey suppresses his own negative feelings about his son's actions while at the same time preaching honest communication. This is classic Model 1 behaviour. The aim is to achieve the desired outcomes with minimal resistance. His conclusion: 'Although Covey advises people to act authentically, he himself does not do so.'

As you may have guessed, self-help is quintessentially American in tone and outlook. The American speaker's circuit is crowded with self-improvement evangelists and straight talking sales gurus. Their number includes the bright-toothed master of motivation Anthony Robbins (whose clients include Andre Agassi and, bizarrely, the city of Sheffield). According to Stephen Covey, Mr. Robbins is 'one of the great influencers of this generation'. Robbins suggests that he knows the route to 'life mastery' – 'Within you is a powerful driving force that, once unleashed, can make your boldest visions, dreams, and desires real.'

Self-improvement twenty-first century style possesses many of the characteristics of self-improvement 1950s-style. Universal messages abound. There are much the same bullet points. And, most of all, there is the same gung-ho positivity which bedevils all such books. Go on, cheer up.

It is easy to knock the self-improvement genre as a whole. It is too gushing, too simplistic, too cheery for its own good. But self-improvement thrives because it is human nature. The genre appeals not to the rational but to the aspirational. We all want to take control. We want to be proactive. We want to be more assertive. We want to be richer and more successful. We want to have balanced fulfilling lives. And we would all like to believe that achieving these objectives requires 10 steps, seven habits, eight essentials or six keys. We want it all and we want it now in a neat bullet-pointed list.

RICHARD CYERT & JAMES MARCH

A Behavioral Theory of the Firm

1963

The authors

James G March is one of the foremost decision-making theorists of the twentieth century. He is co-author (with Herbert Simon) of *Organizations* (1958) and is also author of five volumes of poetry. His other books include *A Primer on Decision-making* (1994).

Richard Cyert was educated at the University of Minnesota and Columbia University. He is a Professor of Economics and Management at Carnegie-Mellon University.

The classic

An entire academic discipline, decision science, is devoted to understanding management decision-making. Much of it is built on the foundations set down by early business thinkers who believed that under a given set of circumstances human behaviour was logical and therefore predictable. The fundamental belief of the likes of computer pioneer Charles Babbage and Scientific Management founder Frederick Taylor was that the decision process (and many other things) could be rationalized and systematized. Based on this premise, models emerged to explain the workings of commerce which, it was thought, could be extended to the way in which decisions were made.

The belief in decision theory persists. Indeed, most management books and ideas are inextricably linked to helping managers make better decisions.

There is now a profusion of models, software packages and analytical tools which seek to distil decision-making into a formula. Decision-making models assume that the distilled mass of experience will enable people to make accurate decisions. They enable you to learn from other people's experiences. Many promise the world. Feed in your particular circumstances and out will pop an answer. The danger is in concluding that the solution provided by a software package is *the* answer.

Whether in a software package or buried in a textbook, decision theorizing suggests that effective decision-making involves a number of logical stages. This is referred to as the 'rational model of decision-making' or the 'synoptic model'. The latter involves a series of steps – identifying the problem; clarifying the problem; prioritizing goals; generating options; evaluating options (using appropriate analysis); comparing predicted outcomes of each option with the goals; and choosing the option which best matches the goals.

Such models rely on a number of assumptions about the way in which people will behave when confronted with a set of circumstances. These assumptions allow mathematicians to derive formulae based on probability theory. These decision-making tools include such things as cost/benefit analysis which aims to help managers evaluate different options.

Alluring though they are, the trouble with such theories is that reality is often more confused and messy than a neat model can allow for. Underpinning the mathematical approach are a number of flawed assumptions – such as that decision-making is consistent, based on accurate information, free from emotion or prejudice, and rational. Another obvious drawback to any decision-making model is that identifying what you need to make a decision about is often more important than the actual decision itself. If a decision seeks to solve a problem, it may be the right decision but the wrong problem.

The reality is that managers make decisions based on a combination of intuition, experience and analysis. As intuition and experience are impossible to measure in any sensible way, the temptation is to focus on the analytical side of decision-making, the science rather than the mysterious art. (The entire management consultancy industry is based on reaching decisions through analysis.) Of course, the manager in the real world does not care whether he or she is practising an art or science. What they do care about is solving problems and reaching reliable, well-informed decisions.

This does not mean that decision theory is redundant or that decision-making models should be cast to one side. Indeed, a number of factors mean that decision-making is becoming ever more demanding. The growth in complexity means that companies no longer encounter simple problems. And complex decisions are now not simply the preserve of the most senior managers but the responsibility of many others in organizations. In addition, managers are having to deal with a flood of information

– a 1996 survey by Reuters of 1,200 managers worldwide found that 43 per cent thought that important decisions were delayed and their ability to make decisions affected as a result of having too much information.

There is little doubt that decision theory and the use of such models is reassuring. They lend legitimacy to decisions which may be based on prejudices or hunches. But the usefulness of decision-making models remains a leap of faith. None are foolproof as none are universally applicable. And none can yet cope with the wilful idiosyncrasies of human behaviour.

As an introduction to the complex world of decision-making, Cyert and March's *A Behavioral Theory of the Firm* remains powerful and useful. Cyert and March contend that business decision-making theory faces a crucial and immediate problem. Individuals have goals; collective groups do not. There is a need, therefore, to create credible and useful organizational goals while not believing there is such a thing as an 'organizational mind'.

Cyert and March regard organizations as coalitions which negotiate goals. Creating goals requires three processes: the bargaining process which establishes the composition and general terms of the coalition; the internal organizational process of control which clarifies and develops the objectives; and the process of adjustment to experience which alters agreements in accord with changing circumstances.

The trouble is that, as circumstances change, short-term issues take precedence over long-term objectives. Goals are inconsistent thanks to decentralized decision-making, short-terms goals taking most managerial attention, and the disparity between the resources available to the organization and the payments required to maintain the coalition.

Cyert and March identify the five principal goals of the modern organization – production, inventory, sales, market share, and profit – and nine steps in the decision process: forecast competitors' behaviour; forecast demand; estimate costs; specify objectives; evaluate plan; re-examine costs; re-examine demand; re-examine objectives; and select alternatives.

To work successfully, this decision-making model demands that there are standard operating procedures, a learned group of behaviour rules. The procedures can be divided into general ones – based on avoiding uncertainty, maintaining the rules, and using simple rules – and specifics – task performance rules, continuing records and reports, information-handling rules, and plans. These procedures are the link between the individual and organization. They are the means by which organizations make and implement choices.

STAN DAVIS & CHRISTOPHER MEYER

Blur

1997

The authors

Stan Davis is the author of *2020 Vision* and *Future Perfect*. Christopher Meyer heads Ernst & Young's Center for Business Innovation (CBI) where Davis is a research fellow. CBI is an 'R&D shop' which aims to identify the issues that will be challenging business in the future and defining responses to them. Meyer also established the Bios Group, Ernst & Young's initiative to develop complexity-based solutions for management.

The classic

From Dale Carnegie to Stephen Covey, Frederick Taylor to Michael Porter, business book readers have been weaned on a diet of prescriptions for success. Books are distilled down to a handful of key points or simple models. 'This is the way to do it', promises the expert author, 'Believe me. I have the case studies to prove that it works.' In most business books, there is little room for the vagaries of reality, the inherent messiness of business life. Readers, publishers appear to believe, want the clinical reassurance of bullet-points. They relish tidiness and order. They want the certainty of being told what to do.

The trouble is that lists of the essential ingredients for success are becoming increasingly more questionable. At a time when uncertainty is a universal business experience whether you are in Tokyo, Munich or Dallas, the certainty of prescriptions has the hollow ring of a placebo. Bullet points have become meaningless wish lists. Tidiness and order (if they ever existed) are elusive.

Without their backbone of certainty most business books collapse in a heap. Uncertainty is uncharted territory. For the first-time traveller, it is bedevilled by ambiguity, abstract thoughts, unusual metaphors, and a distinct unwillingness to launch into a short sharp diagnosis followed by an equally pithy prescription. The journey is harder and as likely to leave the reader with even more questions as to provide any answers. Stan Davis and Christopher Meyer's *Blur* is a book of the new breed. Nowhere is this more evident than in the book's title.[1] *Blur* would not even have been considered as a possible title just a few years ago when blind faith and certainty ruled. It would have been too weak, too suggestive of managerial confusion and impotence; too realistic.

For a book about the future, Davis and Meyer are candid about their lack of answers: 'We are not offering the ultimate word on our topics, but a starting point: provocative ideas, observations, and predictions to get you to think creatively about your business and your future.' There is an array of questions, delivered with a suggestion of urgency in keeping with Davis and Meyer's central themes.

At the heart of *Blur* are three forces: connectivity, speed, and intangibles ('the derivatives of time, space, and mass'). According to Davis and Meyer, this triad 'are blurring the rules and redefining our businesses and our lives. They are destroying solutions, such as mass production, segmented pricing, and standardized jobs, that worked for the relatively slow, unconnected industrial world.' The three forces are shaping the behaviour of the new economy. They are affecting what Davis and Meyer label 'the blur of desires; the blur of fulfilment; and the blur of resources'.

The 'blur of desires' has two central elements: the offer and the exchange. These were once clear-cut. In the product-dominated age, a company offered a product for sale. Money was exchanged and the customer disappeared into the distance. Now products and services are often indistinguishable from each other and buyers and sellers are in a constantly evolving relationship ('mutual exchange') which is driven by information and emotion as well as by money.

The second aspect of the new economic reality is 'the blur of fulfilment'. As organizations change to meet changing demands so, too, must the entire theory and practice of competitive strategy. Connectivity produces different forms of organization operating to different first principles. 'The blur of businesses has created a new economic model in which returns increase rather than diminish; supermarkets mimic stock markets; and you want the market – not your strategy – to price, market, and manage your offer', write Davis and Meyer.

The third leg to the economic stool is that of resources and the emergence of intellectual capital as the key resource. Hard assets have become intangibles; intangibles have become your only assets.

Blur portrays an unsettling world. Strangely, the disturbing element at its core is not the one you most expect. 'Built to last now means built to change', say Davis and Meyer. But change, and the ambiguity it brings, no longer carries the huge weight it did only a few years ago. We may lament the rapidity of change but it was ever thus – a point reinforced when Davis and Meyer quote Joseph Schumpeter's definition of capitalism as 'Gales of creative destruction'. The gales have been howling since time immemorial.

The surprisingly disturbing thing about *Blur* is the concept – and fast emerging reality – of connectivity. Understanding connectivity is like coming to terms with the childhood revelation that we are all, somewhere along the line, related. A whole new family suddenly emerges before you go on to ponder the awful impossibility of it all. In the information economy mapped out by Davis and Meyer, small things are connected in a myriad of ways to create a 'complex adaptive system'. Instantaneous, myriad connections are speeding the economy up and, more critically, changing the way it works.

The trouble is that the connections are so many and so complex that they can bring things to a grinding, inexplicable halt. The randomness is disturbing, but the reality so poignantly mapped out by Stan Davis and Christopher Meyer in *Blur* is one without safety nets.

Note

1   Davis, Stan & Meyer, Christopher, *Blur*, Capstone, Oxford, 1997.

W EDWARDS DEMING

Out of the Crisis

1982

The author

W Edwards Deming (1900–93) has a unique place among management theorists. He had an impact on industrial history in a way others only dream of. Trained as an electrical engineer, Deming then received a PhD in mathematical physics from Yale. Deming visited Japan after World War II on the invitation of General MacArthur and played a key role in the rebuilding of Japanese industry.

His impact was quickly recognized. He was awarded the Second Order of the Sacred Treasure and the Union of Japanese Scientists and Engineers instigated the annual Deming Prize in 1951.

During the fifties, Deming and the other American standard bearer of quality, Joseph Juran, conducted seminars and courses throughout Japan. Between 1950 and 1970 the Japanese Union of Scientists and Engineers taught statistical methods to 14,700 engineers and hundreds of others.

Deming, and Japanese management, were eventually 'discovered' by the West in the 1980s and then only when NBC featured a programme on the emergence of Japan as an industrial power ('If Japan can, why can't we?'). Suddenly, Western managers were seeking out every morsel of information they could find – in October 1991 *Business Week* published a bonus issue devoted exclusively to quality which sold out in a matter of days and ran to two special printings of tens of thousands of copies.

Though by now an old man, Deming travelled the world preaching his gospel to increasingly receptive audiences.

Gary Hamel on *Out of the Crisis*

'Of all the management gurus sandwiched between the covers of this book, there is only one who should be regarded as a hero by every consumer in the world – Dr Deming. He may have taken the gospel of quality to the Japanese first, but thank God his message finally penetrated the smug complacency of American and European companies. I sat in a meeting where a worried American automobile executive inquired of Dr Deming: "When will we catch our Japanese competitors?" "Hrmmph", replied Dr Deming, "do you think they're standing still?" No senior executive ever sat through one of Dr Deming's "the rot starts at the top" harangues without coming away just a little bit more humble and contrite – a good beginning on the road to total quality.'

The classic

Out of the Crisis[1] was published near to the end of W Edwards Deming's life and exists as a rather pallid representation of his lifetime's work. In *Out of the Crisis*, Deming distils quality down to a simple message. 'Profit in business comes from repeat customers, customers that boast about your product and service, and that bring friends with them', he writes. While such beguiling home truths attracted a broader audience, they are only a shadow of Deming's all-encompassing concept of what quality entails. 'The aim of this book is transformation of the style of American management', says Deming.

For Deming, quality was more than statistical control, though this was important. 'His work bridges the gap between science-based application and humanistic philosophy. Statistical quality control is as arid as it sounds. But results so spectacular as to be almost romantic flow from using these tools to improve processes in ways that minimize defects and eliminate the deadly trio of rejects, rework and recalls', stated the British management commentator, Robert Heller.[2]

The quality gospel of *Out of the Crisis* revolves around a number of basic precepts. First, if consistent quality is to be achieved senior managers must take charge of quality. Second, implementation requires a 'cascade' with training beginning at the top of the organization before moving downwards through the hierarchy. Third, the use of statistical methods of quality control is necessary so that, finally, business plans can be expanded to include clear quality goals.

As summarized in his famous Fourteen Points, quality is a way of living, the meaning of industrial life and, in particular, the meaning of management – 'Management for quality' was Deming's constant refrain. *Out of the Crisis* presents a snappy version of Deming's Fourteen Points:

1 Create constancy of purpose for improvement of product and service.
2 Adopt the new philosophy.
3 Cease dependence on inspection to achieve quality.
4 End the practice of awarding business on the basis of price tag alone. Instead, minimize total cost by working with a single supplier.
5 Improve constantly and forever every process for planning, production and service.
6 Institute training on the job.
7 Adopt and institute leadership.
8 Drive out fear.
9 Break down barriers between staff areas.
10 Eliminate slogans, exhortations and targets for the workforce.
11 Eliminate numerical quotas for the workforce and numerical goals for management.
12 Remove barriers that rob people of pride of workmanship. Eliminate the annual rating or merit system.
13 Institute a vigorous program of education and self-improvement for everyone.
14 Put everybody in the company to work to accomplish the transformation.

The simplicity of the Fourteen Points disguises the immensity of the challenge, particularly that facing management. Quality, in Deming's eyes, is not the preserve of the few but the responsibility of all. In arguing this case Deming was anticipating the fashion for empowerment. 'People all over the world think that it is the factory worker that causes problems. He is not your problem', observed Deming in a 1983 lecture. 'Ever since there has been anything such as industry, the factory worker has known that quality is what will protect his job. He knows that poor quality in the hands of the customer will lose the market and cost him his job. He knows it and lives with that fear every day. Yet he cannot do a good job. He is not allowed to do it because the management wants figures, more products, and never mind the quality.'[3]

To Deming, management is 90 per cent of the problem, a problem caused in part by the Western enthusiasm for annual performance appraisals – Deming points out that Japanese managers receive feedback every day of their working lives. 'The basic cause of sickness in American industry and resulting unemployment is failure of top management to manage. He that sells not can buy not', writes Deming.

Indeed, the Japanese culture was uniquely receptive to Deming's message for a number of reasons. Its emphasis on group rather than individual achievement enables the Japanese to share ideas and responsibility, and promotes collective ownership in a way that the West often finds difficult to contemplate let alone understand.

Deming's evangelical fervour has played a part in his work being narrowly interpreted. Managers feel ill-at-ease with his exhortations and broad philosophical goals. Even so, Deming's ideas contain echoes of many current managerial preoccupations. In 1950, for example, Deming was anticipating reengineering with his call to arms: 'Don't just make it and try to sell it. But redesign it and then again bring the process under control ... with ever-increasing quality ... The consumer is the most important part of the production line.'

The longevity of Deming's particular interpretation of quality remains open to debate. The popularity of quality as a generic good thing has tended to dilute the profundity of the changes in thinking and action propounded by Deming. Amid a host of short-lived initiatives and ungainly acronyms, managers and their organizations can appear to have firmly embraced Deming's theories. In practice this is not usually the case.

Even so, there is no questioning the enormous effect Deming's thinking has had – both in Japan and now in the West. The explosion of interest in quality in the 1980s, belated as it was, was principally stirred by Deming. 'Deming didn't invent "quality" ... but his sermons had a uniquely powerful effect because of this first pulpit and congregation: Japan and Japanese managers. Had his fellow Americans responded with the same intense application, post-war industrial history would have differed enormously,' commented Robert Heller after his death.[4]

Notes

1 Deming, W Edwards, *Out of the Crisis*, MIT Center for Advanced Engineering Study, MIT, Cambridge, MA, 1982.
2 Heller, Robert, 'Fourteen points that the West ignores at its peril', *Management Today*, March 1994.
3 Deming, W Edwards, Lecture at Utah State University, 1983.

4 Heller, Robert, 'Fourteen points that the West ignores at its peril', *Management Today*, March 1994.

PETER F DRUCKER

The Practice of Management

1954

The author

In South Korea there is a businessman who has changed his name to Drucker in the expectation that some of the brilliant insights of the Austrian-born thinker will be passed on to him. Such is the influence of Peter Ferdinand Drucker (born 1909), the major management and business thinker of the century. 'In a field packed with egomaniacs and snake-oil merchants, he remains a genuinely original thinker', observes *The Economist*.[1] Drucker has been described as 'the world's most important and influential management thinker … a guru, an international legend, and business icon'. Prolific, even in his nineties, Drucker's work is all-encompassing.

After working as a journalist in London, Drucker moved to America in 1937 and produced *Concept of the Corporation* in 1946. This ground-breaking work examined the intricate internal working of General Motors and revealed the auto-giant to be a labyrinthine social system rather than an economical machine.

His books have emerged regularly ever since. Along the way he has coined phrases such as *privatization* and *knowledge worker* and championed concepts such as *Management By Objectives*. Many of his innovations have become accepted facts of managerial life. He has celebrated huge organizations and anticipated their demise ('The Fortune 500 is over', is one of his more recent aphorisms).

'In most areas of intellectual life nobody can quite agree who is top dog. In management theory, however, there is no dispute. Peter Drucker has produced ground-breaking work in every aspect of the field', says *The Economist*.[2]

Eschewing the academic glamour of the likes of Harvard, Drucker has been a professor at Claremont Graduate School in California since 1971. He also lectures in oriental art and has an abiding passion for Jane

Austen, though his two novels were less successful than his management books.

The classic

The Practice of Management[3] is a book of huge range. Encyclopaedic in its scope and fulsome in its historical perspectives, for the humble practising executive it is both daunting and inspiring. 'Management will remain a basic and dominant institution perhaps as long as Western civilization itself survives', pronounces Peter Drucker. There is a dashing, and infectious, confidence to Drucker's tone. The book, he says in the preface, 'comes from many years of experience in working with managements'. At the time Drucker was in his early forties.

While *The Practice of Management* is important for its ideas, the tools and techniques of management, it is also important for the central role it argues management has in twentieth century society. Drucker places management and managers at the epicentre of economic activity. 'Management is also a distinct and a leading group in industrial society', he writes. 'Rarely, if ever, has a new basic institution, a new leading group, emerged as fast as has management since the turn of the century. Rarely in human history has a new institution proved indispensable so quickly.'

Bold and forthright as it is, *The Practice of Management* is also remarkable in its clarity. Drucker sets huge parameters for the art of management but reins them in through his masterly ability to return to first principles. Management may change the world, but its essence remains the same. In one of the most quoted and memorable paragraphs in management literature, Drucker gets to the heart of the meaning of business life. 'There is only one valid definition of business purpose: to create a customer. Markets are not created by God, nature or economic forces, but by businessmen. The want they satisfy may have been felt by the customer before he was offered the means of satisfying it. It may indeed, like the want of food in a famine, have dominated the customer's life and filled all his waking moments. But it was a theoretical want before; only when the action of businessmen makes it an effective demand is there a customer, a market.'

Drucker argues that, since the role of business is to create customers, its only two essential functions are marketing and innovation. In 1954 he wrote: 'Marketing is not a function, it is the whole business seen from the customer's point of view.' As markets have matured and become more competitive, especially during the 1990s, this 40-year-old concept has become increasingly widely accepted. (In his famous 1960 article 'Marketing myopia', Harvard's Ted Levitt acknowledges his debt to Drucker's championing of marketing.)

Drucker also provides an evocatively simple insight into the nature and *raison d'être* of organizations: 'Organization is not an end in itself, but a means to an end of business performance and business results. Organization structure is an indispensable means, and the wrong structure will seriously impair business performance and may even destroy it ... The first question in discussing organization structure must be: What is our business and what should it be? Organization structure must be designed so as to make possible the attainment of the objectives of the business for five, ten, fifteen years hence.'

In *The Practice of Management* and the equally enormous, *Management: Tasks, Responsibilities and Practices* in 1973, Drucker establishes five basics of the managerial role: to set objectives; to organize; to motivate and communicate; to measure; and to develop people. 'The function which distinguishes the manager above all others is his educational one', he writes. 'The one contribution he is uniquely expected to make is to give others vision and ability to perform. It is vision and moral responsibility that, in the last analysis, define the manager.' This morality is reflected in the five areas identified by Drucker 'in which practices are required to ensure the right spirit throughout management organization:

'1 There must be high performance requirements; no condoning of poor or mediocre performance; and rewards must be based on performance.
'2 Each management job must be a rewarding job in itself rather than just a step on the promotion ladder.
'3 There must be a rational and just promotion system.
'4 Management needs a 'charter' spelling out clearly who has the power to make 'life-and-death' decisions affecting a manager; and there should be some way for a manager to appeal to a higher court.
'5 In its appointments, management must demonstrate that it realizes that integrity is the one absolute requirement of a manager, the one quality that he has to bring with him and cannot be expected to acquire later on.'

At the time, the idea from The *Practice of Management* which was seized upon was what became known as Management By Objectives (MBO). 'A manager's job should be based on a task to be performed in order to attain the company's objectives ... the manager should be directed and

---

Gary Hamel on *The Practice of Management*

'No other writer has contributed as much to the "professionalization" of management as Peter Drucker. Drucker's commitment to
the discipline of management grew out of his belief that industrial
organizations would become, and would continue to be, the world's
most important social organizations – more influential, more encom-
passing, and often more intrusive than either church or state. Professor
Drucker bridges the theoretical and the practical, the analytical and
the emotive, the private and the social more perfectly than any other
management writer.'

---

controlled by the objectives of performance rather than by his boss',
Drucker writes.

Lacking the populist trend of snappy abbreviation, Drucker always
refers to 'management by objectives and self control'. Drucker's inspiration for the idea of MBO was Harold Smiddy of General Electric whom
Drucker knew well. He also acknowledges Alfred Sloan, Pierre DuPont
and Donaldson Brown of DuPont as practitioners of MBO.

As MBO became popularized, interpretations became more narrow
than that proposed by Drucker. 'The performance that is expected of the
manager must be derived from the performance goal of the business, his
results must be measured by the contribution they make to the success
of the enterprise. The manager must know and understand what the
business goals demand of him in terms of performance and his superior
must know what contribution to demand and expect of him – and must
judge him accordingly', he writes.

In practice, the personal element in Drucker's interpretation of
MBO was subsumed by the corporate. Instead of being a pervasive means
of understanding, motivation and satisfaction, MBO became a simplistic
means of setting a corporate goal and heading towards it.

With its examinations of GM, Ford and others, Drucker's audience
and world-view in *The Practice of Management* is resolutely that of the
large corporation. The world has moved on. In *Liberation Management*,
Tom Peters describes the book as 'one long diatribe against intuition
– and one long paean to hyperrational approaches to harnessing large
numbers of people in large organizations'.[4] While this is largely true,
The Practice of Management is critical of overly hierarchical organizations
– Drucker recommends seven layers as the maximum necessary for any
organization.

Drucker also identifies 'seven new tasks' for the manager of the future. Given that these were laid down over 40 years ago, their prescience is astounding. Drucker writes that tomorrow's managers must:

'1 Manage by objectives
'2 Take more risks and for a longer period ahead
'3 Be able to make strategic decisions
'4 Be able to built an integrated team, each member of which is capable of managing and of measuring his own performance and results in relation to the common objectives
'5 Be able to communicate information fast and clearly
'6 Traditionally a manager has been expected to know one or more functions. This will no longer be enough. The manager of the future must be able to see the business as a whole and to integrate his function with it.
'7 Traditionally a manager has been expected to know a few products or one industry. This, too, will no longer be enough.'

In 1973 Drucker re-evaluated some of his conclusions in *Management: Tasks, Responsibilities and Practices,* an equally impressive examination of the role and nature of management. However, *The Practice of Management* remains more complete in that it laid the groundwork for many of the developments in management thinking during the sixties.

Asked about how management has moved on since his first book was published some 60 years ago, Drucker summarized: 'I see four great changes. First, the end of orthodoxy in the management principle, as a way of organizing and managing people. The idea of the Frenchman Henri Fayol, at the beginning of the 20th century, that there was only one single "correct" type of organization, is not useful anymore. Today we don't believe that anymore. The organization is not something by itself: it's a tool. The second big change relates with the shift of the gravity center in the equation of the "information technologies", with the weight of the "T" from technologies shifting to the "I" from information. Broadly speaking, people tend to look "technocratically" at the information society, thinking about computers and the Internet as "technology" tools. But a new information revolution is underway. But it is not mainly a revolution in technology, machines, techniques, software, speed. It's a concept revolution. Not understanding this is why many people in top management positions continue to face IT as data processing, instead of understanding that they are information and knowledge sources, leading to new and different issues, new and different strategies. Back to the changes I foresee. The third one is a return to "casual" times of turbulence. Ongoing stability is the exception in history! The problem is that the great majority of people cannot adapt to this return of history to its "normal" course … of turbulence.'

And finally? 'The understanding that the growth areas of the 20th century in developed countries were not linked to the business world. There were others: governments, liberal professions, health, education, areas where good management is dramatically lacking. And I think that the most promising area in the next century will be the non-profit social industry.'[5]

Notes

1 'Good guru guide', *The Economist*, 25 December–7 January 1994.
2 'Peter Drucker, salvationist', *The Economist*, 1 October 1994.
3 Drucker, Peter F, *The Practice of Management*, Harper & Row, New York, 1954.
4 Peters, Tom, *Liberation Management*, Alfred P Knopf, New York, 1992.
5 Interview with Jorge Nascimento Rodrigues 2000.

PETER F DRUCKER

The Age of Discontinuity

1969

The classic

Most business and management books report on what already exists. They examine and prod the same corporate superstars from similar angles. Few deal convincingly with the future. Instead, the future is left to 'futurists': the business equivalent of sci-fi writers rather than serious novelists. They are flaky and beyond the academic pale.

The trouble with predicting the future is that it requires going out on a limb. Most academics and consultants cling to the safety of the tree. Meanwhile Peter Drucker has been dancing at the furthermost limbs for decades. He has gazed into the future and been proved right – though like anyone so prolific he has also got it wrong and changed his mind along the way.

The highpoint of Drucker's future-gazing was *The Age of Discontinuity*.[1] Published in 1969, the book effectively mapped out the demise of the age of mass, labour-based production and the advent of the knowledge-based, information age. Somewhat inevitably, no-one paid much attention – Drucker's influence has not always been matched by huge book sales. The complacent corporate world of the late 1960s was not ready for change.

In *The Age of Discontinuity*, Drucker coined the term 'knowledge worker'. This, in theory, was a new breed of thoughtful, intelligent executive. The knowledge worker was a highly trained, intelligent managerial professional who realized his or her own worth and contribution to the organization. In effect, Drucker bade farewell to the concept of the manager as mere supervisor or paper shuffler. The manager was reincarnated as a responsible individual (though, in those pre-PC days, not yet as a woman). 'Though the knowledge worker is not a *laborer*, and certainly not *proletarian*, he is not a *subordinate* in the sense that he can be told what

Gary Hamel on *The Age of Discontinuity*

'Peter Drucker's reputation is as a management theorist. He has also been a management prophet. Writing in 1969 he clearly anticipated the emergence of the 'knowledge economy'. I'd like to set a challenge for would-be management gurus: Try to find something to say that Peter Drucker has not said first, and has not said well. This high hurdle should substantially reduce the number of business books clogging the bookshelves of booksellers, and offer managers the hope of gaining some truly fresh insights.'

to do; he is paid, on the contrary, for applying his knowledge, exercising his judgement, and taking responsible leadership', Drucker wrote. As a pithy summary of the role of the manager, this is as applicable now as it was thirty years ago.

Drucker's realization that the role of the manager had fundamentally changed was not a sudden one. Indeed, the foundations of the idea of the knowledge worker can be seen in his description of Management By Objectives in his 1950s *magnum opus, The Practice of Management,* where the worth, motivation and aspirations of the executive are integral to corporate success.

Of course, knowledge management, intellectual capital and the like are now the height of corporate fashion. Our modern perspective on the knowledge worker is of a creature of the technological age, the mobile executive, the hot-desker. Knowledge is easily equated with IT-power and the size of corporate databases. Drucker provided a characteristically broader perspective. He placed the rise of the knowledge worker in the evolution of management into a respectable and influential discipline. (Indeed, Drucker's lifetime of work has been dedicated to nurturing appreciation of the role and influence of management in society.)

'The knowledge worker sees himself just as another *professional,* no different from the lawyer, the teacher, the preacher, the doctor or the government servant of yesterday', Drucker wrote. 'He has the same education. He has more income, he has probably greater opportunities as well. He may well realize that he depends on the organization for access to income and opportunity, and that without the investment the organization has made – and a high investment at that – there would be no job for him, but he also realises, and rightly so, that the organization equally depends on him.' Drucker effectively wrote the obituary for obedient, grey-suited, loyal, corporate man. The only trouble was it took corporate man another 20 years to die.

Typically, Drucker pointed to the social ramifications of this new breed of corporate executive. If knowledge, rather than labour, is the new measure of economic society then the fabric of capitalist society must change: 'The knowledge worker is both the true *capitalist* in the knowledge society and dependent on his job. Collectively the knowledge workers, the employed educated middle-class of today's society, own the means of production through pension funds, investment trusts, and so on.' Drucker recognized that knowledge was not only power, but it was also ownership.

Drucker has since developed his thinking on the role of knowledge – most notably in his 1992 book, *Managing for the Future* in which he observed: 'From now on the key is knowledge. The world is becoming not labor intensive, not materials intensive, not energy intensive, but knowledge intensive.'

The Age of Discontinuity was startlingly correct in its predictions. Much of it would fit easily into business books of today – 'Businessmen will have to learn to build and manage innovative organizations', predicted Drucker, echoing today's familiar refrain from a score of thinkers.

More recently, Drucker has commented: 'With the knowledge worker, the issue of ownership of the production process has been inverted. He now owns the production process which is his own knowledge. The "alienation" the Marxists fought doesn't make sense anymore for the people who own knowledge, mostly a high and specialized knowledge. The manual workers of capitalism did not have this ownership, but they had a great deal of experience, which only had an economic value in the place they worked in, it wasn't "portable". Now knowledge is completely portable and the knowledge worker is not just one more "asset", in the traditional meaning of the word. He cannot be bought or sold.'[2]

The Age of Discontinuity was also notable for Drucker's criticisms of business schools – another theme which he has since developed. 'The business schools in the US, set up less than a century ago, have been preparing well-trained clerks', he wrote. Again, the debate about the role of business school rumbles on. More significantly, Drucker introduced the idea of privatization – though he labelled it, with customary exactitude, *reprivatization*. This was energetically seized upon by politicians in the 1980s, though their interpretation of privatization went far beyond that envisaged by Drucker. He also argued the case for minimal government – a constant political refrain of more recent years.

In *The Age of Discontinuity*, Drucker uncovered fundamental trends which no-one else had even noticed. The book provides a far-reaching insight into the business world which largely now exists. In his 1990 book, *Managing on the Edge*, Richard Pascale simply accepted the accuracy of Drucker's insights, commenting: 'Peter Drucker's book *The Age of Discontinuity* describes the commercial era in which we live.' Drucker was proved right sooner than even he probably expected. Discontinuity – in the shape of the oil crisis – was just around the corner.

Notes

1 Drucker, Peter F, *The Age of Discontinuity*, Heinemann, London, 1969.
2 Interview with Jorge Nascimento Rodrigues, 2000.

HENRI FAYOL

General and Industrial Management

1916

The author

enri Fayol (1841–1925) was educated in Lyon, France and at the National School of Mines in St. Etienne. In 1860 he graduated as a mining engineer and joined the French mining company, Commentry-Fourchamboult-Décazeville. He spent his entire working career with the company and was its managing director between 1888 and 1918. During that time he produced the 'functional principle', the first rational approach to the organization of enterprise. His studies led to lectures at the Ecole Supérieure de la Guerre and to an examination of the public services.

The origins of *General and Industrial Management* can be traced back to 1900 when Fayol delivered a speech at a mining conference. When he gave a developed version of his ideas at a 1908 conference, 2,000 copies were immediately reprinted to satisfy demand. By 1925, 15,000 copies had been printed and a book was published.

Igor Ansoff has noted that Fayol 'anticipated imaginatively and soundly most of the more recent analyses of modern business practice'.[1]

The classic

While, across the Atlantic, Frederick Taylor examined the tasks of steel workers, France's Henri Fayol created a system of management encapsulated in *General and Industrial Management*.[2] Indeed, Fayol put management at the centre of the organization in a way never envisaged by Taylor. 'Management plays a very important part in the government of undertakings; of all undertakings, large or small, industrial, commercial, political, religious or any other', he writes.

Fayol's system was based on acceptance of and adherence to different functions (and was later influential on Alfred P Sloan at General Motors). 'All activities to which industrial undertakings give rise can be divided into the following six groups', writes Fayol. The six functions which he identifies are:

- technical activities
- commercial activities
- financial activities
- security activities
- accounting activities
- managerial activities.

'The management function is quite distinct from the other five essential functions', notes Fayol. 'To manage is to forecast and plan, to organize, to command, to co-ordinate and to control.' This brief résumé of what constitutes management has largely held sway throughout the twentieth century. Only now is it being seriously questioned and challenged.

From his observations, Fayol also produces general principles of management:

- division of work
- authority and responsibility
- discipline
- unity of command
- unity of direction
- subordination of individual interest to general interest
- remuneration of personnel
- centralization
- scalar chain (line of authority)
- order
- equity
- stability of tenure of personnel
- initiative
- *esprit de corps.*

Fayol's methods were later exposed by Drucker who observed: 'If used beyond the limits of Fayol's model, functional structure becomes costly in terms of time and effort.' While this is undoubtedly true, Fayol's observations and conclusions are important. He talks of 'ten yearly forecasts … revised every five years' – one of the first instances of business planning in practice and writes: 'The maxim, "managing means looking ahead", gives some idea of the importance attached to planning in the business world, and it is true that if foresight is not the whole of management at least it is an essential part of it.'

In *The Principles and Practice of Management,* one of the first comprehensive studies of the fledgling years of management thinking, its editor E F L Brech notes: 'The importance of Fayol's contribution lay in two features: the first was his systematic analysis of the process of management; the second, his firm advocacy of the principle that management can, and should, be taught. Both were revolutionary lines of thought in 1908, and still little accepted in 1925.'[4]

Fayol's championing of management was highly important. While Frederick Taylor regarded managers as little more than overseers with limited responsibility, Fayol regarded their role as critical to organizational success. In his faith in carefully defined functions, Fayol was systematizing business organization in ways which worked at the time, but proved too limiting and restraining in the long-term.

Notes

1 'The corporate sages', *Business,* September 1988.
2 Originally published in French as *Administration Industrielle et Générale* (1916) and first published in English as *General and Industrial Management,* Pitman, London, 1949.
3 'The corporate sages', *Business,* September 1988.
4 Brech, E F L (ed.), *The Principles and Practice of Management,* Longman, London, 1953.

MARY PARKER FOLLETT

Dynamic Administration

1941

The author

Born in Quincy, Massachusetts, Mary Parker Follett (1868–1933) attended Thayer Academy and the Society for the Collegiate Instruction of Women in Cambridge (now part of Harvard). She spent time at England's Cambridge University and in Paris. Her first published work was *The Speaker of the House of Representatives* (1896), which she wrote while still a student.

Follett's career was largely spent in social work, though her books appeared regularly – *The New State* (1918), an influential description of Follett's brand of dynamic democracy, and *Creative Experience* (1924), Follett's first business-oriented book. In her later years she was in great demand as a lecturer. After the death of a long-time partner, Isobel Briggs, in 1926, she moved to London.

Follett's work was largely neglected in the West, but she was honoured in Japan, where there is a Follett Society. Her work has now been brought to a wider audience through the UK academic Pauline Graham – in 1994, Graham edited *Mary Parker Follett: Prophet of Management*[1] a compendium of Follett's writings with commentaries from a host of contemporary figures including Kanter, Drucker and Mintzberg.

The classic

Mary Parker Follett's work stands as a humane counterpoint to that of Frederick Taylor and the proponents of Scientific Management. Follett was a female, liberal humanist in an era dominated by reactionary males intent on mechanizing the world of business. 'We should remember that we can never wholly separate the human from the mechanical sides', warns Follett in *Dynamic Administration*.[2] 'The study of human relations in business and the study of the technology of operating are bound up together.'

During her life, Mary Parker Follett's thinking on management was generally ignored – though in Japan there was a great deal of interest in her perspectives. In her advocacy of human relations she was ahead of her time, something acknowledged by E F L Brech in his book *The Principles and Practice of Management*. 'Mary Follett, broadly, was less interested in the practice of management than in the extent to which the everyday incidents and problems reflected the presence or absence of sound principle. She was chiefly concerned to teach principles in simple language, amply illustrated from everyday events – not the mechanics of management, but its special human character, its nature as a social process, deeply embedded in the emotions of man and in the interrelations to which the everyday working of industry necessarily gives rise – at manager levels, at worker levels, and, of course, between the two,' writes Brech. 'Bearing in mind she was speaking of America in the early 1920s, her thinking can be described as little less than revolutionary, and certainly a generation ahead of its time. There is no evidence that Mary Follett had any contact with the persons who sponsored or conducted the Hawthorne Investigations, but the findings of those investigations, when they appeared in their full form in the 1930s, were a striking testimony to the soundness of her teaching.'[3]

Published eight years after her death, *Dynamic Administration* is a collection of Follett's papers on management gathered from 12 lectures between 1925 and 1933. It includes a great deal of forthright and resoundingly contemporary-sounding comments. 'I think we should undepartmentalize our thinking in regard to every problem that comes to us', says Follett. 'I do not think that we have psychological and ethical and economic problems. We have human problems, with psychological, ethical and economical aspects, and as many others as you like.'

Follett advocates giving greater responsibility to people – at a time when the mechanical might of mass production was at its height. 'Responsibility is the great developer of men', she writes. There is also a modern ring to Follett's advice on leadership: 'The most successful leader of all is one who sees another picture not yet actualized.' Follett suggests that a leader is someone who sees the whole rather than the particular, organizes the experiences of the group, offers a vision of the future and trains followers to become leaders. Leading should be a two-way, mutually beneficial process. 'We want worked out a relation between leaders and led which will give to each the opportunity to make creative contributions to the situation', she writes in *Dynamic Administration*.

Gary Hamel on *Dynamic Administration*

'The work of Mary Parker Follett is refreshingly different from that of her peers. She was the first modern thinker to get us close to the human soul of management. She had the heart of a humanist, not an engineer.'

'Follett sent one principal message: relationships matter', says Rosabeth Moss Kanter. 'Underpinning all of her work is the importance of relationships, not just transactions, in organizations. She pointed to the reciprocal nature of relationships, the mutual influence developed when people work together, however formal authority is defined.'[4]

In particular, Follett explores conflict. She argues that, as conflict is a fact of life, 'we should, I think, use it to work for us'. Follett points out three ways of dealing with confrontation: domination, compromise or integration. The latter, she concludes, is the only positive way forward. This can be achieved by first 'uncovering' the real conflict and then taking 'the demands of both sides and breaking them up into their constituent parts'. 'Our outlook is narrowed, our activity is restricted, our chances of business success largely diminished when our thinking is constrained within the limits of what has been called an either-or situation. We should never allow ourselves to be bullied by an "either-or". There is often the possibility of something better than either of two given alternatives', Follett writes.

To some, Follett remains a utopian idealist, out of touch with reality; to others, she is a torchbearer of good sense whose ideas have sadly not had significant impact on organizations. 'Integration requires understanding, in-depth understanding', says Henry Mintzberg. 'It requires serious commitment and dedication. It takes effort, and it depends on creativity. There is precious little of all of these qualities in too many of our organizations today.'[5]

Notes

1 Graham, Pauline (ed.), *Mary Parker Follett: Prophet of Management*, Harvard Business School Press, Cambridge, MA, 1994.
2 Follett, Mary Parker, *Dynamic Administration* (eds Fox, Elliot & Urwick, Lyndall), Harper & Bros., New York, 1941.

3 Brech, E F L (ed.), *The Principles and Practice of Management*, Longman, London, 1953.
4 Graham, Pauline (ed.), *Mary Parker Follett: Prophet of Management*, Harvard Business School Press, Cambridge, MA, 1994.
5 Graham, Pauline (ed.), *Mary Parker Follett: Prophet of Management*, Harvard Business School Press, Cambridge, MA, 1994.

HENRY FORD

My Life and Work

1923

The author

After spending time as a machinist's apprentice, a watch repairer and a mechanic, Henry Ford (1863–1947) built his first car in 1896. Initially, Ford was fascinated by the mechanical possibilities and drove racing cars. Quickly he became convinced of the commercial potential and started his own company in 1899. Through innovative use of new mass production techniques, between 1908 and 1927 Ford produced 15 million Model Ts. In 1919 Ford resigned as the company's President with his son, Edsel, taking over. By then the Ford company was making a car a minute.

The classic

My Life and Work[1] was published in Henry Ford's sixtieth year when he bestrode the modern industrial world like a colossus. It is a robust account of his life and business philosophy. Indeed, it is notable for the dominance of the former and the lack of the latter.

Ford's business thinking is simply expressed: 'Our policy is to reduce the price, extend the operations, and improve the article', he writes. 'You will notice that the reduction of price comes first. We have never considered any costs as fixed. Therefore we first reduce the price to the point where we believe more sales will result. Then we go ahead and try to make the prices. We do not bother about the costs. The new price forces the costs down. The more usual way is to take the costs and then determine the price, and, although that method may be scientific in the narrow sense, it is not scientific in the broad sense, because what earthly use is it to know the cost if it tells you that you cannot manufacture at a price at which the article can be sold?' Ford's commitment to lowering

Gary Hamel on *My Life and Work*

'Henry Ford may have been autocratic and paranoid, but he brought to men and women everywhere a stunningly precious gift – mobility. Whatever his faults, Henry Ford was driven by the dream of every great entrepreneur – to make a real difference in people's lives – and to do it globally.'

prices cannot be doubted. Between 1908 and 1916 he reduced prices by 58 per cent – at a time when demand was such that he could easily have raised prices.

The above extract from *My Life and Work* was quoted by Ted Levitt in his article 'Marketing myopia'. In it, he provides an unconventional interpretation of Ford's gifts. 'In a sense Ford was both the most brilliant and the most senseless marketer in American history. He was senseless because he refused to give the customer anything but a black car. He was brilliant because he fashioned a production system designed to fit market needs. We habitually celebrate him for the wrong reason, his production genius. His real genius was marketing … mass production was the result not the cause of his low prices.'[2]

Ford's masterly piece of marketing lay in his intuitive realization that the mass car market existed – it just remained for him to provide the products the market wanted. In management jargon, Ford stuck to the knitting. Model Ts were black, straightforward and affordable. At the centre of Ford's thinking was the aim of standardization – something continually emphasized by the car makers of today, though they talk in terms of quality, and Ford in quantity.

'I have no use for a motor car which has more spark plugs than a cow has teats', said Ford. The trouble was that, when other manufacturers added extras, Ford kept it simple and dramatically lost ground.

The company's reliance on the Model T nearly drove it to self-destruction even though at one time Ford had cash reserves of $1 billion. Henry Ford is reputed to have kicked a slightly modified Model T to pieces such was his commitment to the unadulterated version. The man with a genius for marketing lost touch with the aspirations of customers.

More conventionally, Ford is celebrated – if that is the right word – for his transformation of the production line into a means of previously unimagined mass production. Production, in the Ford company's huge plant, was based round strict functional divides – demarcations. Ford believed in people getting on with their jobs and not raising their heads above functional parapets. He didn't want engineers talking to salespeople, or people making decisions without his say so.

In *My Life and Work* Ford gives a chilling insight into his own unforgiving logic. He calculates that the production of a Model T requires 78,882 different operations. Of these, 949 require 'strong, able-bodied, and practically physical perfect men' and 3,338 require 'ordinary physical strength'. The remainder, says Ford, could be undertaken by 'women or older children' and 'we found that 670 could be filled by legless men, 2,637 by one-legged men, two by armless men, 715 by one-armed men and 10 by blind men'.

With characteristic forthrightness, management and managers were dismissed by Ford as largely unnecessary. 'Fundamental to Henry Ford's misrule was a systematic, deliberate and conscious attempt to run the billion-dollar business without managers. The secret police that spied on all Ford executives served to inform Henry Ford of any attempt on the part of one of his executives to make a decision,' noted Peter Drucker in *The Practice of Management.*[3] Ford's lack of faith in management proved the undoing of the huge corporate empire he assembled. Without his autocratic belligerence to drive the company forward, it quickly ground to a halt.

Even so, Ford's achievements are not in doubt. 'In some respects Ford remains a good role model', says Ray Wild, principal of Henley Management College. 'He was an improviser and innovator, he borrowed ideas and then adapted and synthesized them. He developed flow lines that involved people; now, we have flow lines without people, but no-one questions their relevance or importance. Though he is seen as having de-humanized work, it shouldn't be forgotten that he provided a level of wealth for workers and products for consumers which weren't previously available.' Among his many innovations was a single human one: Ford introduced the $5 wage for his workers which, at that time, was around twice the average for the industry.

Ford will never be celebrated for his humanity or people management skills. But, in the realms of business, he had an international perspective which was ahead of his time. His plant at Highland Park, Detroit, produced – the world, not just the US, bought. Also, Ford was acutely aware that time was an important competitive weapon – 'Time waste differs from material waste in that there can be no salvage', he observed. Ford's business achievements and contribution to the development of industrialization are likely to be remembered long after his theories on politics, history, motivation or humanity.

Notes

1 Ford, Henry, *My Life and Work*, Doubleday, Page & Co., New York, 1923.
2 Levitt, Ted, 'Marketing myopia', *Harvard Business Review*, July-August 1960.
3 Drucker, Peter F, *The Practice of Management*, Harper & Row, New York, 1954.

HAROLD GENEEN

Managing

1984

The author

arold Geneen (1910–97) was born in Bournemouth, but became the quintessential hard-nosed American business executive. He qualified as an accountant after studying at night school and then began climbing the executive career ladder working at American Can, Bell & Howell, Jones & Laughlin and finally Raytheon, which was taken over by ITT. ITT had started life in 1920 as a Caribbean telephone company. Geneen joined the board of ITT in 1959 and set about turning the company into the world's greatest conglomerate. Along the way, he became, according to *Business Week*, the 'legendary conglomerateur'.

The classic

The management gospel according to Harold Geneen was encapsulated in *Managing*. It was unforgiving, built on a degree of intellectual rigour which borders on ruthlessness. Geneen pinned his managerial faith on hard work and knowing every single figure possible. He was the archetypal workaholic – 'Putting deals together beats spending every day playing golf' – and, even in his late eighties, worked a ten-hour day at his office in New York's Waldorf-Astoria Hotel. For Geneen, detail was all. Once an accountant, always an accountant.

The conglomerate was not Geneen's invention. But he brought an obsessional belief that it could be made to work. He believed that ITT could manage any business in any industry if it knew the figures. His career with ITT, described in *Managing*, is a pageant of acquisition and diversification. Under Geneen, ITT bought companies as casually as a billionaire buys trinkets. ITT's spending spree amounted to 350 companies and included Avis Rent-A-Car, Sheraton Hotels, Continental Baking and Levitt & Sons among many others. By 1970 ITT was composed of 400 separate companies operating in 70 countries. The ball just kept on rolling. One acquisition funded another.

With such huge numbers of companies in such vastly different fields, ITT was hopelessly diversified. To contemporary eyes, in particular, the company was a managerial nightmare. Yet Geneen made the nightmare work. He did so by fanatical attention to detail. He micro-managed – but he only micro-managed the numbers; the people were generally over-looked. 'The very fact that you go over the progression of those numbers week after week, month after month, means that you have strengthened your memory and your familiarity with them so that you retain in your mind a vivid composite picture of what is going on in your company', said Geneen. If you knew the numbers inside out, you knew the company inside out.

Geneen inculcated a remarkable culture within ITT. His success meant that people followed his methods with the unquestioning faith of true believers. Between 1959 and 1977 (when Geneen stepped down as chief executive) ITT's sales went from $765 million to nearly $28 billion. Earnings went from $29 million to $562 million and earnings per share rose from $1 to $4.20. Such success could not be argued with.

As part of Geneen's formula, every month over 50 executives flew to Brussels to spend four days poring over the figures. Day and night they sat, leaving no financial stone unturned. To minimize disorienta-tion, clocks were kept on New York time. It was calculated that over 200 days a year were devoted to management meetings held throughout the world. The point was to amass all the facts available so that the deci-sions became self-evident. If you knew everything, you would then know exactly what to do.

Facts were the lifeblood of the expanding ITT – and executives sweated blood in their pursuit. 'The highest art of professional manage-ment requires the literal ability to *smell* a *real fact* from all others – and, moreover, to have the temerity, intellectual curiosity, guts and/or plain impoliteness, if necessary, to be sure that what you do have is indeed what we will call an *unshakeable fact*', said Geneen.

'I want no surprises', he announced with solemnity – frivolity was not Geneen's style. Indeed, there was a strong strain of dictatorship running through his management. Geneen had a disturbingly strong belief in the rightfulness of his methods. He was blinkered in a similar way to Henry Ford. Geneen hoped to make people 'as predictable and controllable as the capital resources they must manage'. Ford moaned: 'How come when I want a pair of hands I get a human being as well?'

The methods of both worked, for a while at least. Geneen constructed a labyrinthian house of corporate cards. While others would have watched as the deck of cards fell to the ground, Geneen kept adding more cards, while managing to know the pressures and stresses each was under.

Much of Geneen's managerial philosophy and practice would appear to be anathema to the contemporary executive. After all, this is the era of human resource management rather than planning and strategic management. This is only partly true. The obsessional excesses of Geneen – such as his involvement with the CIA in Chile under Allende – are hopefully consigned to history. But his fundamentalist style of management remains. Management consultants, for example, continue to trade their rational models – pour in all the figures you can find and the right decision will emerge. There is still a temptation to manage by numbers rather than through and with people.

On the positive side, Geneen can be said to have elevated management to a new level. His system required a cadre of highly numerate, professional managers. 'Managers must manage', said Geneen. They had to take responsibility.

The Geneen legacy is most notably evident in the conglomerates which continue to survive. General Electric under Jack Welch may be the most lauded corporation of our age, but it is also a conglomerate with interests in everything from financial services to nuclear reactors and washing machines. Harold Geneen would have regarded the survival of such companies as vindication of his methods. Others point to the decline of ITT on his departure as a true measure of the long-term validity of Geneen's approach to management.

ARIE DE GEUS

The Living Company

1997

The author

The ultimate corporate man, Arie de Geus spent 38 years with Royal Dutch/Shell. (Such loyalty runs in the family – de Geus' father also worked for the company for 26 years.) De Geus is a member of the direction of the Center for Organizational Learning of the Sloan School of Management of MIT and of Nijenrode Learning Centre of Nijenrode University, and The Netherlands Business School in Holland. He is also a founding member of Global Business Network and visiting teacher at the London Business School. He is one of the founding members of the Society for Organizational Learning (SOL). Since his retirement from Shell in 1989, de Geus has headed an advisory group to the World Bank and consults with government and private institutions.

The classic

Companies may be legal entities, but they are disturbingly mortal. 'The natural average lifespan of a corporation should be as long as two or three centuries', writes Arie de Geus in *The Living Company*, noting a few prospering relics such as the Sumitomo Group and the Scandinavian company, Stora.[1] But the reality is that companies do not head off into the Florida sunset to play bingo. They usually die young.

De Geus explains the book's gestation: 'When I was at Shell, in 1983, we decided to conduct a study of corporate longevity. In that investigation we examined 27 well-documented cases of long-lived organizations. Some came from the 13th and 17th centuries, like Stora created in Sweden, Sumitomo and Mitsui in Japan. More than ten were born in the early 19th century. Our question was: how could these companies have lived so long? How was that possible? Especially given our points of contrast. For example, we found that of the 500 companies on the *Fortune* magazine list of 1970, thirteen years later one-third had disappeared, because of takeovers, fusion, or liquidation. We found this terrible statistic: on average, corporate life expectancy is less than twenty years. Recently, a student updated this Shell study and found that the average life expectancy of an organization is twelve-and-a-half years. What this means is that the companies die in their teens, in their prime. That represents the liquidation of an enormous potential; and society will pay a dear price for that.'[2]

De Geus quotes a Dutch survey of corporate life expectancy in Japan and Europe which came up with 12.5 years as the average life expectancy of all firms. 'The average life expectancy of a multinational corporation – Fortune 500 or its equivalent – is between 40 and 50 years', says de Geus, noting that one-third of 1970's Fortune 500 had disappeared by 1983. Such endemic failure is attributed by de Geus to the focus of managers on profits and the bottom line rather than the human community which makes up their organization.

In an attempt to get to the bottom of this mystery, de Geus and a number of his Shell colleagues carried out some research to identify the characteristics of corporate longevity. As you would expect, the onus is on keeping excitement to a minimum. More Ronald Reagan than James Dean. The average human centenarian advocates a life of abstinence, caution and moderation, and so it is with companies. The Royal Dutch/Shell team identified four key characteristics. The long-lived were 'sensitive to their environment'; 'cohesive, with a strong sense of identity'; 'tolerant'; and 'conservative in financing'.

Key to de Geus' entire argument is that there is more to companies – and to longevity – than mere money making. 'The dichotomy between profits and longevity is false', he says. His logic is impeccably straightforward. Capital is no longer king; the skills, capabilities and knowledge of people are. The corollary from this is that 'a successful company is one that can learn effectively'. Learning is tomorrow's capital. In de Geus' eyes, learning means being prepared to accept continuous change.

Here, de Geus provides the new deal: contemporary corporate man or woman must understand that the corporation will, and must, change and it can only change if its community of people changes also. Individuals must change and the way they change is through learning. As a result, de Geus believes that senior executives must dedicate a great deal of time nurturing their people. He recalls spending around a quarter of his time on the development and placement of people. Jack Welch claims to spend half of his time on such issues.

According to de Geus, all corporate activities are grounded in two hypotheses: 'The company is a living being; and the decisions for action made by this living being result from a learning process.' With its faith in learning, *The Living Company* represents a careful and powerful riposte to corporate nihilism.

The Living Company proposes that the wisdom of the past be appreciated and utilized rather than cast out in some cultural revolution. Contrast this with reengineering which (as practised, if not necessarily preached) sought to dismiss the past so that the future could be begun anew with a fresh piece of paper. De Geus suggests that the piece of paper already exists and notes are constantly being scrawled in the margins as new insights are added.

De Geus' arguments are probably at their weakest when he contemplates why it is that companies deserve to live long lives. After all, the average entrepreneur would probably accept a life expectancy of 12.5 years. 'Like all organisms, the living company exists primarily for its own survival and improvement: to fulfil its potential and to become as great as it can be', writes de Geus. But life is littered with failed stars. Some fall by the wayside. We can't all be great. We can't all be Shell.

The Living Company is the testimony of someone who practised the human side of enterprise and who believes that companies must be fundamentally humane to prosper, whatever the century.

Notes

1 de Geus, Arie, *The Living Company*, Harvard Business School Press, Boston, 1997.
2 Interview with Jorge Nascimento Rodrigues 2000.

FRANK GILBRETH

Motion Study

1911

The author

T ruth be told, *Motion Study* had two authors: Frank Gilbreth (1868–1924) and his wife Lillian (1878–1972). If every movement needs its zealots, the Gilbreths were the greatest disciples of Scientific Management.

The classic

The Gilbreths put Scientific Management to the test. They made an art of measurement and, in doing so, helped further confuse the borders between measurement and management. In *Fatigue Study* (1916), the Gilbreths wrote: 'The aim of life is happiness, no matter how we differ as to what happiness means. Fatigue elimination, starting as it does from a desire to conserve human life and to eliminate enormous waste, must increase "Happiness Minutes", no matter what else it does, or it has failed in its fundamental aim.'[1]

The angle pursued by the Gilbreths was what they labelled 'motion study'. Most famously, Frank Gilbreth examined bricklayers at work. He was also a bricklayer and builder – among many other accomplishments. The bricklayers were inefficient. In response, Gilbreth designed and patented scaffolding which reduced bending and reaching, and increased output by over 100 per cent. Gilbreth also invented the process flow diagram and worked with the typewriter maker, Remington, and helped develop the more efficient Dvorak keyboard.

Their analysis of motion – aided by photography – led the Gilbreths to conclude there were 16 units of movement. These units they named 'therbligs' – Gilbreth backwards and slightly altered for ease of pronunciation.

When Frank Gilbreth died in 1924, Lillian picked up where he had left off and turned herself into an exemplar of industry. Not only did she bring up their large family, but she also headed the women's division of President Hoover's Organization on Unemployment Relief (1930–32), gained various degrees and, along the way, became famous. In 1938 Gilbreth was named one of twelve women 'capable of holding the office of president of the United States'. In 1944 the *California Monthly* said Lillian was 'a genius in the art of living'.

In fact, after Frank Gilbreth's death, his consulting clients all refused to use Lillian Gilbreth as a consultant simply because she was a woman. Her response was to use this to her advantage. 'If the only way to enter a man's field was through the kitchen door, that's the way she'd enter', wrote Frank Jr and Ernestine Gilbreth in their book *Belles on Their Toes*. Lillian simply applied efficiency theories to her and her family's domestic arrangements. The children were brought up using efficiency techniques. Charts recorded if they had brushed their teeth. The children dusted the furniture before being allowed to play. Two stenographers were on hand to record Lillian's insights.

Though there was a farcical air to many of their endeavours and their blind enthusiasm took them down some unusual avenues, the Gilbreths had a powerful effect on management thinking. They elevated measurement to an all-embracing credo and helped establish it as one of the central tasks of management.

Note

1 Gilbreth, Frank and Lillian, *Fatigue Study*, Hive Publishing Company, Easton, 1973 (reprint of 1916 edn), p. 149.

DANIEL GOLEMAN

Emotional Intelligence

1995

The author

Daniel Goleman (born 1946) works with companies through the emotional intelligence practice of the Hay Group. He is also co-chairman of the Consortium for Social and Emotional Learning in the Workplace, based in the School of Professional Psychology at Rutgers University, which recommends best practices for developing emotional competence.

Goleman is both a clinical psychologist and a distinguished journalist. He has received two Pulitzer Prize nominations for his articles in the *New York Times*, a Career Achievement award for journalism from the American Psychological Association, and was elected a Fellow of the American Association for the Advancement of Science.

The classic

Emotional Intelligence is based on the notion that the ability of managers to understand and manage their own emotions and those of the people they work with is the key to better business performance. Like so many important management breakthroughs, its origins lie outside of business.

Rising rates of aggression and depression in US schools led Daniel Goleman to compile the research summarized in his 1995 book *Emotional Intelligence*. 'While covering brain and behavior research for the *New York Times*, I became aware of how little correlation existed between intelligence tests and what it takes to be successful in life', he explains. 'Study after study showed that success had surprisingly little to do with IQ (Intelligence Quotient) – IQ accounting for only about four to ten per cent of the variance. On the other hand, the ability to handle one's emotions, deal with frustration, self-awareness, self-discipline, persistence, empathy, and being able to get along with people – skills we learn as children – did appear to matter a great deal.'[1]

He concluded that human competencies like self-awareness, self-discipline, persistence and empathy are of greater consequence than IQ in much of life. Goleman asserted that we ignore the emotional competencies at our peril, and that children can – and should – be taught these abilities at school.

The groundbreaking book did much to raise awareness of the concept of Emotional Intelligence in the business community. The new interest is reflected in the growing number of business books and articles on the subject. Goleman himself is now a rising star in the management guru constellation. *Emotional Intelligence* was on *The New York Times* bestseller list for 18 months, and was translated into nearly 30 languages. The term is now finding its way into management development programmes and onto business school curricula.

Goleman, a psychologist by training, built on the ideas of the Harvard-based psychologist Howard Gardner – credited with the development of the multiple intelligence theory – and the Yale psychologist, Peter Salovey. In his book, he adopts Salovey's definition of emotional intelligence. According to Salovey, E.I. can be observed in five key areas: knowing one's emotions; managing emotions; motivating oneself; recognizing emotions in others; and handling relationships.

'The emotional climate is more important to the success of an organization than previously recognized', says Goleman. 'In particular, the emotional dimension is critical in determining the effectiveness of leaders. In jobs where above-average I.Q. is a given, superior emotional capability gives leaders an edge. At senior levels, emotional intelligence rather than rational intelligence marks out the true leader. And the best news is that emotional intelligence can be learned. My previous work had not focused on leaders per se, but on people in jobs of all kinds. Leadership puts unique demands on people that makes how well they handle themselves and others of paramount importance. Leadership is the art of getting work done through other people: it's a relationship capability.'[2]

Goleman has gone on to explore the issue of personal and professional effectiveness. In a business world too often obsessed by cold analysis and intellect, he argues, the emotional climate is more important to the success of an organization than previously recognized. His 1998 book, *Working With Emotional Intelligence* argues that workplace competencies based on emotional intelligence play a far greater role in star performance than do intellect or technical skill, and that both individuals and companies will benefit from cultivating these capabilities.

In particular, he claims that the emotional dimension is critical in determining the effectiveness of leaders, arguing that, in demanding jobs where above average IQ is a given, superior emotional capability gives leaders an edge. At senior levels, 'emotional intelligence' rather than 'rational intelligence' marks out the true leader.

According to Goleman, studies of outstanding performers in organizations show that about two-thirds of the abilities that set star performers apart in the leadership stakes are based on emotional intelligence; only one-third of the skills that matter relate to raw intelligence (as measured by IQ) and technical expertise.

'Our emotions are hardwired into our being', he explains. 'The very architecture of the brain gives feelings priority over thought.' In reality, it is impossible to entirely separate thought from emotion. 'We can be effective only when the two systems – our emotional brain and our thinking brain – work together. That working relationship, which encompasses most of what we do in life, is the essence of emotional intelligence.'

Goleman takes his analysis further, applying it to the elusive role of leadership. He argues that part of the problem is that pontification and hypotheses have generally been the currency of leadership theorists rather than hard data. This, it must be said, is generally true. The average book on leadership is more likely to feature Churchillian quotations than rigorous analysis of the behaviour of leaders. Goleman redresses the balance with his research covering over 3000 executives. From this, Goleman identifies six separate leadership styles:

> 'Coercive leaders demand immediate compliance. Authoritative leaders mobilise people towards a vision. Affiliative leaders create emotional bonds and harmony. Democratic leaders build consensus through participation. Pacesetting leaders expect excellence and self-direction. And coaching leaders develop people for the future.'

These types are useful – and commonsensical. Where Goleman departs from the usual theories is in his belief that leaders need to apply different leadership styles in different situations. Today's coercive leader may need to switch to coaching mode in the next meeting. 'Leaders who have mastered four or more – especially the authoritative, democratic, affiliative, and coaching strategies – have the best climate and business performance', Goleman writes.

This, once again, makes sense. Leaders require a mix of pragmatism and mental agility to survive the mire of organizational politics, not to mention the demands of the markets. This fits neatly with changes in the business world. Companies are re-evaluating the leadership character-istics they require for the future. Some companies talk about an inward journey. Emotional Intelligence is part of that redefinition.

The good news is that, according to Goleman, Emotional Intel-ligence can be learned. There are five dimensions to this, he says. These are:

- Self-awareness: We seldom pay attention to what we feel. A stream of moods runs in parallel to our thoughts. This and previous emotional experiences provide a context for our decision-making.
- Managing emotions: All effective leaders learn to manage their emotions, especially the big three: anger, anxiety, sadness. This is a decisive life skill.
- Motivating others: The root meaning of motive is the same as the root of emotion: to move.
- Showing empathy: The flip side of self-awareness is the ability to read emotions in others.
- Staying connected: Emotions are contagious. There is an unseen transaction that passes between us in every interaction that makes us feel either a little better or a little worse. Goleman calls this a 'secret economy'. It holds the key to motivating the people we work with.

Notes

1 Interview with Stuart Crainer, 2001.
2 Interview with Jorge Nascimento Rodrigues, 2000.

MICHAEL GOOLD, MARCUS ALEXANDER & ANDREW CAMPBELL

Corporate-Level Strategy

1994

The authors

Michael Goold, Andrew Campbell and Marcus Alexander are directors of the Ashridge Strategic Management Centre, London, England. They were previously strategy consultants with either the Boston Consulting Group or McKinsey & Company.

Michael Goold and Andrew Campbell are the authors of the highly influential *Strategies and Styles* (1987). Among the group's other books are *Managing the Multibusiness Company*, (Goold and Kathleen Sommers Luchs,1995); *Strategic Synergy* (Campbell and Luchs,1992); *Strategic Control* (Goold with John J Quinn,1990); and *Break Up!* (Campbell and Richard Koch, 1996).

The classic

The basic, and accurate, realization behind Michael Goold, Marcus Alexander and Andrew Campbell's *Corporate-Level Strategy*[1] is that most large companies are now multibusiness organizations. The logic behind this fact of business life is one which is generally assumed rather than examined in any depth. Multibusiness companies through their very size offer economies of scale and synergies between the various businesses, which can be exploited to the overall good.

While this is a truth universally acknowledged, Goold, Campbell and Alexander's research suggests that this *raison d'être* does not, in reality, exist. They calculate that in over half multibusiness companies the whole is worth less than the sum of its parts. Instead of adding and nurturing

Gary Hamel on *Corporate-Level Strategy*

'Chandler and Drucker celebrated large multi-divisional organizations, but as these companies grew, decentralized and diversified the corporate center often became little more than a layer of accounting consolidation. In the worst cases, a conglomerate was worth less than its break-up value. In writing the definitive book on corporate strategy, Goold, Alexander and Campbell gave hope to corporate bureaucrats everywhere. Maybe it really was possible for the corporate level to add value.'

value, the corporation actually negates value. It is costly and its influence, though pervasive, is often counter-productive.

This condemnation is not restricted to what we would normally consider to be conglomerates. Goold, Campbell and Alexander suggest that the baleful influence of the corporate parent also applies to companies with portfolios in a single industry, or in a series of apparently related areas.

One of the primary causes of this phenomenon is that, while the individual businesses within the organization often have strategies, the corporation as a whole does not. They may pretend otherwise, but the proclaimed strategy is often an amalgam of the individual business strategies given credence by general aspirations.

If corporate level strategy is to add value, Goold, Campbell and Alexander suggest that there needs to be a tight fit between the parent organization and its businesses. Successful corporate parents focus on a narrow range of tasks, create value in those areas and align the structures, processes and central functions of the parent accordingly. Rather than all-encompassing and constantly interfering, the centre is akin to a specialist medical practitioner – intervening in its areas of expertise when it knows it can suggest a cure.

From their detailed analysis of 15 successful multibusiness corporations, Goold, Campbell and Alexander identify three essentials to successful corporate strategies. First, there must be a clear insight about the role of the parent. If the parent does not know how or where it can add value it is unlikely to do so. Second, the parent must have distinctive characteristics. They, too, have a corporate culture and personality. Third, there must be recognition that 'each parent will only be effective with certain sorts of business' – described as their 'heartland'.

'Heartland businesses are also well understood by the parent; they do not suffer from the inappropriate influence and meddling that can damage less familiar businesses. The parent has an innate feel for its heartland that enables it to make difficult judgments and decisions with a high degree of success', say the authors. Heartlands are broad ranging and can cover different industries, markets and technologies. Given this added complexity, the ability of the parent to intervene on a limited number of issues is crucial.

The concept of heartland businesses is, they make clear, distinct from core businesses. Though core businesses may be important and substantial, say Goold, Campbell and Alexander, the parent may not be adding a great deal to them. 'A core business is often merely a business that the company has decided to commit itself to', they write. 'In contrast, the heartland definition focuses on the **fit** between a parent and a business: do the parent's insights and behavior fit the opportunities and nature of this business? Does the parent have specialist skills in assisting this type of business to perform better?'

Corporate strategy should be driven by what Goold, Campbell and Alexander label 'parenting advantage' – 'to create more value in the portfolio of businesses than would be achieved by any rival'. To do so requires a fundamental change in basic perspectives on the role of the parent and of the nature of the multibusiness organization.

'Anyone who reads *Corporate-Level Strategy* will subsequently think and talk about corporate strategy in a different way', noted Bain & Company's Robin Buchanan, adding, 'It is to be hoped that they will act on it, too.'[2]

Notes

1 Goold, Michael; Alexander, Marcus & Campbell, Andrew, *Corporate-Level Strategy*, John Wiley, New York, 1994.
2 Buchanan, Robin, 'Practical parenting', *The Observer*, 23 October 1994.

GARY HAMEL & C K PRAHALAD

Competing for the Future

1994

The authors

C K Prahalad is Harvey C Fruehauf Professor of Business Administration at the University of Michigan's Graduate School of Business Administration. He is co-author, with INSEAD's Yves Doz, of *The Multinational Mission: Balancing Local Responsiveness and Global Vision* and is a consultant to many leading firms including AT&T, Motorola and Philips.

Gary Hamel (born 1954) is Visiting Professor of Strategic and International Management at London Business School. Based in Woodside, California, he is a founder of Strategos, a firm dedicated to helping companies build high performance innovation systems.

Hamel and Prahalad's articles 'Strategic intent' and 'Competing with core competencies' won McKinsey awards in the *Harvard Business Review*. Their article 'The core competence of the corporation' is one of the most reprinted articles in the *Review's* history.

The classic

The debate on the meaning and application of strategy is long-running. Each decade produces its own interpretation and its own voice. The sixties gave us the resolutely analytical Igor Ansoff; the seventies Henry Mintzberg and his cerebral and creative 'crafting strategy'; the 1980s, Michael Porter's rational route to competitiveness, and nominations for the leading strategic thinkers of the 1990s would certainly short-list Gary Hamel and CK Prahalad.

Gary Hamel and C K Prahalad's *Competing for the Future*[1] has been seized on as the blueprint for a new generation of strategic thinking. *Business Week* named it as the best management book of 1994 and it has

Gary Hamel on *Competing for the Future*

'By the 1990s strategy had become discredited. All too often "vision" was ego masquerading as foresight; planning was formulaic, incrementalist and largely a waste of time in a world of discontinuous change; "strategic" investments were those that lost millions, if not billions of dollars. As strategy professors, CK and I had a simple choice: change jobs or try to reinvent strategy for a new age. We chose the latter course. We'll let you judge whether we succeeded.'

sold over 250,000 copies in hardcover. 'At a time when many companies continue to lay off thousands in massive reengineering exercises, this is a book that deserves widespread attention', observed *Business Week's* John Byrne. 'It's a valuable and worthwhile tonic for devotees of today's slash-and-burn school of management.'[2]

Hamel and Prahalad believe strategy has tied itself into a straitjacket of narrow, and narrowing, perspectives: 'Among the people who work on strategy in organizations and the theorists, a huge proportion, perhaps 95 per cent, are economists and engineers who share a mechanistic view of strategy. Where are the theologists, the anthropologists to give broader and fresher insights?'

They argue that strategy is multi-faceted, emotional as well as analytical, concerned with meaning, purpose and passion. While strategy is a process of learning and discovery, it is not looked on as a learning process and this represents a huge blind spot.

Broader perspectives are necessitated by the 'emerging competitive reality' in which the onus is on transforming not just individual organizations but entire industries. The boldness of such objectives is put in perspective when Hamel and Prahalad observe that, for all the research and books on the subject, there remains no theory of strategy creation. Strategy emerges and the real problem, executives perceive, is not in creating strategy but in implementing it.

'We have an enormous appetite for simplicity. We like to believe we can break strategy down to Five Forces or Seven Ss. But you can't. Strategy is extraordinarily emotional and demanding. It is not a ritual or a once-a-year exercise, though that is what it has become. We have set the bar too low,' say Hamel and Prahalad. As a result, managers are bogged down in the nitty-gritty of the present – spending less than three per cent of their time looking to the future.

Instead of talking about strategy or planning, they advocate that companies should talk of *strategizing* and ask, 'What are the fundamental preconditions for developing complex, variegated, robust strategies?' Strategizing is part of the new managerial argot of 'strategic intent', 'strategic architecture', 'foresight' (rather than vision) and, crucially, the idea of 'core competencies'.

Hamel and Prahalad define core competencies as 'the collective learning in the organization, especially how to co-ordinate diverse production skills and integrate multiple streams of technologies' and call on organizations to see themselves as a portfolio of core competencies as opposed to business units. The former are geared to growing 'opportunity share' wherever that may be; the latter narrowly focused on market share and more of the same.

The surge of interest in core competencies has tended to enthusiastic over simplification. 'You need to be cautious about where core competencies will lead you', warns Marcus Alexander of the Ashridge Strategic Management Centre. 'They are a very powerful weapon in some cases but are not the sole basis for a sound corporate strategy. They can encourage companies to get into businesses simply because they see a link between core competencies rather than ones where they have an in-depth knowledge. Similarly, there is a temptation for mature companies to be persuaded to go into growth businesses when that is not necessarily the best option for them.'[3]

In some ways, Hamel and Prahalad's strategic prognosis falls between two extremes. At one extreme are the arch-rationalists, insisting on a constant stream of data to support any strategy; at the other are the 'thriving on chaos' school with their belief in free-wheeling organizations where strategy is a moveable feast.

There is a thin dividing line between order and chaos. 'Neither Stalinist bureaucracy nor Silicon Valley provides an optimal economic system', they caution. 'Silicon Valley is extraordinarily good at creating new ideas but in other ways is extraordinarily inefficient. There are 100 failures for every success and, in fact, you find that smaller companies usually succeed in partnership with large organizations.'

They conclude that small entrepreneurial offshoots are not the route to organizational regeneration. They are too random, inefficient and prone to becoming becalmed by corporate indifference. This does not mean that interlopers can't change the shape of entire industries.

In Europe, they acknowledge the revolutionary impact of entrepreneurial newcomers such as IKEA, Body Shop, Swatch and Virgin. But, the true challenge is to create revolutions when you are large and dominant. This is something which American companies – such as Motorola and Hewlett-Packard – are more successful at than their European counterparts.

This is partly attributable to traditional cultures. 'We are moving to more democratic models of organization to which US corporations appear more attuned. In Europe and Japan there is a much more elitist sense that all knowledge resides at the top. There is a hierarchy of experience, not a hierarchy of imagination. And the half life of experience is very short.'

The two are also long-standing critics of the corporate obsession with downsizing, labelling it 'corporate anorexia'. The golden rules are summed up by Hamel and Prahalad: 'A company surrenders today's businesses when it gets smaller faster than it gets better. A company surrenders tomorrow's businesses when it gets better without getting different.' Downsizing is an easy option – 'There is nothing more short-term than a sixty year old CEO holding a fist full of share options.'

Growth (they prefer to talk of vitality) comes from difference; though they add the caveat that 'there are as many stupid ways to grow as there are to downsize. You might merge with another organization but two drunks don't make a sensible person.' The catch-22 for organizations is that vitality is usually ignited by a crisis – something borne out by the burgeoning literature on spectacular turnarounds.

Perhaps reassuringly, Hamel and Prahalad believe vitality comes from within. If only executives would listen – 'Go to any company and ask when was the last time someone in their twenties spent time with the board teaching them something they didn't know. For many it is inconceivable, yet companies will pay millions of dollars for the opinions of McKinsey's bright 29-year old. What about their own 29-year olds?'

While such questions remain largely unanswered, Hamel and Prahalad are moving on to pose yet more: 'Something new needed to be said about the content of strategy. Now we need to rethink the process of strategy.'

Hamel's sequel, *Leading the Revolution*, calls for companies to throw aside their single-strategy business plans and instead develop a deeply embedded capability for continual, radical innovation. Hamel now talks of 'creative strategizing'. By way of explanation he says: 'First, strategic planning is not strategy. Planning and strategic formulations are very different things. Strategy is discovering and inventing, which makes strategy subversive, and the strategist a rule-breaker, or revolutionary. Second, the real barrier to strategic planning is generally at the top – not in the middle, nor at the bottom. The objective of the revolutionary is to free the process from the tyranny of the past. Its guardians are at the top. And, third, you cannot expect to see the end at the start. The strategic formulation is a discovery process and a moment of invention. It is not selling to those in the middle and at the bottom something already defined by those at the top or from outsiders (the external consultants).'[4]

Notes

1 Hamel, Gary & Prahalad, C K, *Competing for the Future*, Harvard University Press, Cambridge, MA, 1994 .
2 Byrne, John, 'Corporate anorexia: a lack-of-foresight saga', *Business Week*, 19 September 1994.
3 Interview with author.
4 Brown, Tom *et al.*, *Business Minds*, FT Prentice Hall, London, 2001.

CHARLES HANDY

The Age of Unreason

1989

The author

C harles Handy (born 1932) is a writer and broadcaster. Irish-born, he worked for Shell before joining academia. He spent time at MIT and later joined London Business School.

His first book belies the wide-ranging, social and philo-sophical nature of his later work. *Understanding Organizations* (1976) is a comprehensive and readable primer of organizational theory. It is the most conventional of his books. Its sequel was the idiosyncratic *Gods of Management* (1978).

Over the last decade Handy has sealed his reputation as a thinker. His books routinely crop up in bestseller lists and he has spread his wings to become a much-quoted sage on the future of society and work. His articles are as likely to appear in the *Harvard Business Review* as in the lifestyle sections of tabloid newspapers. The cornerstones of his ideas on emerging working structures can be found in *The Age of Unreason*; his 1994 bestseller; *The Empty Raincoat* (called *The Age of Paradox* in the United States); *The Hungry Spirit* (1998); and *The Elephant and the Flea* (2002).

The classic

Charles Handy's *The Age of Unreason*[1] is a disquieting book – and remains so years after its publication. The age of unreason, which Handy predicts is 'a time when what we used to take for granted may no longer hold true, when the future, in so many areas, is there to be shaped, by us and for us; a time when the only prediction that will hold true is that no predictions will hold. A time, therefore, for bold imaginings in private life as well as public, for thinking the unlikely and doing the unreasonable.'

Gary Hamel on *The Age of Unreason*

'There is no contemporary management thinker who is more genuinely, and originally thoughtful than Charles Handy. Charles is one of the few management writers who can step entirely outside the world of management and then look back in. This outside-in perspective yields an uncompromising and unorthodox perspective which will discomfort and enlighten anyone who cares about the future of management and organizations. Where most business authors are intent on giving you the "how", Professor Handy forces us to ask "why?".'

The future, writes Handy, will be one of 'discontinuous change' (a phrase which has now entered the mainstream). The path through time, with society slowly, naturally and radically improving on a steady course, is a thing of the past. The blinkers have to be removed. Handy tells the story of the Peruvian Indians who saw invading ships on the horizon. Having no knowledge of such things, they discounted them as a freak of the weather. They settled for their sense of continuity.

In order to adapt to a society in which mysterious invaders are perpetually on the horizon, the way people think will have to change fundamentally. 'We are all prisoners of our past. It is hard to think of things except in the way we have always thought of them. But that solves no problems and seldom changes anything,' writes Handy. He points out that people who have thought unconventionally, 'unreasonably', have had the most profound impact on twentieth-century living. Freud, Marx and Einstein succeeded through 'discontinuous' (or what Handy labels 'upside down') thinking.

He sees the need for the development of 'a new intelligentsia'. Education will have to alter radically, as the way people think can only be changed by revolutionizing the way they learn and think about learning.

In practice, Handy believes that certain forms of organization will become dominant. These are the type of organization most readily associated with service industries. First, what he calls 'the shamrock organization' – 'a form of organization based around a core of essential executives and workers supported by outside contractors and part-time help'. The consequence of such an organizational form is that organizations in the future are likely to resemble the way consultancy firms, advertising agencies and professional partnerships are currently structured.

The second emergent structure identified by Handy is the federal one. It is not, he points out, another word for decentralization. He provides a blueprint for federal organizations in which the central function co-ordinates, influences, advises and suggests. It does not dictate terms or short-term decisions. The centre is, however, concerned with long-term strategy. It is 'at the middle of things and is not a polite word for the top or even for head office'.

Handy develops his federal thinking in *The Empty Raincoat* and observes: 'Increasingly we are realizing that organizations are not mechanistic devices. They are communities of people and federalism is all about negotiation as to who does what and who has the power and authority for what. It's not hierarchical. In a mechanistic model it's easy for the organization to say the top man does everything and the bottom man has limits to his authority. But it's much more complicated in the federal organization which is often made up of alliances and partnerships, and you actually have to negotiate who has the power to do what and where it really does need to be written down.'[2]

The third type of organization Handy anticipates is what he calls 'the Triple I'. The three 'Is' are Information, Intelligence and Ideas. In such organizations the demands on personnel management are large. Explains Handy: 'The wise organization already knows that their smart people are not to be easily defined as workers or as managers but as individuals, as specialist, as professional or executives, or as leader (the older terms of manager and worker are dropping out of use), and that they and it need also to be obsessed with the pursuit of learning if they are going to keep up with the pace of change.'

Discontinuity demands new organizations, new people to run them with new skills, capacities and career patterns. No one will be able to work simply as a manager: organizations will demand much more.

As organizations change in the age of unreason so, Handy predicts, will other aspects of our lives. Less time will be spent at work – 50,000 hours in a lifetime rather than the present figure of around 100,000. Handy does not predict, as people did in the 1970s, an enlightened age of leisure. Instead he challenges people to spend more time thinking about what they want to do. Time will not simply be divided between work and play – there could be 'portfolios' which split time between fee work (where you sell time), gift work (for neighbours or charities), study (keeping up-to-date with your work), and homework and leisure.

'An age of unreason is an age of opportunity even if it looks at first sight like the end of all ages', says Handy. People must seize the opportunity, not ignore the invaders on the horizon.

Central to Handy's work and The Age of Unreason is his use of metaphors. 'I think they're very helpful to understand things', he says. 'People think visually when they are in a hurry better than they think analytically. My metaphors are basically visual – the latest is the elephant and the flea, referring to large organizations and smaller organizations and individuals. They are also very home-made. I talk about doughnuts and shamrocks and all that sort of stuff. First of all, it intrigues people. Secondly, it is user-friendly. And thirdly, it is terribly useful.

'Now that doesn't tell you what to do, but it does make you look at your organization and yourself in a different way – and I think that's the first step to practicality, to understand where you are and what the possibilities are. Then you have to work out what exactly you do. Now I don't go the next step in my writing. I don't tell people what to do. I think every individual situation is just a little different though they have generalities. I like to leave it at the metaphor level.'[3]

More recently he has become increasingly questioning of the role and nature of capitalism. 'I'm concerned that capitalism is eating itself up', he says. 'I think money is an essential ingredient in successful societies. So I never want to be heard to say that money is not important, but it is a means to another end. And I think the danger with capitalism and with organizations and businesses is that money has become the end.

'I think the purpose of business is not to make money but to do something that is more useful to more people than anybody else. But most capitalists don't think about it that way, I'm afraid. And most managers don't think about it that way. They want promotion because they can make more money to pay off a bigger mortgage and have a bigger house, rather than that they can now be in a position to do something more worthy with their lives.'[4]

Notes

1 Handy, Charles, *The Age of Unreason*, Business Books, London, 1989.
2 Interview with Des Dearlove, June 2002.
3 Interview with Des Dearlove, June 2002.
4 Interview with Des Dearlove, June 2002.

FREDERICK HERZBERG

The Motivation to Work

1959

The author

F rederick Herzberg (born 1923) served in World War II and was posted to Dachau concentration camp after its liberation. This proved a powerful experience. On his return to the US, Herzberg studied at the University of Pittsburgh and worked for the US Public Health Service in his area of expertise, clinical psychology.

Along with Maslow and McGregor, he was identified with the Human Relations School of the 1950s. His most influential publication was an article in the *Harvard Business Review* in 1968. 'One More Time: How Do You Motivate Employees?' has sold over one million copies in reprints making it the *Review's* most popular article ever. The article introduced the acronym KITA (kick in the ass) and argued: 'If you have someone on a job, use him. If you can't use him get rid of him.' Herzberg also coined the now popular phrase 'job enrichment'. He believes that business organizations could be an enormous force for good, provided they liberate both themselves and their people from the thrall of numbers, and get on with creative expansion of individuals' roles within them.

Herzberg eventually became a Professor of Management at the University of Utah. His co-authors for *Motivation to Work* were his co-researchers Mausner and Snyderman.

The classic

Frederick Herzberg received a grant to investigate the entire field of attitudes to work when he was research director at Psychological Services in Pittsburgh. A review of the literature left Herzberg bemused. 'We could make no sense out of it', Herzberg later recalled. 'It seemed that the human being was forever debarred from rational understanding as

Gary Hamel on *The Motivation to Work*

'Pay-for-performance, employee stock ownership plans, end-of-year bonuses – too many organizations seem to believe that the only motivation to work is an economic one. Treating knowledge assets like Skinnerian rats is hardly the way to get the best out of people. Herzberg offered a substantially more subtle approach – one that still has much to recommend it. The next time you hear the glib phrase, "people are our most important asset", roll off the tongue of an executive who still regards people as a variable cost, dig out a copy of *The Motivation to Work* and suggest a little bed-time reading.'

to why he worked. We looked again at some of the data describing what people wanted from their jobs and noticed that there was a hint that the things people said positively about their job experiences were not the opposite of what they said negatively about their job experiences; the reverse of the factors that seemed to make people happy in jobs did not make them unhappy. So what happens in science, when your research leads to ambiguity? You begin to suspect your premises. In my Public Health School days I had conceived the concept that mental health was not the opposite of mental illness; that mentally healthy people were not just the obverse of mentally sick people. So I took a stab on the basis of mental health not being the opposite of mental illness and came up with a new concept.'[1]

Researching *The Motivation to Work*[2] Frederick Herzberg and his co-authors, Mausner and Snyderman, asked 203 Pittsburgh engineers and accountants about their jobs and what pleased and displeased them.

As a result, Herzberg separates the motivational elements of work into two categories – those serving people's animal needs (hygiene factors) and those meeting uniquely human needs (motivation factors). In *The Motivation to Work*, Herzberg and his co-authors write: 'Hygiene operates to remove health hazards from the environment of man. It is not a curative; it is, rather, a preventative … Similarly, when there are deleterious factors in the context of the job, they serve to bring about poor job attitudes. Improvements in these factors of hygiene will serve to remove the impediments to positive job attitudes.'

Hygiene factors – also labelled maintenance factors – are determined to include supervision, interpersonal relations, physical working conditions, salary, company policies and administrative practices, benefits, and job security. 'When these factors deteriorate to a level below that which the employee considers acceptable, then job dissatisfaction ensues', observes Herzberg. Hygiene alone is insufficient to provide the 'motivation to work'. Indeed, the book argues that the factors which provide satisfaction are quite different from those leading to dissatisfaction.

True motivation, says Herzberg, comes from achievement, personal development, job satisfaction and recognition. The aim should be to motivate people through the job itself rather than through rewards or pressure.

Herzberg went on to broaden his research base. This further confirmed his conclusion that hygiene factors are the principle creator of unhappiness in work and motivational factors the route to satisfaction.

Herzberg's work has had a considerable effect on the rewards and remuneration packages offered by corporations. Increasingly, there is a trend towards 'cafeteria' benefits in which people can choose from a range of options. In effect, they can select the elements which they recognize as providing their own motivation to work.

Similarly, the current emphasis on self-development, career management and self-managed learning can be seen as having evolved from Herzberg's insights. Ultimately, motivation comes from within the individual rather than being created by the organization according to some formula.

Notes

1 'An Interview with Frederick Herzberg: Managers or Animal Trainers?', Management Review, 1971, pp. 2–5.
2 Herzberg, Frederick (with Mausner, B & Snyderman, B), *The Motivation to Work*, John Wiley, New York, 1959.

ELLIOTT JAQUES

The Changing Culture of a Factory

1951

The author

E lliott Jaques (born 1917), the Canadian-born psychologist, has ploughed an idiosyncratic furrow throughout his career. His work is based on exhaustive research and has generally been ignored by the mass managerial market. He was one of the founders of the Tavistock Institute of Human Relations in London. Jaques worked at Brunel University in the UK and later at George Washington University.

The classic

Elliott Jaques is best known for his involvement in an extensive study of industrial democracy in practice at the UK's Glacier Metal Company between 1948 and 1965. The experiment was driven forward by the vision and political ideas of the company's chairman and managing director, Wilfred Brown. Brown served in the Labour government of Harold Wilson and later became Lord Brown. He died in 1985.

Glacier introduced a number of highly progressive changes in working practices. A works council was introduced. This was far removed from the usually toothless attempts at worker representation. Indeed, no change of company policy was allowed unless all members of the works council agreed. Any single person on the council had a veto. Contrary to what experts and observers anticipated, the company did not grind to an immediate halt. Other innovations at Glacier included the abolition of 'clocking on', the traditional means of recording whether someone had turned up for work.

The emphasis was on granting people responsibility and of understanding the dynamics of group working. 'I'm completely convinced of the necessity of encouraging everybody to accept the maximum amount of personal responsibility, and allowing them to have a say in every problem in which they can help', said Jaques. He was brought into the project as a facilitator, though his role was more expansive than that. 'We spent the first month just having widespread discussions through the company and gradually we worked through things', is how Jaques remembers his introduction.[1]

The Glacier research led to Jaques' 1951 book *The Changing Culture of a Factory*. 'The project itself produced none of the successors we had anticipated. It was a decade ahead of any form of organizational development', said Eric Trist. What the experiment did successfully highlight was the redundancy of conventional organization charts; the potential power of corporate culture (a concept then barely understood); and the potential benefits of running organizations in a fair and mutually beneficial way.

Later in *A General Theory of Bureaucracy* (1976), Jaques presented his theory of the value of work. This was ornate, but aimed to clarify something Jaques had observed during his research: 'The manifest picture of bureaucratic organization is a confusing one. There appears to be no rhyme or reason for the structures that are developed, in number of levels, in titling, or even in the meaning to be attached to the manager-subordinate linkage.'

His solution was labelled the *time span of discretion*, which contended that levels of management should be based on how long it was before their decisions could be checked, and that people should be paid in accordance with that time. This meant that managers were measured by the long-term impact of their decisions.

The site of the Glacier factory in Alperton is now a supermarket car park. Jaques remains convinced of the merits of Glacier's approach and is roundly dismissive of current managerial fashions: 'The consultants and the gurus and so on continue to play around with these fantasy fads; empowerment and self-managed teams, and now it's competency theory and God knows what. It goes on and on. I think it's the same issue as why modern natural science hadn't developed until the seventeenth century and the answer is that they hadn't as they were ensconced in alchemy. I think the major point we're talking about now, and Wilfred [Brown] was deeply aware of this, was the need for a scientifically based approach, and that we've not achieved. The field consultancy and gurus and so on is very much like alchemy; no concepts, no rigorous definition and just waffle and fiddling around.'[2]

Notes

1 'Here comes the boss', BBC Radio Four, 1 August 1997.
2 'Here comes the boss', BBC Radio Four, 1 August 1997.

JOSEPH M JURAN

Planning for Quality

1988

The author

The Romanian-born Joseph M Juran – with W Edwards Deming – was instigator of the Japanese discovery of quality after the end of World War II. Born in 1904, Juran is an American electrical engineer who worked for Western Electric in the 1920s and then AT&T. In 1953 he arrived in Tokyo, by which time Deming was already making waves with his quality philosophy. At the invitation of the Japanese Federation of Economic Associations and the Japanese Union of Scientists and Engineers, Juran was asked to spend two months analysing Japanese approaches to quality.

From his experience, Juran believed Japan's success was built on quality products. This message was ignored as Western businesses continued with their, by then mistaken, belief that Japan was succeeding through lower prices and nothing else. In the 1960s Juran could be found attempting to awaken US executives to the emergence of Japan.

With the 'discovery' of quality in the 1980s, Juran and his work through the Juran Institute came to greater prominence – while remaining slightly in the shadow of Deming. Juran's weighty *Quality Control Handbook* was published in 1951. Juran was awarded the Second Class Order of the Sacred Treasure by the Emperor of Japan – the highest honour for a non-Japanese citizen – for 'the development of quality control in Japan and the facilitation of US and Japanese friendship'.

The classic

Talking to Japanese audiences in the 1950s, Joseph Juran's message was enthusiastically absorbed by groups of senior managers. In the West, his audiences were made up of engineers and quality inspectors. Therein,

Gary Hamel on *Planning for Quality*

'A senior executive at an American car company once told me that the company had just finished its twentieth annual study of Toyota. After 20 years, was the company still learning something new about its adversary, I asked. The answer was illuminating. "For the first five years," the American manager replied, "we thought we had a data problem. No-one's quality could be that good. For the next five years, we thought we thought it must have something to do with being Japanese – docile workers, group-ism and so on. For the next five years we thought it must be their technology – robots, supply systems, etc. Only in the last five years have we come to realize that they have a fundamentally different philosophy about customers and workers." The impact of Juran, and of Deming as well, went far beyond quality. By drawing the attention of Western managers to the successes of Japan, they forced Western managers to challenge some of their most basic beliefs about the capabilities of their employees and the expectations of their customers.'

argues Juran, lies the problem. While the Japanese have made quality a priority at the top of the organization, in the West it is delegated downwards, an operational rather than a managerial issue.

In the post-war years, Juran believes US businesses were caught unawares because of two reasons: they assumed their Asian adversaries were copycats rather than innovators, and their chief executives were too obsessed with financial indicators to notice any danger signs.

Juran's quality philosophy, laid out in *Planning for Quality*[1] and his other books, is built around a quality trilogy: quality planning, quality management and quality implementation. While Juran is critical of Deming as being overly reliant on statistics, his own approach is based on the forbiddingly entitled Company-Wide Quality Management (CWQM) which aims to create a means of disseminating quality to all.

Juran insists that quality cannot be delegated and was an early exponent of what has come to be known as empowerment: for him quality has to be the goal of each employee, individually and in teams, through self-supervision.

His approach is less mechanistic than Deming and places greater stress on human relations (though Deming adherents disagree with this interpretation).

Juran places quality in a historical perspective. Manufacturing products to design specifications and then inspecting them for defects to protect the buyer, he points out, was something the Egyptians had mastered 5,000 years previously when building the pyramids. Similarly, the ancient Chinese had set up a separate department of the central government to establish quality standards and maintain them. Juran's message – encapsulated in *Planning for Quality* – is that quality is nothing new. This is a simple, but daunting message. If quality is so elemental and elementary, why had it become ignored in the West? Juran's unwillingness to gild his straightforward message is attractive to some, but has made the communication of his ideas less successful than he would have liked.

Where Juran is innovative is in his belief that there is more to quality than specification and rigorous testing for defects. The human side of quality is regarded as critical. The origins of Juran's thoughts can be traced to his time at Western Electric. Juran analysed the large number of tiny circuit breakers routinely scrapped by the company. Instead of waiting at the end of a production line to count the defective products, Juran looked at the manufacturing process as a whole. He came up with a solution and offered it to his bosses. They were not impressed and told Juran that this wasn't his job: 'We're the inspection department and our job is to look at these things after they are made and find the bad ones. Making them right in the first place is the job of the production department.'

In response, Juran developed his all-embracing theories of what quality should entail. 'In broad terms, quality planning consists of developing the products and processes required to meet the customers' needs. More specifically, quality planning comprises the following basic activities:

- identify the customers and their needs
- develop a product that responds to those needs
- develop a process able to produce that product.'

Quality planning, says Juran, can be produced through 'a road map … an invariable sequence of steps'. These are:

- identify who are the customers
- determine the needs of those customers
- translate those needs into our language
- develop a product that can respond to those needs
- optimize the product features so as to meet our needs as well as customers' needs
- develop a process which is able to produce the product

- optimize the process
- prove that the process can produce the product under operating conditions
- transfer the process to the operating forces.

As with so many other recipes for quality, Juran's is more far-reaching and difficult to achieve than a list of bullet-points can ever suggest.

Note

1 Juran, Joseph M, *Planning for Quality*, Free Press, New York, 1988.

ROSABETH MOSS KANTER

The Change Masters

1983

The author

R osabeth Moss Kanter was born in 1943. She graduated from Bryn Mawr and has a PhD from the University of Michigan. After a spell as associate professor at Brandeis University, she joined Harvard's Organization Behavior program in 1978. She has also worked at Yale and MIT and is now a Harvard professor. She is the former editor of the *Harvard Business Review* (1989–92).

She is co-founder of the Boston-based consultancy firm Goodmeasure. Her more recent books, *When Giants Learn to Dance* (1989), *World Class* (1995) and *Evolve!* (2000), have cemented her already secure reputation.

The classic

Rosabeth Moss Kanter's *The Change Masters*[1] has been dubbed the 'thinking man's *In Search of Excellence*'. *The Change Masters* also became a bestseller, but comparisons with Peters and Waterman's opus are largely futile. (Indeed, the authoritative *Sloan Management Review* concluded it was 'of immeasurably higher quality than such competitors as Peters and Waterman's best-selling *In Search of Excellence*'.) Kanter's analysis of 'corporate entrepreneurs at work' is thoroughly academic. Its prose is slow and occasionally cumbersome, its references lengthy and intricate. It oozes authority.

Kanter defines change masters as 'those people and organizations adept at the art of anticipating the need for, and of leading, productive change'. At the opposite end to the change masters are the 'change resisters' intent on reining in innovation.

Gary Hamel on *The Change Masters*

'In a turbulent and inhospitable world, corporate vitality is a fragile thing. Yesterday's industry challengers are today's laggards. Entropy is endemic. Certainly *The Change Masters* is the most carefully researched, and best argued, book on change and transformation to date. While Rosabeth may not have discovered the eternal fountain of corporate vitality, she certainly points us in its general direction.'

The starting point of Kanter's research was a request to 65 vice-presidents of human resources in large companies to name companies which were 'progressive and forward thinking in their systems and practices with respect to people'. Forty-seven companies emerged as leaders in the field. They were then compared to similar companies. The companies with a commitment to human resources were 'significantly higher in long-term profitability and financial growth'. The message is that if you manage your people well, you are probably managing your business well.

The book's sub-title is 'Innovation and entrepreneurship in the American corporation'. Innovation is identified by Kanter as the key to future growth; and the key to developing and sustaining innovation is, says Kanter, an 'integrative' approach rather than a 'segmentalist' one. American woes are firmly placed at the door of 'the quiet suffocation of the entrepreneurial spirit in segmentalist companies'.

'Three new sets of skills are required to manage effectively in such integrative, innovation-stimulating environments', writes Kanter. 'First are "power skills" – skills in persuading others to invest information, support, and resources in new initiatives driven by an "entrepreneur". Second is the ability to manage the problems associated with the greater use of teams and employee participation. And third is an understanding of how change is designed and constructed in an organization – how the microchanges introduced by individual innovators relate to macro-changes or strategic reorientations.'

Kanter, through *The Change Masters* and her follow-up *When Giants Learn to Dance*, was partly responsible for the rise in interest – if not the practice – of empowerment. (In *The Change Masters* empowerment had yet to be added to the management vocabulary and is not even listed in the index – participation, however, gains a lengthy list of references.) People are put at centre stage – 'The degree to which the opportunity to use power effectively is granted to or withheld from individuals is one operative difference between those companies which stagnate and those which innovate.'

In this sense, Kanter's work forms a contemporary development from the Human Relations School of the late 1950s and 1960s. 'Above all, Ms Kanter is too quick to assume that "people-sensitive" strategies must also be "growth-boosting" ones. The most salient fact about the past decade is not the camaraderie of brown-bag lunches, but the epidemic of downsizing,' observed *The Economist* in a profile of Kanter's work.[2]

Professor Kanter's work – which also includes *When Giants Learn to Dance*, *World Class* and *Evolve* – combines academic rigour with a degree of idealism not usually found in the bottom-line fixated world of management thinking. She does not consider idealism and business as mutually exclusive.

Unlike some other commentators, her world-view is not confined to the boardroom. Her thesis examined nineteenth-century Utopian communities including the Shakers. Such was her enthusiasm that in the early 1970s she compared IBM to a Utopian culture. Trained as a sociologist, she found the business world beguiling. 'Business became increasingly interesting to me because it is so pivotal. It is the bedrock. The idealistic entrepreneurs of the 1960s and 1970s changed things so that business became a great arena for experimentation.'[3]

Rather than leaving her youthful Utopian idealism behind, Professor Kanter brought it to bear on the big management issues. While business school academics often eschew any agenda other than their own careers, Kanter is different. She seeks out involvement. She wants her ideas to work. 'Companies looked at *Change Masters* when it came out in 1983 and said its ideas were unrealistic. Five years later they were practising them', she says. 'I am interested in being an actor, not just a bystander, perhaps close to power.'

In her quest to get close to the corporate action, Kanter first tackled the narrow-minded, hierarchy-heavy, corporation of the 1970s. In her 1977 book, *Men and Women of the Corporation*, she effectively sounded the death knell for the traditional corporation. Unfortunately, as the bell tolled, the men and women of the corporation were too busy signing forms in triplicate, sending meaningless memos to each other and jockeying for position in the ornate hierarchy to actually hear anything. The book was a powerful obituary though the victim kept on breathing for a while longer (and can still be viewed gasping for breath in many places).

To charges of idealism, she pleads guilty with a caveat. 'I am a very realistic idealist. The ideas I have put forward work. The ideas are useful and effective. We sometimes think of idealists as setting out a utopian vision, but my work is very empirically grounded. It is based on research not on an artificial model.'

Despite the lip service often paid to ideas like empowerment, flexible working and stakeholder organizations, she remains optimistic. 'Organizations have improved – though it is easy to slip. Organizations are now faster and more diverse. Most have professionally trained managers and more women. There is much more emphasis on leadership. New organizational models are now accepted. There is, for example, less hierarchy, more emphasis on alliances and partnerships, and encouragement of innovation.'

She calls for capitalism with a human face – and has been doing so for a considerable time. Kanter's book, *World Class,* outlined many of the issues now being violently aired by anti-capitalist protestors. She describes it as 'an activist's book'. It looked at the need among companies, communities and regions to create an infrastructure for collaboration. It suggests that globalization can only be a force for good if it delivered at a local and regional level.

The change master still wants to change the world.

Notes

1 Kanter, Rosabeth Moss, *The Change Masters,* Simon & Schuster, New York, 1983.
2 'Moss Kanter, corporate sociologist', *The Economist,* 15 October 1994.
3 Interview with Stuart Crainer, June 2001.

ROBERT S KAPLAN & DAVID P NORTON

The Balanced Scorecard

1996

The authors

R obert Kaplan is the Marvin Bower Professor of Leadership Development at Harvard Business School.

David Norton is co-founder of the consulting company, Renaissance Solutions.

Their other books include *The Strategy-Focused Organization: How Balanced Scorecard Companies Thrive in the New Business Environment* (2000).

The classic

Measurement has lain at the heart of twentieth-century management. Indeed, measurement has often appeared to be the central function of management. The man who put the measure into the hands of managers was Frederick Taylor, the inventor of Scientific Management which involved measuring the performance of workers against pre-determined optimum times. Throughout the twentieth century, managers found different things to measure and more sophisticated means of measurement. And, as every manager knows, what gets measured gets done.

The most fruitful area for this mania for quantification has been finance. Managers once simply talked of sales and profits. But over the years a complex array of ratios, measures, analytical tools and software packages has evolved. Every penny a company spends or produces can be analysed in an infinite number of ways. Such are their powers of persuasion, that entire companies can be driven by such financial measures. The most famous instance of this was ITT in the 1960s under the control of

Harold Geneen. Geneen took management by financial measurement to its limits, creating an elaborate system of financial reporting. When he left the company, the deck of cards collapsed.

The obvious conclusion to be drawn from Geneen's approach was that, if you concentrated solely on financial measures, you could achieve short-term, even medium-term success, but such narrow constraining measures were unlikely to yield long-term prosperity. The trouble was that financial ratios and performance were the easiest things to measure. Other elements of corporate performance – such as customer loyalty or employee satisfaction – were more abstract and measurement appeared to pose more questions than answers.

At the same time as companies were considering how to measure 'softer' elements of their performance, they became increasingly addicted to managerial fads and fashions. Throughout the last twenty years in particular, there has been a steady stream of bright ideas which have all been seized upon by companies as the holy grail. Most, whether reengineering, total quality or just in time production, have disappeared without a trace.

So, organizations are faced with the dilemmas of unwieldy financial measurement systems, few reliable means of measuring other elements of their performance, and a predilection for short-lived fads whose impact is rarely measured in any way whatsoever.

The answer to these imbalances is proposed by David Norton and Robert Kaplan as the Balanced Scorecard ('a strategic management and measurement system that links strategic objectives to comprehensive indicators').[1]

The duo developed the Balanced Scorecard concept at the beginning of the 1990s in research sponsored by KPMG.

The result was an article in the *Harvard Business Review* ('The balanced scorecard', January/February 1993). This had a simple message for managers: what you measure is what you get. Kaplan and Norton compared running a company to flying a plane. The pilot who relies on a single dial is unlikely to be safe. Pilots must utilize all the information contained in their cockpit. 'The complexity of managing an organization today requires that managers be able to view performance in several areas simultaneously', said Kaplan and Norton. 'Moreover, by forcing senior managers to consider all the important operational measures together, the balanced scorecard can let them see whether improvement in one area may be achieved at the expense of another.'

Kaplan and Norton suggested that four elements need to be balanced. First is the customer perspective. Companies must ask how they are perceived by customers. The second element is 'internal perspective'.

Companies must ask what it is that they must excel at. Third is the 'innovation and learning perspective'. Companies must ask whether they can continue to improve and create value. Finally is the financial perspective. How does the company look to shareholders?

According to Kaplan and Norton, by focusing energies, attention and measures on all four of these dimensions, companies become driven by their mission rather than by short-term financial performance. Crucial to achieving this is applying measures to company strategy. Instead of being beyond measurement, the Balanced Scorecard argues that strategy must be central to any process of measurement – 'A good Balanced Scorecard should tell the story of your strategy.'

Identifying the essential measures for an organization is not straightforward. One company produced 500 measures on its first examination. This was distilled down to seven measures – 20 is par for the course. According to Kaplan and Norton, a 'good' Balanced Scorecard contains three elements. First, it establishes 'cause and effect relationships'. Rather than being isolated figures, measures are related to each other and the network of relationships makes up the strategy. Second, a Balanced Scorecard should have a combination of lead and lag indicators. Lag indicators are measures, such as market share, which are common across an industry and, though important, offer no distinctive advantage. Lead indicators are measures which are company (and strategy) specific. Finally, an effective Balanced Scorecard is linked to financial measures. By this, Kaplan and Norton mean that initiatives such as reengineering or lean production need to be tied to financial measures rather than pursued indiscriminately.

In many ways, the concept of the Balanced Scorecard is brazen commonsense. Balance is clearly preferable to imbalance. (The counter intuitive reality is that unbalanced companies, usually driven by a single dominant individual, have often proved short-term successes.) The Balanced Scorecard is now widely championed by a variety of companies. Indeed, it has somewhat ironically become a management fad. Its argument that blind faith in a single measurement or a small range of measures is dangerous is a powerful one. However, effective measures of elements, such as management competencies or intellectual capital, remain elusive.

Note

1 Kaplan, Robert S & Norton, David P, *The Balanced Scorecard: Translating Strategy into Action*, Harvard Business School Press, 1996.

PHILIP KOTLER

Marketing Management

1967

The author

Philip Kotler (born 1931) is the SC Johnson Distinguished Professor of International Marketing at the JL Kellogg Graduate School of Management, Northwestern University. Kotler is one of the leading authorities on marketing. He received his master's degree from the University of Chicago and has a Ph.D from MIT – both in economics. He has worked at Harvard, where he studied mathematics as a postdoctoral student, and at the University of Chicago where he worked on behavioural science.

He is a prolific author. As well as *Marketing Management: Analysis, Planning, Implementation and Control*, the most widely used marketing book in business schools, his books include *Principles of Marketing*; *Marketing Models*; *Strategic Marketing for Non-Profit Organizations*; *The New Competition and High Visibility*; *Social Marketing: Strategies for Changing Public Behavior and Marketing Places*.

The classic

An advertisement for a Philip Kotler seminar features four neat aphorisms by way of a summary of contemporary marketing: 'Companies pay too much attention to the cost of doing something. They should worry more about the cost of not doing it'; 'Every company should work hard to obsolete its own product line ... before its competitors do'; 'Your company does not belong in any market where it can't be the best'; and 'Marketing takes a day to learn. Unfortunately it takes a life time to master'.

Such observations distil Kotler's massive productiveness down to a few memorable phrases. This is grossly unrepresentative. Kotler's books are text books in the best sense and *Marketing Management*[1] the definitive marketing textbook of our times. It is now in its eighth edition.

Describing the genesis of his thinking and career, Kotler says:

> 'My training was in economics all the way through. I studied under Milton Friedman and then my PhD at MIT was under Paul Samuelson. Both were Nobel Prize winners but with very different perspectives. They couldn't agree on economics. So I thought that I would work at the level of micro economics, how things work in the market place. I went back to the early literature – people like Edward Robinson at Cambridge – who said that price was everything and you needed to look at sales forces and advertising. I then went onto a special Harvard program for one year which trained economists in mathematics. This involved 60 of the best people they could find from business schools. On that program I met the eight or nine top guys in marketing, accounting and so on. I got into the marketing group and found the problems fascinating.
>
> 'I then looked at the marketing textbooks which were, at the time, heavily prescriptive but lacked analysis.
>
> 'My first book looked at the big decisions. I was the first academic to look at these questions and then the logic of the answers. Then I went from marketing management to recognizing that there was so much marketing in society. I went into social marketing – how do you market causes, places, etc – and found that there was no literature on those subjects. Then I moved into personality marketing, looking at how fame is produced in our society. Are there marketing techniques at work or is it accidental? I focused on how organizations and individuals gain attention.'[2]

Marketing Management is tightly argued and all-encompassing. Through its various editions, its content has been expanded and brought up-to-date. The emerging challenge to all those involved in marketing is potently mapped out by Kotler in the eighth edition, published in 1994. 'The marketing discipline is redeveloping its assumptions, concepts, skills, tools, and systems for making sound business decisions', writes Kotler. 'Marketers must know when to cultivate large markets and when to niche; when to launch new brands and when to extend existing brand names; when to push products through distribution and when to pull them through distribution; when to protect the domestic market and when to penetrate aggressively into foreign markets; when to add more

Gary Hamel on *Marketing Management*

'There are few MBA graduates alive who have not plowed through Kotler's encyclopedic textbook on marketing, and have not benefited enormously from doing so. I know of no other business author who covers his (or her) territory with such comprehensiveness, clarity and authority as Phil Kotler. I can think of few other books, even within the vaunted company of this volume, whose insights would be of more practical benefit to the average company than those found in *Marketing Management*.'

benefits to the offer and when to reduce the price; and when to expand and when to contract their budgets for salesforce, advertising, and other marketing tools.' The scope of marketing is expanding exponentially as is demonstrated by the size and scope of *Marketing Management* – its contents range from industry and competitor analysis to designing strategies for the global marketplace, from managing product life cycle strategies to retailing, wholesaling and physical-distribution systems.

Kotler examines the shift in emphasis from 'transaction oriented' marketing to 'relationship marketing'. 'Good customers are an asset which, when well managed and served, will return a handsome lifetime income stream to the company. In the intensely competitive marketplace, the company's first order of business is to retain customer loyalty through continually satisfying their needs in a superior way,' says Kotler.

For the aspiring or practising marketer, the attraction of *Marketing Management* lies in the clarity of its definitions of key phrases and roles. It defines marketing as 'a social and managerial process by which individuals and groups obtain what they need and want through creating, offering, and exchanging products of value with others'. Kotler goes on to explain the concept of a market as consisting 'of all the potential customers sharing a particular need or want who might be willing and able to engage in exchange to satisfy that need or want'. Marketing management, therefore, 'is the process of planning and executing the conception, pricing, promotion, and distribution of goods, services, and ideas to create exchanges with target groups that satisfy customer and organizational objectives'.

The clarity of *Marketing Management* enables Kotler to return to the fundamentals. His examination of what makes up a product is typical. Kotler defines a product as 'anything that can be offered to a market for attention, acquisition, use, or consumption that might satisfy a want or need'. He says that a product has five levels: the core benefit ('Marketers must see themselves as benefit providers'); the generic product; the expected product (the normal expectations the customer has of the product); the augmented product (the additional services or benefits added to the product); and, finally, the potential product ('all of the augmentations and transformations that this product might ultimately undergo in the future').

Kotler explores what he labels 'customer delivered value' which he defines as 'the difference between total customer value and total customer cost. And total customer value is the bundle of benefits customers expect from a given product or service.' Total customer value is made up of product value, service value, personnel value and image value. Total customer cost is made up of monetary price, time cost, energy cost and psychic cost. The two are combined to produce customer delivered value.

Given the scale and challenge of modern marketing outlined by Kotler, it is perhaps little wonder that he laments that so few companies are actually adept and committed to marketing. His list of successful marketing organizations is notable for its brevity. In the United States he identifies Procter & Gamble, Apple, Disney, Nordstrom, Wal-Mart, Milliken, McDonald's, Marriott Hotels and Delta Airlines as true marketing organizations. Elsewhere, the list is even shorter. In Europe, Kotler highlights Ikea, Club Med, Ericsson, Bang & Olufsen and Marks & Spencer and, in Japan, only Sony, Toyota and Canon.

In order to become marketing-oriented, Kotler believes organizations encounter three common hurdles:

1 **Organized resistance** – entrenched functional behaviour tends to oppose increased emphasis on marketing as it is seen as undermining functional power bases.
2 **Slow learning** – most companies are only capable of slowly embracing the marketing concept. In the banking industry, Kotler says that marketing has passed through five stages. In the first marketing was regarded as sales promotion and publicity. Then it was taken to be smiling and providing a friendly atmosphere. Banks moved on to segmentation and innovation, and then regarded marketing as positioning. Finally, they came to see marketing as marketing analysis, planning and control.
3 **Fast forgetting** – companies which embrace marketing concepts tend, over time, to lose touch with core marketing principles. Various US companies have sought to establish their products in Europe with little knowledge of the differences in the marketplace.

For all the practical difficulties and the limitations of our concept of marketing, Kotler regards it as the essence of business and more. 'Good companies will meet needs; great companies will create markets', he writes. 'Market leadership is gained by envisioning new products, services, lifestyles, and ways to raise living standards. There is a vast difference between companies that offer me-too products and those that create new product and service values not even imagined by the marketplace. Ultimately, marketing at its best is about value creation and raising the world's living standards.'

Notes

1 Kotler, Philip, *Marketing Management: Analysis, Planning, Implementation and Control*, Prentice Hall, Englewood Cliffs, NJ, 1967.
2 Interview with Stuart Crainer, June 2002.

JOHN KOTTER

Leading Change

1996

The author

John Kotter (born 1947) was among the youngest Harvard faculty members ever given tenure and a full professorship. He celebrated 30 years at Harvard in 2002.

His books include *What Leaders Really Do* (1999); *Matsushita Leadership* (1996); *The New Rules* (1995); *Corporate Culture and Performance* (1992); *Force for Change* (1990); and *The General Managers* (1982).

The classic

While some of his Harvard Business School colleagues are prolific contributors to the *Harvard Business Review*, John Kotter has written only six articles. At first sight, it seems a slender basis for an academic career. But Kotter's timing has been impeccable. His ideas have struck a chord. Kotter was on the leadership trail at the right time. Then it was change management. Then culture. Then careers. If success was measured in article reprints, Kotter is a success. Then there are his bestselling books, *Leading Change*, *Corporate Culture and Performance*, and *A Force for Change*.

Kotter explains the genesis of his work as follows: 'My first book on leadership, *The Leadership Factor*, came out in 1988. Then I figured out that differentiating between management and leadership was important – 90 per cent of people doing management stuff thought that it was leadership. The system didn't support leadership so I did a culture study. Then I looked at economical and environmental changes, discontinuities. I saw how they were affecting the careers of Harvard Business School graduates. From there I increasingly understood that leadership and change were closely related. I looked at a whole bunch of situations involving transformations.

'The next step was to do an in-depth study of a fascinating leader so I did a biography of Konosuke Matsushita who no-one, in the United States at least, knew anything about. It was another cut at the whole thing. Some big insights came out of that which I'm still working through.'

If you were to pick a central theme to Kotter's work it would be change. He argues that a mobilizing, inspiring vision is central to any change initiative. 'The key is to go beyond the downsizing clichés – talking only of lean and nice. And carefree statements like "I see a smaller firm in the future" are not a vision that allows people to see a light at the end of the tunnel, that mobilizes people, or that makes them endure sacrifices', he says.[1]

Practically, Kotter suggests that executives 'be creative, be genuine, and most of all, know why you're doing what you're doing. Communicate that and the organization will be stronger. Anything short of this will breed the cynicism that results when we see inconsistencies between what people say and what they do, between talk and practice.'

While allowing that the desire for change may start with one person – the Lee Iacocca, Sam Walton, or Lou Gerstner – Kotter argues that no-one can provoke great changes alone. Successful change requires the efforts of a critical mass of key individuals – a group of two to fifty people, depending on the size of the corporation – in order to move the organization in significantly different directions. If the minimum of critical mass is not reached in the first stages, nothing really important will happen.

Failing to establish a sense of urgency is one of the key mistakes made by change leaders. In *Leading Change*, Kotter identifies seven additional steps in successful change efforts. In addition to establishing a sense of urgency, organizations need to create a powerful, guiding coalition; develop vision and strategy; communicate the change vision; empower broad-based action; celebrate short-term wins; continuously reinvigorate the initiative with new projects and participants; and anchor the change in the corporate culture.

The guiding coalition mentioned by Kotter needs to have four characteristics. First, it needs to have what he calls, 'position power' – the group needs to consist of a combination of individuals who, if left out of the process, are in positions to block progress. Second, the group needs a variety of skills, perspectives, experiences, and so forth relative to the project. Third, it must have credibility. When the group announces initiatives will its members have reputations that get the ideas taken seriously? And fourth, leadership. The group needs to be composed of proven leaders. 'Remember, in all of this the guiding coalition should not be assumed to be composed exclusively of managers. Leadership is found throughout the organization, and it's leadership you want – not management,' he says.

He warns against including individuals with large egos – 'The bigger the ego, the less space there is for anyone else to think and work. And snakes are individuals who destroy trust. They spread rumors, talk about other group members behind their backs, nod yes in meetings but condemn project ideas as unworkable or short-sighted when talking with colleagues. Trust is critical in successful change efforts, and these two sorts of individuals put trust in jeopardy.'

Kotter is dedicated to finding the formula for effective leadership. He considers it critical to any business or organization. As he says in his Preface to *Leading Change*, leadership is the critical ingredient for driving change. 'A purely managerial mindset', he argues, 'inevitably fails, regardless of the quality of people involved.'

Notes

1 Interview with Stuart Crainer, June 2002.

TED LEVITT

Innovation in Marketing

1962

The author

B orn in Germany in 1925, Ted Levitt is the leading marketing guru of the last thirty years. He is a Professor at Harvard Business School and former editor of the *Harvard Business Review*.
Levitt is the author of *The Marketing Mode* (1969); *The Marketing Imagination* (1983); and *Thinking About Management* (1991). His recent work has charted the emergence of global brands.

The classic

Ted Levitt's fame was secured early in his career with 'Marketing myopia',[1] a *Harvard Business Review* article which enjoyed unprecedented success and attention, selling over 500,000 reprints. It has since been reproduced in virtually every collection of key marketing texts – and by Levitt in his 1962 book *Innovation in Marketing.*[2]

In 'Marketing myopia' Levitt argues that the central preoccupation of corporations should be with satisfying customers rather than simply producing goods. Companies should be marketing-led rather than production-led and the lead must come from the chief executive and senior management – 'Management must think of itself not as producing products but as providing customer-creating value satisfactions.' (In his ability to coin new management jargon, as well as his thinking, Levitt was ahead of his time.) 'Marketing myopia' is, as Levitt later admitted, a manifesto rather than a deeply academic article. It embraces ideas which had already been explored by others – Levitt acknowledges, for example, his debt to Peter Drucker's *The Practice of Management*.

At the time of Levitt's article, the fact that companies were production-led is not open to question. Henry Ford's success in mass production

Gary Hamel on *Innovation in Marketing*

'If Ted Levitt had done nothing else in his career – and he did plenty – he would have earned his keep on this planet with the article, "Marketing myopia". Managers get wrapped up inside their products (railroads) and lose sight of the fundamental benefits customers are seeking (transportation). Equally provocative was Ted's 1983 *Harvard Business Review* article, 'The globalization of markets'. While some argue that markets will never become truly global, there are few companies that are betting against the general trend.'

had fuelled the belief that low-cost production was the key to business success. Ford persisted in his belief that he knew what customers wanted, long after they had decided otherwise. (Even so, Levitt salutes Ford's marketing prowess, arguing that the mass production techniques he used were a means to a marketing end rather than an end in themselves.)

Levitt observes that production-led thinking inevitably leads to narrow perspectives. He argues that companies must broaden their view of the nature of their business. Otherwise their customers will soon be forgotten. 'The railroads are in trouble today not because the need was filled by others ... but because it was not filled by the railroads themselves', writes Levitt. 'They let others take customers away from them because they assumed themselves to be in the railroad business rather than in the transportation business. The reason they defined their industry wrong was because they were railroad-oriented instead of transportation-oriented; they were product-oriented instead of customer oriented.' The railroad business was constrained, in Levitt's view, by a lack of willingness to expand its horizons.

Levitt goes on to level similar criticisms at other industries. The film industry failed to respond to the growth of television because it regarded itself as being in the business of making movies rather than providing entertainment. (Interestingly, this can be applied to the resurgence of Disney in recent years – once the company began to regard itself as a provider of family entertainment in a variety of formats, rather than a children's film maker, it became spectacularly successful.)

Growth, writes Levitt, can never be taken for granted – 'In truth, there is no such thing as a growth industry.' Growth is not a matter of being in a particular industry, but of being perceptive enough to spot where future growth may lie. History, says Levitt, is filled with companies which fall into 'undetected decay' usually for a number of reasons. First, they assume that the growth in their particular market will continue so long as the population grows in size and wealth. Second is the belief that a product cannot be surpassed. Third, there is a tendency to place faith in the ability of improved production techniques to deliver lower costs and, therefore, higher profits. 'Mass production industries are impelled by a great drive to produce all they can. The prospect of steeply declining unit costs as output rises is more than most companies can usually resist. The profit possibilities look spectacular. All effort focuses on production. The result is that marketing gets neglected', Levitt writes. Finally, there is concentration on the product as this lends itself to measurement and analysis.

These insights have proved themselves depressingly accurate. Indeed, many of today's leading thinkers, such as Pascale and Peters, continually re-emphasize Levitt's message that there is no such thing as a growth industry. Success breeds complacency and complacency leads to failure. This is a fact of business life as true in the early 2000s as it was in the early 1960s.

In 'Marketing myopia' Levitt also makes a telling distinction between the tasks of selling and marketing. 'Selling concerns itself with the tricks and techniques of getting people to exchange their cash for your product. It is not concerned with the values that the exchange is all about. And it does not, as marketing invariably does, view the entire business process as consisting of a tightly integrated effort to discover, create, arouse, and satisfy customer needs,' he writes. This was picked up again in the 1980s when marketing underwent a resurgence and companies began to heed Levitt's view that they were overly oriented towards production.

Levitt's article and his subsequent work pushed marketing to centre stage. Indeed, in some cases it led to what Levitt labelled 'marketing mania' with companies 'obsessively responsive to every fleeting whim of the customer'. The main thrust of the article has stood the test of time ('I'd do it again and in the same way', commented Levitt in 1975).

Levitt's analysis of the problem was clearly accurate – companies were production-led – though his prognosis for potential solutions was less so. If the railroads had decided they were in the transportation business it is unlikely they would have succeeded, but if they had looked at the needs and aspirations of their customers they may well have stemmed the tide.

Notes

1 Levitt, Ted, 'Marketing myopia', *Harvard Business Review,* July-August 1960 .
2 Levitt, Ted, *Innovation in Marketing,* McGraw Hill, New York, 1962.

RENSIS LIKERT

New Patterns of Management

1961

The author

The American psychologist Rensis Likert (1903–81) was a pioneer of attitude surveys and poll design, as well as social research as a whole. From Cheyenne, Wyoming, Likert studied civil engineering at the University of Michigan. He then changed tack to major in sociology and economics. He completed a doctorate in psychology at Columbia University.

Likert then joined the psychology faculty at New York University before leaving academia as director for research at the Life Insurance Sales Research Bureau in Hartford, Connecticut. Likert moved on to work on statistics at the United States Department of Agriculture before returning to academia to form the Survey Research Center at the University of Michigan in Ann Arbor. This developed into the Institute for Social Research. Likert was also professor of psychology and sociology at the university.

The classic

While a doctoral student at Columbia University, Rensis Likert's 1932 doctoral thesis was entitled 'A Technique for the Measurement of Attitudes'. This introduced a straightforward five-point scale by which attitudes could be measured. (The now well-known scale ranges from strongly agree to strongly disagree.) This became known as the Likert Scale. Later Likert examined supervision styles in the insurance industry and interviewed farmers to discover their attitudes to government programmes. During World War II, Likert was highly active in studies related to the war effort. Most notably, Likert was involved in the Strategic Bombing Survey in which he examined the effect on morale of bombing campaigns. (The conclusions had a major effect on government policy in the post-war years – Likert's groups found that light bombing decreased morale while heavy bombing was likely to have little effect on morale. This conclusion has provided justification for such campaigns as that waged in Kosovo in 1999.)

Likert's business research focused on the ways in which participative groups could improve management and performance; and the human systems which exist in organizations. 'The greater the loyalty of a group toward the group, the greater is the motivation among the members to achieve the goals of the group, and the greater the probability that the group will achieve its goals', he wrote. Likert identified four types – systems 1 to 4 – of management style. The first is exploitative and authoritarian; the second, 'benevolent autocracy'; the third, 'consultative'; and the fourth 'participative'. The latter was seen by Likert as the best option – both in a business and a personal sense. He also proposed System 5 in which there was no formal authority. 'Each system tends to mold people in its own image. Authoritarian organizations tend to develop dependent people and few leaders. Participative organizations tend to develop emotionally and socially mature persons capable of effective interaction, initiative and leadership', writes Likert in his key book, *New Patterns of Management*.

New Patterns of Management (1961) bids farewell to the world of blind obedience and corporate man. Likert picks up the mood of individualism which was to sweep the world later in the 1960s. 'Managers with the best records of performance in American business and government are in the process of pointing the way to an appreciably more effective system of management than now exists', writes Likert in the book's opening. 'With the assistance of social science research, it is now possible to state a generalized theory of organization based on the management practices of these highest producers.'

Likert paints a picture of increased participation in the workplace and individualism. This, he argues, is a necessary consequence of increased competition and fast accelerating technological improvement – 'There is much greater need for cooperation and participation in managing the enterprise than when technologies were simple and the chief possessed all the technical knowledge needed.'

While this is contemporary sounding, Likert's prescription is of its time: management can make a difference and the route to understanding managerial performance is improved measurement. While Frederick Taylor measured movement, Likert measured minds.

Rensis Likert provides a blueprint of the ideal organization which has largely stood the test of time – though it has not, except in a few cases, become reality. Likert's description of the organizational ideal would be at home in an issue of *Fast Company*. 'An organization should be outstanding in its performance if it has competent personnel, if it has leadership which develops highly effective groups and uses the overlapping group form of structure, and if it achieves effective communication and influence, decentralized and co-ordinated decision-making, and high performance goals coupled with high motivation', Likert writes. In *New Patterns of Management* Likert established the standards which enlightened humane organizations needed to aspire to.

NICOLÓ MACHIAVELLI

The Prince

1513

The author

Nicoló Machiavelli (1469–1527) served as an official in the Florentine government. During 14 years as Secretary of the Second Chancery, he became known as the 'Florentine secretary' and served on nearly 30 foreign missions. His work brought him into contact with some of Europe's most influential ministers and government representatives. His chief diplomatic triumph occurred when Florence obtained the surrender of Pisa.

Machiavelli's career came to an end in 1512 when the Medicis returned to power. He was then exiled from the city and later accused of being involved in a plot against the government. For this he was imprisoned and tortured on the rack. He then retired to a farm outside Florence and began a successful writing career, with books on politics as well as plays and a history of Florence.

The classic

The late twentieth century has more than its fair share of self-improvement books. Publications promising the secrets of time management, stunning presentations and interviews fill countless bookshelves. Nearly 500 years ago, the first publication of its type was produced. Nicolo Machiavelli's *The Prince*[1] is the sixteenth century equivalent of Dale Carnegie's *How to Win Friends and Influence People*. Embedded beneath details of Alexander VI's tribulations lies a ready supply of aphorisms and insights which are, perhaps sadly, as appropriate to many of today's managers and organizations as they were half a millennium ago. (Indeed, Antony Jay's 1970 book, *Management and Machiavelli*, developed the comparisons.)

Gary Hamel on *The Prince*

'We occasionally need reminding that leadership and strategy are not twentieth-century inventions. It's just that in previous centuries they are more often the concerns of princes than industrialists. Yet power is a constant in human affairs, and a central theme of Machiavelli's *The Prince*. It is currently out of fashion to talk about power. We are constantly reminded that in the knowledge economy, capital wears shoes and goes home every night. No place here for the blunt instrument of power politics? But would Sumner Redstone, Bill Gates or Rupert Murdoch agree? What is interesting is that after 500 years, Machiavelli is still in print. What modern volume on leadership will be gracing bookstores in the year 2500? Does Machiavelli's longevity tell us anything about what are the deep, enduring truths of management?'

'Like the leaders Machiavelli sought to defend, some executives tend to see themselves as the natural rulers in whose hands organizations can be safely entrusted', says psychologist Robert Sharrock of consultants YSC. 'Theories abound on their motivation. Is it a defensive reaction against failure or a need for predictability through complete control? The effect of the power-driven Machiavellian manager is usually plain to see.'

'It is unnecessary for a prince to have all the good qualities I have enumerated, but it is very necessary to appear to have them', Machiavelli advises, adding the suggestion that it is useful 'to be a great pretender and dissembler'. But *The Prince* goes beyond such helpful presentational hints. Like all great books, it offers something for everyone. Take Machiavelli on managing change: 'There is nothing more difficult to take in hand, more perilous to conduct, or more uncertain in its success, than to take the lead in the introduction of a new order of things.' Or on sustaining motivation: 'He ought above all things to keep his men well-organized and drilled, to follow incessantly the chase.'

Machiavelli even has advice for executives acquiring companies in other countries: 'But when states are acquired in a country differing in language, customs, or laws, there are difficulties, and good fortune and great energy are needed to hold them, and one of the greatest and most real helps would be that he who has acquired them should go and reside there ... Because if one is on the spot, disorders are seen as they spring up, and one can quickly remedy them; but if one is not at hand, they are heard of only when they are great, and then one can no longer remedy them.' Executives throughout the world will be able to identify with Machiavelli's analysis.

Machiavelli is at his best in discussing leadership. Success, he says, is not down to luck or genius, but 'happy shrewdness'. In Machiavelli's hands, this is a euphemism. Elsewhere, he advises 'a Prince ought to have no other aim or thought, nor select anything else for his study, than war and its rules and discipline; for this is the sole art that belongs to him who rules'.

The Prince also examines the perils facing the self-made leader when they reach the dizzy heights: 'Those who solely by good fortune become princes from being private citizens have little trouble in rising, but much in keeping atop; they have not any difficulties on the way up, because they fly, but they have many when they reach the summit.'

Above all, Machiavelli is the champion of leadership through cunning and intrigue, the triumph of force over reason. An admirer of Borgia, Machiavelli had a dismal view of human nature. Unfortunately, as he sagely points out, history has repeatedly proved that a combination of being armed to the teeth and devious is more likely to allow you to achieve your objectives. It is all very well being good, says Machiavelli, but the leader 'should know how to enter into evil when necessity commands'.

Note

1 Machiavelli, Nicoló, *The Prince*, Penguin, London, 1967.

DOUGLAS McGREGOR

The Human Side of Enterprise

1960

The author

D ouglas McGregor was born in Detroit in 1906. The son of a clergyman, he graduated from the City College of Detroit (now Wayne University) in 1932 and did his PhD at Harvard. He taught social philosophy at Harvard before moving to the Massachusetts Institute of Technology (MIT), where he became an assistant professor in psychology. In 1962, after a brief spell at Antioch College, in Ohio, he returned to MIT in 1954. In 1962 he became Sloan Fellows Professor of Industrial Management, a post he held up until his death in 1964.

The classic

In the preface to *The Human Side of Enterprise*[1] Douglas McGregor writes: 'This volume is an attempt to substantiate the thesis that the human side of enterprise is "all of a piece" – that the theoretical assumptions management holds about controlling its human resources determine the whole character of the enterprise.'

The Human Side of Enterprise remains a classic text of its time. McGregor's study of work and motivation fitted in with the concerns of the middle and late 1960s when the large monolithic corporation was at its most dominant, and the world at its most questioning. The book sold 30,000 copies in its peak year of 1965, at that time an unprecedented figure.

McGregor was a central figure in the Human Relations School which emerged at the end of the 1950s (and which included Maslow and Herzberg among its other luminaries).

Gary Hamel on *The Human Side of Enterprise*

'Over the last forty years we have been slowly abandoning a view of human beings as nothing more than warm-blooded cogs in the industrial machine. People can be trusted; people want to do the right thing; people are capable of imagination and ingenuity – these were McGregor's fundamental premises, and they underlie the work of modern management thinkers from Drucker to Deming to Peters, and the employment practices of the world's most progressive and successful companies.'

'McGregor was a role model, and in many ways I emulated his career', says Warren Bennis. 'McGregor had a gift of getting toward the zone of understanding that would truly affect practitioners. Doug was not a great scholar, but he had that quality of unbridled lucidity for taking what was then referred to as behavioral science research and deploying it in a way that it really would have resonance for practitioners.'[2]

McGregor's great contribution was to examine how people behave within organizations and to question man's fundamental relationship with work. 'The essential task of management', he said, 'is to arrange organizational conditions and methods of operation so that people can achieve their own goals *best* by directing *their own* efforts towards organizational objectives.'

At a time when trade union disputes and industrial strife cast a lengthening shadow, it was a bold pronouncement. At MIT, too, McGregor worked with Joseph Scanlon, a former steel worker and trade union leader, contributing to and whole-heartedly endorsing The Scanlon Plan, a philosophy of worker-management participation.

In *The Human Side of Enterprise*, McGregor presents two ways of describing managers' thinking: Theory X and Theory Y.

Theory X is traditional carrot and stick thinking built on 'the assumption of the mediocrity of the masses'. This assumes that workers are inherently lazy, need to be supervised and motivated, and regard work as a necessary evil to provide money. The premises of Theory X, writes McGregor, are '(1) that the average human has an inherent dislike of work and will avoid it if he can; (2) that people, therefore, need to be coerced, controlled, directed, and threatened with punishment to get them to put forward adequate effort toward the organization's ends; and (3) that the typical human prefers to be directed, wants to avoid responsibility, has relatively little ambition, and wants security above all.'

McGregor lamented that Theory X 'materially influences managerial strategy in a wide sector of American industry', and observed 'if there is a single assumption that pervades conventional organizational theory it is that authority is the central, indispensable means of managerial control.'

'The human side of enterprise today is fashioned from propositions and beliefs such as these', writes McGregor, before going on to conclude that 'this behavior is not a consequence of man's inherent nature. It is a consequence rather of the nature of industrial organizations, of management philosophy, policy, and practice.' It is not people who have made organizations, but organizations which have transformed the perspectives, aspirations and behaviour of people.

The other extreme is described by McGregor as Theory Y, which is based on the principle that people want and need to work. If this is the case, then organizations need to develop the individual's commitment to its objectives, and then to liberate his or her abilities on behalf of those objectives. McGregor described the assumptions behind Theory Y: '(1) that the expenditure of physical and mental effort in work is as natural as in play or rest – the typical human doesn't inherently dislike work; (2) external control and threat of punishment are not the only means for bringing about effort toward a company's ends; (3) commitment to objectives is a function of the rewards associated with their achievement – the most important of such rewards is the satisfaction of ego and can be the direct product of effort directed toward an organization's purposes; (4) the average human being learns, under the right conditions, not only to accept but to seek responsibility; and (5) the capacity to exercise a relatively high degree of imagination, ingenuity, and creativity in the solution of organizational problems is widely, not narrowly, distributed in the population.'

Theories X and Y are not simplistic stereotypes. McGregor is realistic: 'It is no more possible to create an organization today which will be a full, effective application of this theory than it was to build an atomic power plant in 1945. There are many formidable obstacles to overcome.'

The Human Side of Enterprise also explores a number of other areas. For example, McGregor examines the process of acquiring new skills and identifies four kinds of learning relevant for managers: intellectual knowledge; manual skills; problem-solving skills; social interaction. The last element is, says McGregor, outside the confines of normal teaching and learning methods. 'We normally get little feedback of real value concerning the impact of our behavior on others. If they don't behave as we desire, it is easy to blame their stupidity, their adjustment, their peculiarities. Above all, it isn't considered good taste to give this kind of feedback in most social settings. Instead, it is discussed by our colleagues when we are not present to learn about it.' McGregor recommends the use of T-groups, then in their early stages, in which group participation was used to help people extend their insights into their own and other people's behaviour.

The common complaint against McGregor's Theories X and Y is that they are mutually exclusive, two incompatible ends of an end-less spectrum. To counter this, before he died in 1964, McGregor was developing Theory Z, a theory which synthesized the organizational and personal imperatives. The concept of Theory Z was later seized upon by William Ouchi. In his book of the same name, he analysed Japanese working methods. Here, he found fertile ground for many of the ideas McGregor was proposing for Theory Z – lifetime employment, concern for employees including their social life, informal control, decisions made by consensus, slow promotion, excellent transmittal of information from top to bottom and bottom to top with the help of middle management, commitment to the firm and high concern for quality.

In another development from McGregor's original argument, John Morse and Jay Lorsch argued that 'the appropriate pattern of organiza-tion is contingent on the nature of the work to be done and the particular needs of the people involved'. They labelled their approach 'contingency theory', a pragmatic juxtaposition of Theories X and Y.[3]

It is worth noting that Theory Y was more than mere theorizing. In the early 1950s, McGregor helped design a Proctor & Gamble plant in Georgia. Built on the Theory Y model with self-managing teams, its performance soon surpassed other P&G plants. This suggests that Theory Y works, though it has largely remained consigned to textbooks rather than being put into practice on the factory floor.

As Peter Drucker, the veteran management commentator, has observed: 'With every passing year, McGregor's message becomes ever more relevant, more timely, and more important.'

'McGregor was my mentor at MIT', Ed Schein has said. 'I think he has always been misunderstood. He observed that the more efficient manager tends to be the one that who values and trusts people upfront. The inefficient manager is cynical and mistrusts people. The inference from this was that McGregor was HR-oriented. But he was simply stating a fact of life rather than a prescription.'

Many managers won't even have heard of McGregor, or if they have will probably associate him with some arcane management philosophy of yesteryear. Yet to disregard McGregor's work is to ignore the central dichotomy of management: whether workers are self-actualizing, self-motivating individuals, or whether they are fundamentally lazy and require constant policing. It is a question that defines the role of managers. It also goes right to the heart of the human condition.

Notes

1 McGregor, Douglas, *The Human Side of Enterprise*, McGraw Hill, New York, 1960.
2 Bennis, Warren, *Organization Frontier*, 93/3.
3 Morse, John & Lorsch, Jay, 'Beyond Theory Y', *Harvard Business Review*, May–June 1970.

ABRAHAM MASLOW

Motivation and Personality

1954

The author

braham Maslow (1908–70) was an American behavioural psychologist. Born in Brooklyn, he trained at the University of Wisconsin. His career involved spells in management and academia. As an academic, he was initially interested in the social behaviour of primates and worked at Columbia University as a research fellow, Brooklyn College as an associate professor, the Western Behavioral Sciences Institute and later at Brandeis University in Massachusetts. It was while working at Brandeis that he wrote *Motivation and Personality*. His other books included *Towards a Psychology of Being* (1962); *Eupsychian Management* (1965); *The Psychology of Science* (1967); and *The Farther Reaches of Human Nature* (1971).

In two spells in industry, he worked as a plant manager at the Maslow Cooperage Corporation in Pleasanton, California, in the late 1940s and later he worked with a Southern Californian electronics company.

The classic

Abraham Maslow was a member of the Human Relations School of the late fifties. *Motivation and Personality*[1] is best known for its 'hierarchy of needs' – a concept which was first published by Maslow in 1943. In this, Maslow argues that there is an ascending scale of needs which need to be understood if people are to be motivated.

First are the fundamental physiological needs of warmth, shelter and food. 'It is quite true that man lives by bread alone – when there is no bread. But what happens to man's desires when there is plenty of bread and when his belly is chronically filled?' Maslow asks.

Gary Hamel on *Motivation and Personality*

'However subtle and variegated the original theory, time tends to reduce it to its most communicable essence: hence Maslow's 'hierarchy of needs', Pascale's 'seven Ss', Michael Porter's 'five forces', and the Boston Consulting Group's growth/share matrix. Yet there is no framework that has so broadly infiltrated organizational life as Maslow's hierarchy of needs. Perhaps this is because it speaks so directly to the aspirations each of us holds for ourself.'

Once basic physiological needs are met, others emerge to dominate. 'If the physiological needs are relatively well gratified, there then emerges a new set of needs, which we may categorize roughly as the safety needs', writes Maslow. 'A man, in this state, if it is extreme enough and chronic enough, may be characterized as living almost for safety alone.'

Next on the hierarchy are social or love needs, and ego, or self-esteem, needs. Ultimately, as man moves up the scale, with each need being satisfied comes what Maslow labels 'self-actualization': the individual achieves their own personal potential. (Later, Maslow created the word 'Eupsychian' to describe 'the culture that would be generated by 1,000 self-actualizing people on some sheltered island where they would not be interfered with'.)

While the hierarchy of needs provides a rational framework for motivation, its flaw lies in the nature of humanity. Man always wants more. When asked what salary they would be comfortable with, people routinely – no matter what their income – name a figure which is around twice their current income.

Even so, Maslow's hierarchy of needs contributed to the emergence of human relations as a discipline and to a sea change in how motivation was perceived. Instead of being simplistically regarded as driven by punishment and deprivation, motivation became intrinsically linked to rewards. Maslow's concept of 'self-actualization' is increasingly the subject of managerial texts.

Note

1 Maslow, Abraham, *Motivation and Personality*, Harper & Row, New York, 1954.

KONOSUKE MATSUSHITA

Quest for Prosperity

1988

The author

K onosuke Matsushita (1894–1989) was brought up in poverty in a small village near Wakayama. He had seven brothers and sisters. His once relatively prosperous family lived in straitened circumstances after his father lost money betting on commodities. He left school in 1904 and was apprenticed to a maker of charcoal grills. Matsushita later worked his way up to become an inspector in the Osaka Electric Light Company and, in 1917, founded his own company, Matsushita Electric. By 1932 Matsushita had over 1000 employees, ten factories and 280 patents.

During the war he made ships and planes as part of the Japanese war effort – even though he had no experience in either area. In 1958 Matsushita Electric was given an award for the quality of its factory operations and, in 1990, Matsushita bought MCA, a year after Sony bought Columbia Pictures. Matsushita created a $42 billion revenue business from nothing. He also created one of the world's most successful brands, Panasonic, and amassed a personal fortune of $3 billion.

The classic

'We are going to win and the industrial West is going to lose out; there's not much you can do about it because the reasons for your failure are within yourselves', said Konosuke Matsushita. For Western managers one of the most chilling passages in management literature must be that when Konosuke Matsushita mapped out why the West was destined to lose and the Japanese were inevitably going to emerge victorious in the battle for industrial supremacy. Matsushita spoke from a position of remarkable strength. His story tells of one of the most impressive industrial achievements of the twentieth century.

Matsushita's first product was a plug adaptor. He had suggested the idea to his previous employers but they had shown no interest – this was hardly surprising as Matsushita had little idea of how to actually make the product. It took Matsushita and four others, four months to figure out how to make the adaptor. No-one bought them.

Matsushita's first break was an order to made insulator plates. The order was delivered on time and was high quality. Matsushita began to make money. He then developed an innovative bicycle light. Again retailers were unimpressed. Then Matsushita had his salesmen leave a switched-on light in each shop. This simple product demonstration impressed and the business took off.

Matsushita's success story contains a huge number of managerial lessons (analysed most helpfully in John Kotter's 1997 book, *Matsushita Leadership*). First, Matsushita understood customer service before anyone in the West had even thought about it. 'Don't sell customers goods that they are attracted to. Sell them goods that will benefit them', he said. 'After-sales service is more important than assistance before sales. It is through such service that one gets permanent customers.'

Second, Matsushita – who admired Henry Ford – emphasized efficient production and quality products. 'To be out of stock is due to carelessness. If this happens, apologize to the customers, ask for their address and tell them that you will deliver the goods immediately.'

The third factor in Matsushita's success was pure entrepreneurism. He took risks and backed his beliefs at every stage. The classic example of this is the development of the video cassette. Matsushita developed VHS video and licensed the technology. Sony developed Betamax, which was immeasurably better, and failed to license the technology. The world standard is VHS and Betamax is consigned to history.

Finally, Matsushita advocated business with a conscience. This was manifested in his paternalistic employment practices. During a recession early in its life the company did not make any people redundant. This cemented loyalty. 'It's not enough to work conscientiously. No matter what kind of job, you should think of yourself as being completely in charge of and responsible for your own work,' he said, going on to describe how he approached his work – 'Big things and little things are my job. Middle-level arrangements can be delegated.' He also explained the role of the leader in more cryptic style – 'The tail trails the head. If the head moves fast, the tail will keep up the same pace. If the head is sluggish, the tail will droop.'

Matsushita mapped out the broader spiritual aims he believed a business should have. Profit was not enough. 'The mission of a manufacturer should be to overcome poverty, to relieve society as a whole from misery, and bring it wealth.' Matsushita's 'basic management objective', coined in 1929, said: 'Recognizing our responsibilities as industrialists, we will devote ourselves to the progress and development of society and the well-being of people through our business activities, thereby enhancing the quality of life throughout the world.'

And failure to make a profit was regarded by him as 'a sort of crime against society. We take society's capital, we take their people, we take their materials, yet without a good profit, we are using precious resources that could be better used elsewhere.'

To Matsushita business was demanding, serious and crucial: 'Business, we know, is now so complex and difficult, the survival of firms so hazardous in an environment increasingly unpredictable, competitive and fraught with danger, that their continued existence depends on the day-to-day mobilization of every ounce of intelligence.'

ELTON MAYO

The Human Problems of an Industrial Civilization

1933

The author

T he Australian Elton Mayo (1880–1949) had an interestingly diverse career though he remains best known – if known at all – for his contribution to the famous Hawthorne experiments into motivation.

Mayo's route to becoming involved in the Hawthorne experiments was circuitous. The early part of his career was spent in a variety of places and occupations. He underwent medical training in London and Edinburgh; spent time in Africa; worked in an Adelaide printing company; and taught at Queensland University. He also worked on psychoanalysing sufferers of shell shock after the First World War.[1] Mayo arrived in the United States in 1923 and worked at the University of Pennsylvania before joining Harvard. It was at Harvard that Mayo cemented his long-term contribution to business thinking.

The classic

The Hawthorne Studies were carried out at Western Electric's Chicago plant between 1927 and 1932. The studies offered important insights into the motivation of workers. It was found, for example, that changes in working conditions led to increased output – even if the changes weren't obviously for the betterment of working conditions.

The Hawthorne experiments were celebrated as a major event. Their significance lay not so much in their results and discoveries, though these were clearly important, but in the statement they made – whatever the dictates of mass production and Scientific Management, people and their motivation were critical to the success of any business – and in their legacy – the Human Relations school of thinkers which emerged in the forties and fifties.

The experiments were carried out in the Relay Assembling Test Room of Western Electric's Hawthorne Works. Mayo was not the only academic involved in the project. The experiments were also written about by a variety of others including Harvard's Fritz Roethlisberger and William Dickson. (Truth be told, none of the books written on the research are particularly accessible. Mayo's book is selected as much as a mark of his leading role in the Hawthorne project as for its literary value.)

The researchers were interested in exploring the links between morale and output. Five women workers were removed to a test room and observed as they worked. The research initially restricted itself to physical and technical variables. Sociological factors were not expected to be of any significance. The results proved otherwise. Removed from their colleagues, the morale of the guinea pigs improved. By virtue of their selection, the women felt that more attention was being paid to them. They felt chosen, and so responded positively. The second important fact which emerged was that the feeling of belonging to a cohesive group led to an increase in productivity. 'The desire to stand well with one's fellows, the so-called human instinct of association, easily outweighs the merely individual interest and the logic of reasoning upon which so many spurious principles of management are based', commented Mayo.

Mayo's belief that the humanity needed to be restored to the workplace struck a chord at a time when the dehumanizing side of mass production was beginning to be more fully appreciated. 'So long as commerce specializes in business methods which take no account of human nature and social motives, so long may we expect strikes and sabotage to be the ordinary accompaniment of industry', Mayo notes. He champions the case for teamworking and for improved communications between management and the workforce. The Hawthorne research revealed informal organizations between groups as a potentially powerful force which companies could utilize or ignore.

While Mayo offered a humanistic view of the workplace, it was still one which assumed that the behaviour of workers was dictated by the 'logic of sentiment' while that of the bosses was by the 'logic of cost and efficiency'. A Japanese manager, quoted in Richard Pascale's *Managing on the Edge*, made an important observation: 'There is nothing wrong with the findings. But the Hawthorne experiments look at human behaviour from the wrong perspective. Your thinking needs to build from the idea of empowering workers, placing responsibility closest to where the knowledge resides, using consistently honoured values to draw the separate individuals together. The Hawthorne experiments imply smug superiority, parent-to-child assumptions. This is not a true understanding.'

Even so, Mayo's work, and that of his fellow Hawthorne researchers, redressed the balance in management theorizing. The scientific bias of earlier researchers was put into a new perspective. This is part of a cyclical pattern as management theorizing swings from science to humanity or art. The yin and yang of thinking have rarely mixed. The humanists (from Mary Parker Follett, Mayo, Douglas McGregor, and Abraham Maslow to Charles Handy and Tom Peters) have shared little or no common ground with the scientists (Frederick Taylor, Alfred P Sloan, Igor Ansoff, Alfred Chandler, Michael Porter and contemporary gurus of reengineering). Mayo's work served as a foundation for all who followed on the humanist side of the divide.

Note

1 War time has provided a range of influences on management thinkers: Frederick Herzberg was deeply affected by the Dachau concentration camp; Ed Schein studied the brainwashing of prisoners of war during the Korean War; Tom Peters served in Vietnam.

HENRY MINTZBERG

The Nature of Managerial Work

1973

The author

Henry Mintzberg is 'perhaps the world's premier management thinker', says Tom Peters.[1] Mintzberg is Professor of Management at McGill University, Montreal and at INSEAD in Fontainebleau, France. He has recently been overseeing a venture by five business schools in Canada, the UK, France, India and Japan to create a next-generation master's programme for the development of managers. Mintzberg's original training was in mechanical engineering. He has a PhD in management from MIT in Boston and honorary degrees from the Universities of Venice, Lund, Lausanne, and Montreal.

His reputation has been made not by popularizing new techniques, but by rethinking the fundamentals of strategy and structure, management and planning. He takes an idiosyncratic, sometimes eccentric, always interesting, view on virtually every aspect of managerial life. His work on strategy, in particular his ideas of 'emergent strategy' and 'grassroots strategy making', has been highly influential.

He has won McKinsey prizes for the best article in the Harvard Business Review and is the author of *Mintzberg on Management: Inside Our Strange World of Organizations* (1989); *Structures in Fives* (1983); *The Nature of Managerial Work* (1973); *The Rise and Fall of Strategic Planning* (1994); and *Why I Hate Flying* (2001).

The classic

What managers actually do, how they do it and why, are fundamental questions. There are a number of generally accepted answers. Managers have a vision of themselves – which they largely persist in believing and propagating – that they sit in solitude contemplating the great strategic issues of the day, that they make time to reach the best decisions and that their meetings are high-powered, concentrating on the meta-narrative rather than the nitty-gritty.

The reality largely went unexplored until Henry Mintzberg's *The Nature of Managerial Work*.[2] Instead of accepting pat answers to perennial questions, Mintzberg went in search of the reality. He simply observed what a number of managers actually did. The resulting book blew away the managerial mystique.

Instead of spending time contemplating the long-term, Mintzberg found that managers were slaves to the moment, moving from task to task with every move dogged by another diversion, another call. The median time spent on any one issue was a mere nine minutes. In *The Nature of Managerial Work*, Mintzberg identifies the characteristics of the manager at work:

- performs a great quantity of work at an unrelenting pace
- undertakes activities marked by variety, brevity and fragmentation
- has a preference for issues which are current, specific and non-routine
- prefers verbal rather than written means of communication
- acts within a web of internal and external contacts
- is subject to heavy constraints but can exert some control over the work.

From these observations, Mintzberg identified the manager's 'work roles' as:

- **Interpersonal roles**
  - Figurehead: representing the organization/unit to outsiders
  - Leader: motivating subordinates, unifying effort
  - Liaiser: maintaining lateral contacts
- **Informational roles**
  - Monitor: of information flows
  - Disseminator: of information to subordinates
  - Spokesman: transmission of information to outsiders
- **Decisional roles**
  - Entrepreneur: initiator and designer of change
  - Disturbance handler: handling non-routine events
  - Resource allocator: deciding who gets what and who will do what
  - Negotiator: negotiating.

Gary Hamel on The Nature of Managerial Work

'Five reasons I like Henry Mintzberg: He is a world-class iconoclast. He loves the messy world of real companies (see *The Nature of Managerial Work*). He is a master storyteller. He is conceptual *and* pragmatic. He doesn't believe in easy answers.'

'All managerial work encompasses these roles, but the prominence of each role varies in different managerial jobs', writes Mintzberg.

Strangely, *The Nature of Managerial Work* has produced few worthwhile imitators. Researchers appear content to rely on neat case studies filled with retrospective wisdom and which are outdated as soon as they are written, or general interviews in which managers pontificate generally without being tied down to particulars. The actual work of managing enterprises often goes unnoticed behind the fashion and hyperbole.

Notes

1 Peters, Tom 'Strategic planning, RIP', 25 March, 1994.
2 Mintzberg, Henry, *The Nature of Managerial Work*, Harper & Row, New York, 1973.

HENRY MINTZBERG

The Rise of Fall of Strategic Planning

1994

The classic

H enry Mintzberg's *The Rise and Fall of Strategic Planning*[1] reflects a general dissatisfaction with the process of strategic planning – research by the US Planning Forum found that only 25 per cent of companies considered their planning processes to be effective and OC&C Strategy Consultants observed in a pamphlet that 'the humane thing to do with most strategic planning processes is to kill them off'.

Mintzberg has long been a critic of formulae and analysis-driven strategic planning. In *The Rise and Fall of Strategic Planning,* he remorselessly destroys much conventional wisdom and proposes his own interpretations.

He defines planning as 'a formalized system for codifying, elaborating and operationalizing the strategies which companies already have'. In contrast, strategy is either an 'emergent' pattern or a deliberate 'perspective'. Mintzberg argues that strategy cannot be planned. While planning is concerned with analysis, strategy making is concerned with synthesis. Today's planners are not redundant but are only valuable as strategy finders, analysts and catalysts. They are supporters of line managers, forever questioning rather than providing automatic answers. Their most effective role is in unearthing 'fledgling strategies in unexpected pockets of the organization so that consideration can be given to (expanding) them'.

Mintzberg identifies three central pitfalls to today's strategy planning practices.

First, the assumption that discontinuities can be predicted. Forecasting techniques are limited by the fact that they tend to assume that the future will resemble the past. This gives artificial reassurance and creates strategies which are liable to disintegrate as they are overtaken by events.

Gary Hamel on *The Rise of Fall of Strategic Planning*

'Henry views strategic planning as a ritual, devoid of creativity and meaning. He is undoubtedly right when he argues that planning doesn't produce strategy. But rather than use the last chapter of the book to create a new charter for planners, Henry might have put his mind to the question of where strategies actually do come from!'

He points out that our passion for planning mostly flourishes during stable times such as in the 1960s. Confronted by a new world order, planners are left seeking to re-create a long-forgotten past.

Second, that planners are detached from the reality of the organization. Mintzberg is critical of the 'assumption of detachment'. 'If the system does the thinking', he writes, 'the thought must be detached from the action, strategy from operations, (and) ostensible thinkers from doers. … It is this disassociation of thinking from acting that lies close to the root of (strategic planning's) problem.'

Planners have traditionally been obsessed with gathering hard data on their industry, markets, competitors. Soft data – networks of contacts, talking with customers, suppliers and employees, using intuition and using the grapevine – have all but been ignored.

Mintzberg points out that much of what is considered 'hard' data is often anything but. There is a 'soft underbelly of hard data', typified by the fallacy of 'measuring what's measurable'. The results are limiting, for example a pronounced tendency 'to favor cost leadership strategies (emphasizing operating efficiencies, which are generally measurable) over product leadership strategies (emphasizing innovative design or high quality, which tends to be less measurable)'.

To gain real and useful understanding of an organization's competitive situation, soft data needs to be dynamically integrated into the planning process. 'Strategy-making is an immensely complex process involving the most sophisticated, subtle and at times subconscious of human cognitive and social processes', writes Mintzberg. 'While hard data may inform the intellect, it is largely soft data that generate wisdom. They may be difficult to "analyze", but they are indispensable for synthesis – the key to strategy making.'

The third and final flaw identified by Mintzberg is the assumption that strategy making can be formalized. The left side of the brain has dominated strategy formulation with its emphasis on logic and analysis. Overly structured, this creates a narrow range of options. Alternatives which do not fit into the pre-determined structure are ignored. The right side of the brain needs to become part of the process with its emphasis on intuition and creativity. 'Planning by its very nature', concludes Mintzberg, 'defines and preserves categories. Creativity, by its very nature, creates categories or rearranges established ones. This is why strategic planning can neither provide creativity, nor deal with it when it emerges by other means.' Mould-breaking strategies 'grow initially like weeds, they are not cultivated like tomatoes in a hothouse ... (They) can take root in all kinds of places.'

Strategy-making, as presented by Mintzberg:

- is derived from synthesis
- is informal and visionary, rather than programmed and formalized
- relies on divergent thinking, intuition and using the subconscious. This leads to outbursts of creativity as new discoveries are made.
- is irregular, unexpected, *ad hoc*, instinctive. It upsets stable patterns
- requires managers who are adaptive information manipulators, opportunists, rather than aloof conductors
- is done in time of instability characterized by discontinuous change
- results from an approach which takes in broad perspectives and is, therefore, visionary, and involves a variety of actors capable of experimenting and then integrating.

The Rise and Fall of Strategic Planning attracted a great deal of attention and some vituperative debate. 'In many ways, the book's title should be reversed to the fall and rise of planning', observed Christopher Lorenz in the *Financial Times*, arguing that the book represented the 'mellowing of Mintzberg'.[2]

Mintzberg's work brought a spirited response from the defenders of strategy. Andrew Campbell, co-author of *Corporate-Level Strategy*, wrote: 'Strategic planning is not futile. Research has shown that some companies – both conglomerates and more focused groups – have strategic planning processes that add real value.' The solution, according to Campbell, is not to deem planning an inappropriate corporate activity, but for it only to occur when 'the corporate center develops a value-creating, corporate-level strategy and builds the management processes needed to implement it'.[3]

As the debate rumbles on, Mintzberg has increasingly expanded his intellectual horizons. He now talks about what he calls 'nuanced managing' – 'I don't think it is a better way of managing, I think it *is* managing', he explains. 'I think all decent management is nuanced. Bad management is not nuanced; bad management is categorical. Nuanced management is about getting involved, knowing the business, knowing what's going on day-to-day. For me it's all about getting past all the nonsense that passes for management. It's getting in touch, knowing what's really going on, being responsive – and responsible.'

Mintzberg has reflected that he has spent his public life dealing with organizations, and his private life escaping from them. 'I just don't like big hierarchical organizations', he says. 'In the past some large organizations treated people paternalistically, but reasonably decently. But many have destroyed that contract. It's significant that the two most popular management techniques of all time – Taylor's work study methods – to control your hands – and strategic planning – to control your brain – were adopted most enthusiastically by two groups, communist governments and American corporations.'[4]

Notes

1 Mintzberg, Henry, *The Rise and Fall of Strategic Planning*, Prentice Hall International, Hemel Hempstead, 1994.
2 Lorenz, Christopher, 'The mellowing of Mintzberg', *Financial Times*, 15 March 1994.
3 Campbell, Andrew, 'The point is to raise the game', *Financial Times*, 14 September 1994.
4 Interview with Des Dearlove, June 2002.

JAMES MOONEY & ALAN REILEY

Onward Industry

1931

The authors

J ames D Mooney (1884–1957) was trained as an engineer and then became a senior executive with General Motors. After graduating from the Case School of Applied Sciences in Mining and Metallurgy, he spent time gold mining. He then found a more lucrative though duller career at Westinghouse, BF Goodrich and the Hyatt Roller Bearing Company. He then became president and general manager of the General Motors subsidiary the Remy Electric Company and, in 1922, was appointed a vice president of GM and president of GM Overseas. After becoming heavily involved in wartime activities —including meetings with German leaders to seek out peace – Mooney became chairman and president of Willys-Overland Motors.

Mooney's co-author was Alan Reiley. In his introduction, Mooney describes how their joint authorship came about: 'When I presented this conception of organization [to Reiley] I could see that a light was beginning to burn in his eye … That the book is at all possible is due largely to Mr Reiley's research.'

The classic

Onward Industry – later re-titled *The Principles of Organization* – provides an organization model.[1] It is a model which is firmly of its time, applying the reasoned science of Frederick Taylor to the broader organizational canvas.

Mooney and Reiley's book is notable in a number of ways. First, it argues that organization is a universal phenomenon. 'Organization is as old as human society itself', they write. Mooney and Reiley consider the scalar organization of the Catholic Church, governmental organization, and the evolution of different forms of organization from Roman times to Medieval times, through to the company of the early twentieth century. Their conclusion is simply put by the title of the book's first chapter: 'Men love to organize'.

The second important strand to Mooney and Reiley's argument is that the organization of businesses is crucial to overall standards of living. They make a direct link between industrial prosperity, built on modern management techniques, and the affluence of society as a whole. 'The highest development of the techniques both of production and distribution will be futile to supply the material wants of those who, because of poverty, are unable to acquire through purchase', they write. 'The final task of industry, therefore, is to organize participation in these activities, even in the most backward communities and countries, through which alone can purchasing capacity be created and extended.'

A third element in Mooney and Reiley's argument is that production without distribution is worthless. This marks something of a watershed. Prior to the 1930s, production was the overarching driving force; from the Second World War the emphasis shifted to finding new markets and enhancing and expanding distribution to make inroads into these markets. Size, note Mooney and Reiley, isn't everything – 'Modern business leadership has been generally characterized by the capacity to create large organizations, but by failure in knowing exactly what to do with them.'

Mooney and Reiley's theory of organizations identified three central organizational principles – the co-ordinative principle, the scalar process, and the functional effect.

	Principle	Process	Effect
The co-ordinative principle	Authority or co-ordination per se	Processive co-ordination	Effective co-ordination
The scalar process	Leadership	Delegation	Functional definition
The functional effect	Determinative functionalism (legislative)	Applicative functionalism (executive)	Interpretative functionalism (judicial)

Note

1 The book's sub-title is 'The principles of organization and their significance to modern industry'.

AKIO MORITA
Made in Japan
1986

The author

A kio Morita (born 1921) was the co-founder of Sony and the best known of the new wave of Japanese businessmen who rose to prominence in the West in the 1980s. Morita was an officer in the Japanese Navy during World War II. Trained as a physicist and scientist, Morita could have followed family tradition and gone into sake production. (He refers to himself as 'the first son and fifteenth generation heir to one of Japan's finest and oldest sake-brewing families'.) Instead, he founded a company with Masaru Ibuka (1908–97) immediately after the end of the war.

The classic

Made in Japan is the story of Sony and, to a large extent, the central text of post-war business history.[1]

The company was christened Tokyo Tsushin Kogyo KK (Tokyo Telecommunications Engineering Corporation). Not a good name to put on a product, Morita later ruminated. Ibuka was the technical expert, Morita the salesman. Initially, the company made radio parts and a rice cooker, among other things. Its rice cooker was unreliable.

In 1949 the company developed magnetic recording tape and, in 1950, sold the first tape recorder in Japan. In 1957 the company produced a pocket-sized radio and a year later renamed itself Sony (*sonus* is Latin for sound). In 1960 it produced the first transistor TV in the world.

And, increasingly, the world was Sony's market. Its combination of smaller and smaller products at the leading edge of technology proved irresistible. In 1961 Sony Corporation of American was the first Japanese company to be listed on Wall Street and, in 1989, Sony bought Columbia Pictures so that by 1991 it had more foreigners on its 135,000 payroll than Japanese.

Morita became famous as the acceptable face of Japanese industry. Sophisticated and entrepreneurial, he did not fit the Western stereotype. (He also advocated a more assertive Japanese approach in *The Japan That Can Say No*, which he wrote with a Japanese politician, Ishihara Shintaro.)

In 1993 Morita resigned as Sony chairman after suffering a cerebral haemorrhage playing tennis. In the same year, the company wrote off $3.2 billion for its movie operations – the major misadventure in its history. Even so, the modern Sony is a $37 billion company.

Morita and Sony's story parallels the rebirth of Japan as an industrial power. 'We in the free world can do great things. We proved it in Japan by changing the image of Made in Japan from something shoddy to something fine', says Morita. When Sony was first attempting to make inroads into Western markets it cannot be forgotten that Japanese products were sneered at as being of the lowest quality. Surmounting that obstacle was a substantial business achievement.

Morita and Sony's gift was to invent new markets. Describing what he called Sony's 'pioneer spirit', Morita said: 'Sony is a pioneer and never intends to follow others. Through progress, Sony wants to serve the whole world. It shall be always a seeker of the unknown … Sony has a principle of respecting and encouraging one's ability, and always tries to bring out the best in a person. This is the vital force of Sony.' While companies such as Matsushita were inspired followers, Sony set a cracking pace with product after product, innovation after innovation.

Sony brought the world the hand-held video camera, the first home video recorder and the floppy disk. The blemishes on its record were the Betamax video format, which it failed to license, and colour television systems.

Its most famous success was the brainchild of Morita, the Walkman. The evolution of this now ubiquitous product is the stuff of corporate legend. Morita noticed that young people liked listening to music wherever they went. He put two and two together and made a Walkman. 'I do not believe that any amount of market research could have told us that it would have been successful', he said adding the rider – 'The public does not know what is possible, we do.'

Such brilliant marketing was no mere accident. 'If you go through life convinced that your way is always best, all the new ideas in the world will pass you by', says Morita who argues that analysis and education do not necessarily get you to the best business decisions. 'You can be totally rational with a machine. But if you work with people, sometimes logic often has to take a backseat to understanding', he says. Morita is also the author of *Never Mind School Records*.

Apart from his marketing prowess, Morita has emphasized the cultural differences in Japanese attitudes towards work. 'Never break another man's rice bowl', he advises and observes: 'Japanese people tend to be much better adjusted to the notion of work, any kind of work, as honourable.' Management is regarded by Morita as where the buck stops and starts: 'If we face a recession, we should not lay off employees; the company should sacrifice a profit. It's management's risk and management's responsibility. Employees are not guilty; why should they suffer?'

Note

1 Morita, Akio, *Made in Japan*, Dutton & Co., New York, 1986.

JOHN NAISBITT

Megatrends

1982

The author

J ohn Naisbitt (born 1930) worked as an executive with IBM and Eastman Kodak, and has been a distinguished international fellow at the Institute of Strategic and International Studies in Kuala Lumpur. He is a futurologist whose books have sold in their millions. Naisbitt was educated at Cornell. Indeed, at one time Cornell could boast the top three authors in the bestseller lists as alumni – Naisbitt with his *Megatrends*, Kenneth Blanchard with *The One Minute Manager* and Tom Peters with *In Search of Excellence*.

The classic

The book which really established Naisbitt as someone worth listening to was the 1982 publication of *Megatrends*. It has sold over eight million copies and Naisbitt has also produced, *Megatrends Asia*.

'The most reliable way to anticipate the future is by understanding the present', says Naisbitt and, in *Megatrends*, he identifies ten 'critical restructurings'. While some have proved accurate predictions of what has happened in intervening years, others have proved less accurate:

- 'Although we continue to think we live in an industrial society, we have in fact changed to an economy based on the creation and distribution of information' – This has become accepted and is now a hackneyed truism. In the early 1980s, however, traditional issues, such as production methods, still held sway. Naisbitt was ahead of the game. The technological possibilities in information exchange and transfer were contemplated by a small group in west coast laboratories.

- 'We are moving in the dual directions of high tech/high touch, matching each new technology with a compensatory human response' – This is a theme Naisbitt has returned to and developed in more recent years. 'The acceleration of technological progress has created an urgent need for a counter ballast – for high touch experiences. Heart transplants have led to new interest in family doctors and neighborhood clinics; jet airplanes have resulted in more face-to-face meetings. High touch is about getting back to a human scale', he says. 'All change is local and bottom-up ... If you keep track of local events, you can see the shifting patterns. Also, remember that high-tech/high-touch isn't an either/or decision. You can't stop technological progress, but by the same token, you can hardly go wrong with a high-touch response. Give out your home phone number. Send a handwritten letter. FedEx has all the reliability and efficiency of modern electronics, but its success is built on a form of high touch: hand delivery.'

- 'No longer do we have the luxury of operating within an isolated, self- sufficient, national economic system; we must now acknowledge that we are part of a global economy. We have begun to let go of the idea that the US is and must remain the world's industrial leader as we move on to other tasks' – Naisbitt was right to identify the emergence of globalization as a powerful force. His perception of a change in America's perception of itself is open to doubt. Naisbitt has gone on to explore what he calls the 'global paradox' which he believes is that 'The bigger the world economy, the more powerful its smallest player'.

- 'We are restructuring from a society run by short-term considerations and rewards in favor of dealing with things in much longer-term time frames' – There is little evidence, some sixteen years on, that this trend has become a reality.

- 'In cities and states, in small organizations and subdivisions, we have rediscovered the ability to act innovatively and to achieve results – from the bottom up' – Naisbitt anticipated the fashion in the late eighties and early nineties for empowerment with responsibility being spread more evenly throughout organizations rather than centred on a coterie of managers.

- 'We are shifting from institutional help to more self-reliance in all aspects of our lives' – Trends in working patterns, such as employability, suggest that this is becoming the case for a select few professionals with marketable skills.

- 'We are discovering that the framework of representative democracy has become obsolete in an era of instantaneously shared information'

– Alvin Toffler was suggesting this in his 1970 book *Future Shock,* though there are few signs of reform.
- 'We are giving up our dependence on hierarchical structures in favor of informal networks. This will be especially important to the business community' – This has become one of the great trends of the last decade as networks are developed in a bewildering variety of ways – with suppliers, between competitors, internally, globally. Technology has enabled networks never previously anticipated – with important repercussions. 'When everyone hears about everything at the same time, everyone else hears about it, and we all know that. Instantly. But we still have the same old system. So we're going through a big period of correction', says Naisbitt.[1] Linked to this is the entire question of speed which Naisbitt identified early on as a competitive weapon – 'Economies of scale are giving way to economies of scope, finding the right size for synergy, market flexibility, and above all, speed', he says in *The Global Paradox.*
- 'More Americans are living in the South and West leaving behind the old industrial cities of the North' – In the era of Silicon Valley et al. this is stating the obvious, but in the eighties it was less so.
- 'From a narrow either/or society with a limited range of personal choices, we are exploding into a free-wheeling multiple option society' – To this, Naisbitt could have added the caveat that this society would offer multiple options but only for a few.

Aside from these trends, Naisbitt has championed the role of small business in generating the wealth of the future. 'Small companies, right down to the individual, can beat big bureaucratic companies ten out of ten times. Unless big companies reconstitute themselves as a collection of small companies, they will just continue to go out of business. It's the small companies who are creating the global company', he says.[2]

Now in his seventies, Naisbitt prefers to think of himself as a social forecaster rather than a futurist. 'There's a lot of nonsense under the futurist banner', he says. 'People ask me "What's going to happen in 2005?" I say I've no idea. There are so many variations. The global economy is incredibly complex. This is good news. If you don't know how it works you can't even begin to try to fix it.'

Rather than being focused on the future, Naisbitt's latest work argues that 'authenticity' will increasingly be a competitive advantage. Instead of inventing the future, companies are set on reinventing the past – some with more guile and commitment than others (witness the term 'genuine reproduction'). 'There is an increasing degree of fuzziness between what is real and what is fake', observes John Naisbitt. 'The authenticity of a company's product or service is now all-important. They need to establish intimacy with consumers.' Some companies have already re-introduced people answering their telephones rather than having automated systems. The cold mechanical hand of technology will only get you so far. The warm hand of humanity is required to maximize the business potential of technology. 'It is embracing technology that preserves our humanness and rejecting technology that intrudes upon it', says Naisbitt.

The trouble is that such reality can be elusive. The corporate world's love affair with technology means that technology rather than humanity tends to set the agenda. It is easier to order up a new software package than discover the tastes and preferences of urban teenagers. Naisbitt laments: 'Companies feel pressured into keeping up with technology because they fear falling behind their competitors. They feel they have to be on the Internet so move as fast as they can to make the Internet their strategy. In effect the promise of the Internet is running their businesses.' Not that Naisbitt is a high-tech Luddite – 'I am very much pro-technology, but more discretion is needed.' Mr. Naisbitt notes that America finds itself in a zone of technological intoxication – more soberly he judges that 'Europe is generally more appreciative of life's essential pleasures'.

Technological intoxication is characterized by an addiction to quick fixes; the increasing acceptance of violence; confusion as to what is real; and a confused relationship with technology in which fear and worship are combined. The end result is that consumer technology and the escape from consumer technology – through holidays for example – are the two biggest markets in the American economy. Often, however, we seek to escape through buying and using more technology. 'We are tethered to work through mobile phones and the like. We're allowing technology to take over our leisure time,' says Naisbitt.

In this environment where the next big thing is likely to be found on an inner city street, where consumers are addicted to technology, and the ability to connect with reality is paramount, small entrepreneurial companies have a clear advantage. The Fortune 500 – a mere nine per cent of the US economy – is no longer where it's at.

Notes

1 Interview with John Naisbitt, *Star Tribune*, November 1996.
2 Gibson, Rowan (editor), *Rethinking the Future*, Nicholas Brealey, London, 1996.

KENICHI OHMAE

The Mind of the Strategist

1982

The author

K enichi Ohmae (born 1943) is a Japanese who was first Americanized (Kenichi became Ken to his US colleagues) and then globalized. Ohmae is enormously gifted. A concert-standard flautist, he is also a nuclear physicist, prodigious author with dozens of books to his credit, politician and long-time star of the consulting firm, McKinsey and Company. Indeed, when he left McKinsey to stand for the governorship of Tokyo in 1995, the consultancy firm's departure announcement noted Ohmae was 'a great consultant, a compelling speaker, an incredibly prolific writer, a musician and a motorcyclist'. The significance of the latter accomplishment is difficult to determine.

Ohmae is a graduate of Waseda University, the Tokyo Institute of Technology, and has a PhD in nuclear engineering from Massachusetts Institute of Technology. He joined McKinsey in 1972, becoming managing director of its Tokyo office. He has been an adviser to the former Japanese Prime Minister Nakasone.

He is the founder and managing director of Ohmae & Associates, JASDICK (a software development house), EveryD.com Home (an Internet platform for living rooms), and Business Breakthrough (an interactive satellite network for business). Ohmae is also the dean of two private schools in Tokyo: Isshinjuku, which studies public policy, and Attacker's Advantage, which studies entrepreneurship. He is also the Chancellor's Professor of Public Policy at the UCLA School of Public and Social Research.

The *Financial Times* described him as 'a personality in a land where outspoken personalities are rare. And while most Japanese are anxious not to offend, Ohmae is blunt and often downright rude ... he is Japan's only successful management guru.'

Gary Hamel on *The Mind of the Strategist*

'I loved this book! At a time when most strategy savants were focused either on the process of planning (Ansoff and his followers) or on the determinants of successful, i.e. profitable, strategies (Michael Porter), Kenichi Ohmae challenged managers to think in new ways. Strategy doesn't come from a calendar-driven process; it isn't the product of a systematic search for ways of earning above average profits; strategy comes from viewing the world in new ways. Strategy starts with an ability to think in new and unconventional ways.'

His best-known books, in the West at least, include *Japan Business: Obstacles and Opportunities* (1983); *Triad Power* (1985); *Beyond National Borders* (1987); and *The End of the Nation State* (1995). *The Invisible Continent: Four Strategic Imperatives of the New Economy* (2001) examines hot industries such as e-commerce, banking, and telecommunications, distinguishing between the old-world 'titans' such as IBM, GM, and CBS, and the new world 'Godzillas' like AOL, Dell, Cisco, and Microsoft.

The classic

The Mind of the Strategist[1] by Kenichi Ohmae was published in Japan in 1975, but did not reach the American market until 1982. 'The author's sometimes imperfect English combines with a simple, personal style to give this book a great deal of charm', observed the *Harvard Business Review* in patronizing mood.

The sub-title in the first edition was 'The art of Japanese business' and the book was published in the West at the height of enthusiasm and interest in Japanese management methods – when the book was first published in Japan, the West remained studiously uninterested in the possibility of learning from Japanese best practice.

In *The Mind of the Strategist* Ohmae challenges the simplistic, but then widely held belief, that Japanese management was a matter of company songs and lifetime employment. Instead, Ohmae argues that Japanese success could be significantly attributed to the nature of Japanese strategic thinking. This, says Ohmae, is 'basically creative and intuitive and rational' – though none of these characteristics were evident in the usual Western stereotype of Japanese management. Offering solace to the bemused and increasingly uncompetitive West, Ohmae suggests that the necessary creativity can be learned.

Ohmae points out that, unlike large US corporations, Japanese businesses tend not to have large strategic planning staffs. Instead they often have a single, naturally talented strategist with 'an idiosyncratic mode of thinking in which company, customers, and competition merge in a dynamic interaction out of which a comprehensive set of objectives and plans for action eventually crystallizes'.

Ohmae explains that an effective business strategy is one by which a company can gain significant ground on its competitors at an acceptable cost to itself. This can be achieved in four ways: by focusing on the key factors for success, by building on relative superiority, through pursuing aggressive initiatives, and through utilizing strategic degrees of freedom – focusing on innovation in areas, which are untouched by competitors. While the outcome or objective is the same from East to West, Japanese entrepreneurs use holistic and intuitive approach at the beginning, as opposed to statistics and surveys often used in large Western corporations.

Another area of fundamental difference explored by Ohmae is the role of the customer who is at the heart of the Japanese approach to strategy and key to corporate values. At the time, customers were generally noticeable by their absence from Western strategic planning and corporate values. 'In the construction of any business strategy, three main players must be taken into account: the corporation itself, the customer, and the competition. Each of these "strategic three Cs" is a living entity with its own interests and objectives. We shall call them, collectively, the "strategic triangle",' says Ohmae. 'Seen in the context of the strategic triangle, the job of the strategist is to achieve superior performance, relative to competition, in the key factors for success of the business. At the same time, the strategist must be sure that his strategy properly matches the strengths of the corporation with the needs of a clearly defined market. Positive matching of the needs and objectives of the two parties involved is required for a lasting good relationship; without it, the corporation's long-term viability may be at stake.'

The central thrust of the book is that strategy as epitomized by the Japanese approach is irrational and non-linear. (Previously, the Japanese had been fêted in the West for the brilliance of their rationality and the far-sighted remorselessness of their thinking.) 'In strategic thinking, one first seeks a clear understanding of the particular character of each element of a situation and then makes the fullest possible use of human brain power to restructure the elements in the most advantageous way', writes Ohmae.

'Phenomena and events in the real world do not always fit a linear model. Hence the most reliable means of dissecting a situation into its constituent parts and reassembling them in the desired pattern is not a step-by-step methodology such as systems analysis. Rather, it is that ultimate non-linear thinking tool, the human brain. True strategic thinking thus contrasts sharply with the conventional mechanical systems approach based on linear thinking. But it also contrasts with the approach that stakes everything on intuition, reaching conclusions without any real breakdown or analysis.'

The Mind of the Strategist is not an unquestioning eulogy to the Japanese approach to strategy. Indeed, Ohmae notes the decline in naturally strategic thinkers in both Japan and the West. Both systems, he says, encourage orthodoxy to the extent that innovative strategic thinking is neither encouraged nor possible.

An effective business strategy, Ohmae says, 'is one by which a company can gain significant ground on its competitors at an acceptable cost to itself'. There are four main ways of achieving this – 'In each of these four methods, the principal concern is to avoid doing the same thing, on the same battle-ground, as the competition', Ohmae explains.

The first method is through focusing on the key factors for success (KFSs). Certain functional or operating areas within every business are more critical for success in that particular business environment than others. If you concentrate effort into these areas and your competitors do not, this is a source of competitive advantage. The problem, of course, is identifying what these key factors for success are. 'The most effective shortcut to major success seems to be to jump quickly to the top of the rank by concentrating major resources early on a single strategically significant function', says Ohmae. 'All of today's industry leaders, without exception, began by bold deployment of strategies based on KFS.'

The second route is by building on relative superiority. When all competitors are seeking to compete on the KFSs, a company can exploit any differences in competitive conditions. For example, it can make use of technology or sales networks not in direct competition with its rivals.

The third method is through pursuing aggressive initiatives. Frequently, the only way to win against a much larger, entrenched competitor is to upset the competitive environment, by undermining the value of its KFSs – changing the rules of the game by introducing new KFSs.

The final route to an effective strategy is through utilizing strategic degrees of freedom. By this, Ohmae means that the company can focus upon innovation in areas which are 'untouched by competitors'.

The Mind of the Strategist began the process of questioning the then pervasive Japanese mythology through providing interpretations of strategy which were not hidebound by habitual cultural or traditional behaviour. In his subsequent works, Ohmae's perspectives have broadened and developed the highly original ideas of *The Mind of the Strategist* still further.

Note

1 Ohmae, Kenichi, *The Mind of the Strategist*, McGraw Hill, New York, 1982.

KENICHI OHMAE

The Borderless World

1990

The classic

*T*he *Borderless World*[1] is an ambitious book exploring 'the new logic of the global marketplace' as well as what Kenichi Ohmae calls 'power and strategy in the interlinked economy'.

To the three Cs of his previous works (commitment, creativity and competitiveness), Ohmae adds two more – country (rather tortuously defined as 'the various government-created environments in which global organizations must operate') and currency ('the exposure of such organizations to fluctuations in foreign exchange rates'). These two additional elements are now key to the formulation of any strategy – 'When a sudden fluctuation in trade policy or exchange rates can turn an otherwise brilliant strategy into a seemingly irreparable haemorrhage of cash, making arrangements to deal with such fluctuations must lie at the very heart of strategy.'

Ohmae now defines strategy as 'creating sustaining values for the customer far better than those of competitors. It therefore means first of all invention and the commercialization of invention. Most people in big companies have forgotten how to invent.' As a result, Ohmae argues that 'it's time for big companies to relearn the art of invention. But this time they must learn to manage invention in industries or businesses that are global, where you have to get world-scale economies and yet tailor products to key markets.'

Strategy, says Ohmae, is about more than being better than the competition. This encourages companies to become fixated with the competition so that in formulating their strategy, they are driven by the strategy of their competitors. 'Competitive realities are what you test possible strategies against; you define them in terms of customers. Tit-for-tat responses to what competitors do may be appropriate, but they are largely reactive. They come second, after your real strategy. Before

Gary Hamel on *The Borderless World*

'So the world is becoming interdependent. Hardly news to companies like Dow Chemical, IBM, Ford or Nestlé. But in 1990 this was still news to Japanese companies (and politicians) who typically defined "globalization" as big open export markets, and maybe a factory in Tennessee. Kenichi challenged Japanese companies, and myopic executives elsewhere, to develop a more sophisticated view of what it means to be global. Just what balance will ultimately be struck between the forces of globalization and the forces of nationalism and tribalism remains to be seen.'

you test yourself against competition, your strategy should encompass the determination to create value for customers', states Ohmae.

To Ohmae, countries are mere governmental creations. In the Inter-linked Economy (made up of the Triad of the US, Europe and Japan) consumers are not driven to purchase things through nationalistic senti-ments – no matter what politicians suggest or say. 'At the cash register, you don't care about country of origin or country of residence. You don't think about employment figures or trade deficits', Ohmae writes. This, he argues, also applies to industrial consumers.

The Borderless World concludes with a 'Declaration of Interdepend-ence toward the world' signed by Ohmae and McKinsey's Fred Gluck and Herbert Henzler. It is immodestly noted below that 'this statement … is one we each embrace and believe to be the best possible course for all countries and governments to follow'.

In the declaration, the trio contend that the role of central govern-ments must change to 'allow individuals access to the best and cheapest goods and services from anywhere in the world; help corporations provide stable and rewarding jobs anywhere in the world regardless of the corpo-ration's national identity; coordinate activities with other governments to minimize conflicts arising from narrow interests; and avoid abrupt changes in economic and social fundamentals'. It calls on governments to 'deal collectively with traditionally parochial affairs' including taxation.

This manifesto for the future is as broad ranging as it is, in political reality, unlikely. *The Borderless World* has, however, fuelled debates about the role of governments and the relationship between governments and the business world which have yet to be resolved. Ohmae has since gone on to explore the role of nations still further and now suggests that we have reached a time when 'the end of the nation state' is imminent.

Note

1 Ohmae, Kenichi, *The Borderless World*, William Collins, London, 1990.

TAIICHI OHNO

Toyota Production System

1978

The author

he architect of the Toyota Production System, Taiichi Ohno
worked for Toyota – originally for Toyota Spinning and Weav-
ing. He later became a consultant.

The classic

During the last forty years, Western car makers have lurched from one
crisis to another. They have always been a step behind. And the company
they have been following is the Japanese giant, Toyota. The reasons why
are pithily explained by Taiichi Ohno in his brief book, *Toyota Production
System: Beyond Large-Scale Production.*

The roots of the Toyota Production System lie in the immediate
post-war years.

Toyoda Kiichiro, president of Toyoda Motor Company, demanded
that the company caught up with America. He gave his company three
years to do so otherwise, he anticipated, the Japanese car industry would
cease to exist. At that time, an average American worker produced around
nine times as much as a Japanese worker.

The Toyota Production System evolved by Ohno was strikingly different from approaches used in the West. The basic objective was seen as
being different. In the West selling price was regarded as the combination
of actual costs plus profit. Toyota, believing that the consumer actually
sets the price, concluded that profit resulted when costs were subtracted
from the selling price. The emphasis was on reducing costs rather than
increasing the selling price.

Three simple principles underlie the Toyota system. The first is
that of just-in-time production. There is no point in producing cars,

or anything else, in blind anticipation of someone buying them. Waste ('muda') is bad. Production has to be closely tied to the market's requirements. Second, responsibility for quality rests with everyone and any quality defects need to be rectified as soon as they are identified. The third, more elusive, concept was the 'value stream'. Instead of seeing the company as a series of unrelated products and processes, it should be seen as a continuous and uniform whole, a stream including suppliers as well as customers.

Another central element in Ohno's system was the process of the 'five whys'. This suggested that by asking why five times and discovering the answer at each stage, the root of any problem can be discovered and solved.

The concepts were brought to mass Western audiences thanks to work carried out at the Massachusetts Institute of Technology as part of its International Motor Vehicle Program. The MIT research took five years, covered 14 countries and looked exclusively at the worldwide car industry.

The research concluded that, while American car makers remained fixed in the mass production techniques of the past, Japanese car makers managed to square the manufacturing circle: management, workers and suppliers worked to the same goals - resulting in increased production, high quality, happy customers and lower costs. The research spawned the 1990 bestseller by James Womack, Daniel Jones and Daniel Roos, *The Machine That Changed the World*. (Womack and Roos were from MIT while Jones was from Cardiff Business School.) From lean production, Womack and Jones went on to propose 'the lean enterprise' (based on research covering 25 American, Japanese and German companies) and 'lean management'.

Lean production became fashionable. As with most management fads, it was wilfully misinterpreted. It became linked to re-engineering and, more worryingly, with downsizing.

The reality is that lean production as introduced by Ohno and Toyota is a highly effective concept. 'Lean production is a superior way for humans to make things', argue Womack and Jones. They are right. If, as Toyota has largely done, you get it right, lean production gives the best of every world – the economies of scale of mass production; the sensitivity to market and customer needs usually associated with smaller companies; and job enrichment for employees.

The trouble is that getting it right has proved difficult. In many cases, Western organizations were so committed to their very different ways of working that the changes required were impossibly all-embracing. The obese cannot transform themselves into sylphs overnight.

But it is not only that lean production requires large-scale changes in practice and attitude. The West continues to equate leanness with numbers. Lean production is seen as a means of squeezing more production from fewer people. This is a fundamental misunderstanding. Reduced numbers of employees is the end rather than the means. Western companies have tended to reduce numbers and then declare themselves as lean organizations. This overlooks all three of the concepts which underlie genuine lean production (just-in-time manufacturing; responsibility for quality; and the company as value stream). Womack argues that, while lean production requires fewer people, the organization should then accelerate product development to tap new markets to keep the people at work.

Inevitably, lean production is not without its downside. The most obvious one is that its natural home is the mass manufacturing world of car making. It has been translated into other industries – retailing, for example – but there are other areas where it is more difficult to apply. It is not a universal panacea.

The second obvious problem with lean production is that it fails to embrace innovation and product development. It is one thing being able to make a product efficiently, but how do you actually originate exciting and marketable products in the first place? Womack and Jones would suggest that 'the critical starting point for lean thinking is value', but this is effectively one stage beyond the initial one of generating ideas.

Even so, lean production has moved the debate about quality forwards. It has raised awareness, provided a new benchmark and brought operational efficiency to a wider audience. 'Organizations did well to employ the most up-to-date equipment, information technology and management techniques to eliminate waste, defects and delays', says Harvard Business School's Michael Porter. 'They did well to operate as close as they could to the productivity frontier. But while improving operational effectiveness is necessary to achieving superior profitability, it is not sufficient.'

DAVID PACKARD

The HP Way

1995

The author

avid Packard (1912–96) was half of the partnership which created one of the business and management benchmarks of the century: Hewlett-Packard.

The classic

In 1937, with a mere $538 and a rented garage in Palo Alto, Bill Hewlett and David Packard created one of the most successful corporations in the world. The two had met while students at nearby Stanford. Their ambitions were typical of many young people starting a business. 'We thought we would have a job for ourselves. That's all we thought about in the beginning,' said Packard. 'We hadn't the slightest idea of building a big company.' The garage was the birthplace of Silicon Valley.

When they were assembling their list of 'excellent' companies in the late 1970s, Tom Peters and Robert Waterman included Hewlett-Packard. It was one of their least controversial choices. Similarly, when Jerry Porras and James Collins wrote *Built to Last*, their celebration of long-lived companies, there was no doubt that Hewlett-Packard was worthy of inclusion. In 1985, *Fortune* ranked Hewlett-Packard as one of the two most highly admired companies in America. The company is ranked similarly in virtually every other poll on well-managed companies or ones which would be good to work for. Hewlett-Packard has pulled off an unusual double: it is admired and successful.

In their first year of business Hewlett and Packard achieved sales of $5,100 with $1,300 in profits. Hewlett-Packard's first success was a device for measuring sound waves, which they sold to Walt Disney. An automatic lettuce thinner and a shock machine to help people lose weight followed. They also pondered on the market opportunities for automatic urinal flushers, bowling alley sensors and air-conditioning equipment. The duo left the garage for good in 1940.

During wartime the business flourished, employing 144 people at its height. Immediately after the war, sales fell off – by half in 1946 alone. Undaunted, Hewlett and Packard hired technical talent. The business revived. By 1948, the company's sales were $2.1 million.

Their secret, said Hewlett and Packard, lay in the simplicity of their methods. 'Professors of management are devastated when I say we were successful because we had no plans. We just took on odd jobs,' said Hewlett. But their legacy is not the efficiency of their lettuce thinner or the quality of their urinal flusher, it lies in the culture of the company they created and the management style they used to run it, the H-P way.

From the very start, Hewlett-Packard worked to a few fundamental principles. It did not believe in long-term borrowing to secure the expansion of the business. Its recipe for growth was simply that its products needed to be leaders in their markets. It got on with the job. 'Our main task is to design, develop and manufacture the finest [electronic equipment] for the advancement of science and the welfare of humanity. We intend to devote ourselves to that task,' said Packard in a 1961 memo to employees.

The duo eschewed fashionable management theory. 'If I hear anybody talking about how big their share of the market is or what they're trying to do to increase their share of the market, I'm going to personally see that a black mark gets put in their personnel folder', Packard said in a 1974 speech.

The company believed that people could be trusted and should always be treated with respect and dignity. 'We both felt fundamentally that people want to do a good job. They just need guidelines on how to do it', said Packard.

H-P believed that management should be available and involved – Managing By Wandering About was the motto. Indeed, rather than the administrative suggestions of management, Packard preferred to talk of leadership.

If there was conflict, it had to be tackled through communication and consensus rather than confrontation.

'Their legacy, and the achievement that Packard was most proud of, is a management style based on openness and respect for the individual', noted Louise Kehoe of the *Financial Times* in Packard's obituary.[1]

Hewlett-Packard was a company built on very simple ideas. While all about were turning into conglomerates, Hewlett and Packard kept their heads down and continued with their methods. When their divisions grew too big – and by that they meant around 1500 people – they split them up to ensure that they didn't spiral out of control.

They kept it simple. Nice guys built a nice company. They didn't do anything too risky or too outlandish. (Packard was sceptical about pocket calculators though, in the end, the company was an early entrant into the market.) They didn't bet the company on a big deal or get into debt. Indeed, in his research Richard Pascale identified 'terminal niceness' as a potential problem for the company. Being criticized for being too good could only happen in the business world. For living up to their simple standards, Hewlett-Packard deserve acknowledgement.

Indeed, their values worked to save the company when times were hard. During the 1970s recession, Hewlett-Packard staff took a 10 per cent pay cut and worked 10 per cent fewer hours. If the company hadn't had a long-term commitment to employee stock ownership perhaps they wouldn't have been so keen to make sacrifices.

Commitment to people clearly fostered commitment to the company. 'The most extraordinary trait at Hewlett-Packard is uniformity of commitment, the consistency of approach and attitude. Wherever you go in the H-P empire, you find people talking product quality, feeling proud of their division's achievements in that area. H-P people at all levels show boundless energy and enthusiasm,' observed Peters and Waterman in *In Search of Excellence*.

David Packard was also involved in politics. He was deputy defence secretary in the Nixon administration (1969 to 1971) and also worked on a variety of government commissions. A devout Republican to the end, he supported George Bush against Bill Clinton and warned of being 'caught in the updraft of Bill Clinton's hot air balloon'.

Both Packard and Hewlett felt that Stanford engineering professor Frederick Terman had launched their careers. They gave donations of over $300 million to Stanford. Packard also gave $40 million to found the Monterey Bay Aquarium. It is estimated that his private family foundation has given $480 million to good causes.

Packard retired as chairman in 1993. On his death in 1996, the company had 100,000 employees in 120 countries with revenues of $31 billion. The H-P Way worked.

Note

1 Kehoe, Louise, 'Radical who built group with open management style', *Financial Times*, 28 March 1996.

C N PARKINSON

Parkinson's Law

1958

The author

C Northcote Parkinson (1909–93) studied history at Cambridge and then undertook a PhD at King's College London. He subsequently held a variety of academic posts in the UK and the US, and later in his career was Raffles Professor of History at the University of Malaya. His theories on the machinations of administrative life were developed during five years of army service during the Second World War.

Parkinson's sequel to *Parkinson's Law* was *The Law and the Profits* (1960), which introduces Parkinson's Second Law: expenditure rises to meet income.

The classic

Parkinson's Law[1] is an amusing interlude in management literature. It was written by C Northcote Parkinson in the late 1950s when the Human Relations School in the United States was beginning to flower and thinkers were actively questioning the bureaucracy which had grown up alongside mass production. Max Weber's model of a paper-producing bureaucratic machine appeared to have been brought to fruition as the arteries of major organizations became clogged with layer upon layer of managerial administrators.

Parkinson's Law is simply that work expands to fill the time available for its completion. As a result, companies grow without thinking of how much they are producing. Even if growth in numbers doesn't make them more money, companies grow and people become busier and busier. Parkinson observes that 'an official wants to multiply subordinates, not rivals' and 'officials make work for each other'.

Gary Hamel on *Parkinson's Law*

'Yes, I know that bureaucracy is dead. We're not managers any more, we're leaders. We're not slaves to our work, we've been liberated. And all those layers of paper-shuffling administrators between the CEO and the order-takers – they're all gone, right? Well then, why does a re-reading of *Parkinson's Law,* written in 1958, at the apex of corporate bureaucracy, still ring true? *Parkinson's Law* was to the fifties what *The Dilbert Principle* is to the 1990s.'

If only Frederick Taylor had met Charles Northcote Parkinson the history of managerial thinking might have been dramatically altered. Parkinson wryly and accurately debunks the notion of a particular task having an optimum time for completion. There are no rules – it depends on the person doing the job and their unique situation. 'An elderly lady of leisure can spend an entire day in writing and dispatching a postcard to her niece at Bognor Regis', writes Parkinson. 'An hour will be spent in finding the postcard, another in hunting for spectacles, half-an-hour in a search for the address, an hour and a quarter in composition, and twenty minutes in deciding whether or not to take an umbrella when going to the pillar-box in the next street. The total effort which would occupy a busy man for three minutes all told, may, in this fashion, leave another person prostrate after a day of doubt, anxiety and toil.'

Parkinson is at his best when describing the life of the humble administrator. Faced with the decreasing energy of age and a feeling of being overworked, he observes that administrators face three options: resign, halve the work with a colleague or ask for two more subordinates. 'There is probably no instance in civil service history of choosing any but the third alternative', Parkinson reflects.

The theory is not simply an exercise in superficial cynicism. Parkinson backs it up with statistics. He points out, for example, that the number of admiralty officials in the British Navy increased by 78 per cent between 1914 and 1928 while the number of ships fell by 67 per cent and the number of officers and men by 31 per cent. Parkinson concludes that the expansion of administrators tends to take on a life of its own – 'The Officials would have multiplied at the same rate had there been no actual seamen at all.' (In the 1990s, Parkinson's Law can perhaps be applied to the preponderance of management jargon in the Navy, which has increased as numbers have plummeted.)

What makes *Parkinson's Law* memorable is the sympathy Parkinson evokes for the humble administrators who know no other way. He waxes lyrical as administrator 'A' leaves work: 'The last of the office lights are being turned off in the gathering dusk which marks the end of another day's administrative toil. Among the last to leave, A reflects, with bowed shoulders and a wry smile, that late hours, like grey hairs, are among the penalties of success.'

Parkinson does not propose solutions. 'It is not the business of the botanist to eradicate the weeds. Enough for him if he can tell us just how fast they grow', he explains. *Parkinson's Law* is a kind of Catch-22 of the business world, by turns irreverent and humorous, but with a darker underside of acute observation.

Parkinson warns of the perils of taking any book on the subject of business seriously: 'Heaven forbid that students should cease to read a book on the science of public or business administration provided that these works are classified as fiction.'

Note

1 Parkinson, C Northcote, *Parkinson's Law*, John Murray, London, 1958.

RICHARD PASCALE & ANTHONY ATHOS

The Art of Japanese Management

1981

The authors

R ichard Pascale (born 1938) was a member of the faculty of Stanford's Graduate School of Business for 20 years and taught the most popular course in its MBA programme – a course on organizational survival. He is also the author of *Managing on the Edge* (1990) and *Surfing the Edge of Chaos* (with Mark Milleman and Linda Gioja).

Anthony Athos was a member of the Harvard Business School faculty for many years.

The classic

The Art of Japanese Management,[1] which Richard Pascale co-authored with Harvard's Anthony Athos, was one of the first business bestsellers. It played a crucial role in the discovery of Japanese management techniques as Pascale and Athos considered how a country the same size as Montana could be outstripping the American industrial juggernaut. 'In 1980, Japan's GNP was third highest in the world and, if we extrapolate current trends, it would be number one by the year 2000', warn Pascale and Athos.

The roots of the book lie in Pascale's work with the US National Commission on Productivity. Having initially thought that lessons from Japan were limited for cultural reasons, Pascale decided that more fertile ground lay in looking at Japanese companies in the US. The research for the book eventually covered 34 companies over six years.

Gary Hamel on *The Art of Japanese Management*

'Japan-phobia has subsided a bit, helped by a strong yen, inept Japanese macro economic policy, and the substantial efforts of many Western companies to rebuild their competitiveness. While Pascale and Athos undoubtedly overstated the unique capabilities of Japanese management (is Matsushita really that much better managed than Hewlett-Packard?), they successfully challenged the unstated assumption that America was the font of all managerial wisdom. Since *The Art of Japanese Management* hit the bookstores, American companies have learned much from Japan. Pascale and Athos deserve credit for setting the learning agenda.'

'I was consulting with the National Commission on Productivity – a board of industry and union leaders', he recalls. 'Though I had been in Japan with the US Navy, I assumed that the reasons we couldn't learn from Japan was because the culture was so different. But then I thought I could study Japanese companies in the US – they did enough differently to encourage me to challenge my basic assumptions. I didn't define myself as a Japan scholar, but I was interested in making Western organizations more productive and in helping huge organizations change. For me, Japan was a new lens on how best to operate. The idea of vision statements, for example, came out of that. The Japanese thought that it was obvious. At the time in the West it was not politically correct for an organization to have a vision. For a company to have a position on something bigger than their results was seen as dangerously quasi-religious. The concept of shared values in the Seven-S model was not an easy sell at the time. Now it is accepted.'

For the American readership, *The Art of Japanese Management* provides harsh home truths. 'If anything, the extent of Japanese superiority over the United States in industrial competitiveness is underestimated', say Pascale and Athos, observing that 'a major reason for the superiority of the Japanese is their managerial skill'. In its comparisons of US and Japanese companies, *The Art of Japanese Management* provides rare insights into the truth behind the mythology of Japanese management and the inadequacy of much Western practice.

Among the key components of Japanese management identified by Pascale and Athos is that of vision, something they found to be notably lacking in the West. 'Our problem today is that the tools are there but our "vision" is limited. A great many American managers are influenced by beliefs, assumptions, and perceptions about management that unduly constrain them', write Pascale and Athos. The book, they say, is 'not an assault on the existing tools of management, but upon the Western vision of management which circumscribes our effectiveness'.

Pascale and Athos's championing of vision proved highly influential. Pascale now attributes much of this to his co-author: 'It was Athos who really started the entire visioning industry in the US. Back in the seventies no one had really thought about it.' Soon after *The Art of Japanese Management* a flurry of books appeared highlighting so-called visionaries. Today, corporate visions are a fact of life though many fail to match the Japanese practice mapped out by Pascale and Athos in which visions are dynamic, vivifying *modus operandi* rather than pallid or generic statements of corporate intent.

The Art of Japanese Management is, however, best known for its central concept: the Seven S framework. This emerged from a series of meetings during June 1978 between Pascale, Athos and the authors of *In Search of Excellence,* Tom Peters and Robert Waterman, who were already involved in their research into excellent companies. The story of the evolution of the framework is given in *The Art of Japanese Management.*

Initially a meeting was arranged between the quartet. 'Athos said we needed an agenda for the five days otherwise we'd be driven round the bend by Peters – he's so energetic, such a scatter-shot. Otherwise we wouldn't survive the five days,' Pascale now recalls. 'Athos said he had given it some thought and said there was a guy at Harvard, Chuck Gibson, who had a scheme – strategy, structure and systems. He had developed these three Ss for Harvard's PMD Program which he and Tony were in charge of. So why didn't we start with strategy on Monday then move on to structure on Tuesday and systems on Wednesday? Athos said he had a couple of his own to add – superordinate goals and shared values. I was working on *The Art of Japanese Management* so was interested in the idea of shared values.

'Athos insisted on superordinate goals and I contributed style. So we walked in with five of the Seven Ss.'[2]

Athos and Pascale persuaded Waterman and Peters to use alliteration. Peters and Pascale then suggested another variable was needed, one concerned with timing and implementation. Athos and Pascale proposed calling it 'sequencing'.

Julian Phillips of McKinsey, who also joined the group, argued vigorously for replacing 'sequencing' with 'staff'. 'Since everyone was having trouble with sequencing it was easy to drop', say Athos and Pascale. 'And since Peters was proposing that "people" and "power" needed somehow to be included (Athos was adding "aggregates of people" at Harvard), it was also possible to agree that staff was an addition which resolved various concerns, Thus, the final Seven S Framework came into being.'

The Seven Ss (strategy, structure, skills, staff, shared values, systems and style) are a kind of *aide memoire*, a useful memory jogger of what concerns organizations. The Seven S framework gained a great deal of attention though, as a generic statement of the issues facing organizations, it is unremarkable. (Tom Peters himself initially thought it 'corny' – though Peters and Waterman used it a year later in *In Search of Excellence*.) 'The framework is nothing more than seven important categories that managers pay attention to', Pascale later noted in *Managing on the Edge*. 'There is nothing sacred about the number seven. There could be six or eight Ss. The value of a framework such as the Seven Ss is that it imposes an interesting discipline on the researcher.'

The Seven Ss presents a way into comparisons between US and Japanese management. Pascale and Athos conclude that the Japanese succeeded largely because of the attention they gave to the soft Ss – style, shared values, skills and staff. In contrast, the West remained preoccupied with the hard Ss of strategy, structure and systems.

Since *The Art of Japanese Management* the general trend of Western managerial thinking has been directed towards the soft Ss. Whether this has led to the West correcting the imbalance identified by Pascale and Athos is a matter of continuing debate.

Notes

1 Pascale, Richard T & Athos, Anthony, *The Art of Japanese Management*, Penguin, London, 1981.
2 Interview with author.

RICHARD PASCALE

Managing on the Edge

1990

The classic

'When we finished *The Art of Japanese Management,* there was pressure to produce another book', says Richard Pascale. 'I wrote a three-page outline on what I thought the next issue would be. I had observed the vulnerability of the companies designated as excellent throughout *In Search of Excellence.* Because they were so coherent internally they were ill-equipped to deal with a radical shift in the environment. I had stumbled on a law of cybernetics which says that variety in organizations shows up as contention. In most companies, because of turf wars, egos and the like, we are relatively inept in dealing with contention. I found that contention and contradiction were seen as mismanagement. I thought I could write the book in six months but all the data and interviews I had didn't help on what I wanted to write about. I had to go back to the start.'[1]

The result was *Managing on the Edge,*[2] which begins with the line 'Nothing fails like success'. 'Great strengths are inevitably the root of weakness', writes Pascale, pausing only to point out that, from the *Fortune 500* of 1985, 143 had departed five years later.

Managing on the Edge presents a formidably researched and argued challenge to complacency and timidity. 'American managerial history is largely inward-focused and self-congratulatory', writes Pascale, echoing his criticisms first aired in *The Art of Japanese Management* nine years previously.

Change, says Pascale, is a fact of business life. The trouble is we are ill-equipped to deal with it and our traditional approach to managing change is no longer applicable. 'The incremental approach to change is effective when what you want is more of what you've already got. Historically, that has been sufficient because our advantages of plentiful resources, geographical isolation, and absence of serious global competi-

Gary Hamel on *Managing on the Edge*

'In *Managing on the Edge,* Richard Pascale provides a number of useful observations on the sources of corporate vitality. One of the things I've always admired about Richard Pascale is that he focuses not on tools and techniques, but on principles and paradigms. While management bookshelves groan with the weight of simplistic how-to books (e.g. *The One Minute Manager)*, Pascale challenges managers to think, and to think deeply. Pascale forces managers to deconstruct the normative models on which they base their beliefs and actions.'

tion defined a league in which we competed with ourselves and everyone played by the same rules.'

Pascale bids farewell to easy options. He is vehement in his criticism of Peters and Waterman's *In Search of Excellence:* 'Simply identifying attributes of success is like identifying attributes of people in excellent health during the age of the bubonic plague.' And argues that 'passions and obsession frequently degenerate into simplistic formulae e.g. acronyms such as KISS (Keep it simple, stupid). This book advocates wisdom and coolness at a higher level of complexity.'

Best known is Pascale's chart of the profusion of management fads. He calculates that there have been more than two dozen since the 1950s – and, of these, a dozen emerged in the five years prior to 1990.

Going on to further examine the malaise he identifies in management, Pascale contends that four factors 'drive stagnation and renewal in organizations':

1 **Fit** – pertains to an organization's internal consistency (unity).
2 **Split** – describes a variety of techniques for breaking a bigger organization into smaller units and providing them with a stronger sense of ownership and identity (plurality).
3 **Contend** – refers to a management process that harnesses (rather than suppresses) the contradictions that are inevitable by-products of organizations (duality).
4 **Transcend** - alerts us to the higher order of complexity that successfully managing the renewal process entails (vitality).

Pascale calls for a fundamental shift in perspective. 'Managerial behavior is predicated on the assumption that we should rationally order the behavior of those we manage. That mindset needs to be challenged,' he writes. Orderly answers are no longer appropriate. Instead, the new emphasis should be on asking questions (the book's final chapter is entitled 'The question is the answer'). 'Strategic planning, at best, is about posing questions, more than attempting to answer them', Pascale suggests.

Pascale argues that successful organizations undergo a continual process of renewal. (Later he developed this theme, calling for 'corporate transformation'.) Central to achieving this is a willingness to ask questions constantly and to harness conflict for the corporate good through systems that encourage questioning. Companies must become 'engines of inquiry'.

The trouble is that managers are ill-equipped to deal with the contention that arises when fundamental questions are posed. If we are to succeed in managing on the edge then 'contention management is essential to orchestrate tensions that arise'. The book's sub-title is 'How the smartest companies use conflict to stay ahead' and Pascale estimates that 50 per cent of the time when contention arises it is smoothed over and avoided. 'The forces that we have historically regarded as locked in opposition can be viewed (through a different mindset, or paradigm) as apparent opposites generating inquiry and adaptive responses', writes Pascale. 'This is because each point of view represents a facet of reality, and these realities tend to challenge one another and raise questions. If we redefine the manager's job as maintaining a constructive level of debate, we are, in effect, holding the organization in the question. This leads to identifying blind spots and working around obstacles.' Truth – personally and organizationally – lies in the openness of vigorous debate and, as Pascale writes: 'Organizations are, in the last analysis, interactions among people.'

Managing on the Edge set the tone for much of the management thinking of the decade. Its emphasis on the need for constant change has since been developed by Pascale. He now argues that the issue of managing the way we change is a competence rather than an episodic necessity. The capability to change is a core competence in its own right.

During the last decade, Pascale's work has embraced complexity theory. 'I found that incremental change was not enough. The traditional models of how to govern organizations didn't do what's necessary,' he says. 'Then I began working with the CSC consulting firm on the subject of organizational change. Linda Gioja – then with CSC and one of my co-authors on *Surfing the Edge of Chaos* – suggested that there was stuff on systems and complexity which would be relevant. I was very skeptical but signed up to go to the Santa Fe Institute to a business network meeting. Their speaker couldn't make it, and they asked whether I could speak. The only thing I could think of talking about was the irrelevance of their ideas to business. They thought this sounded like fun and afterwards asked me to become a visiting scholar so that if I had a different view at least I would know what I was talking about. I got to know Brian Arthur, Murray Gell-Mann and Stuart Kaufmann. It took a while, but I slowly realized that organizations are living things. It is just that we have a strong mindset about organizations being mechanical. Most executives have a very mechanistic view of change.'

Notes

1 Interview with Stuart Crainer, June 2001.
2 Pascale, Richard, *Managing on the Edge*, Viking, London, 1990.

LAURENCE PETER

The Peter Principle

1969

The author

 aurence J Peter (1919–90) was a Canadian academic. Being a man of the world in possession of sight and the normal faculties, he observed incompetence everywhere he looked.

The classic

The bestselling business book of recent years has not been some weighty study of best management practice by a fashionable consultant. It has been *The Dilbert Principle* by Scott Adams. Adams' humorous, human and, for some, all too real cartoons of corporate life caught the managerial imagination. Indeed, the book is reputed to be the bestselling business book of all time. To some, Dilbertian frivolity is a needless distraction. Gary Hamel, co-author of Dilbert's predecessor as a business blockbuster, *Competing for the Future*, regards Dilbert as engendering an infectious strain of cynicism among managers – 'It is cynical about management. Never has there been so much cynicism', he laments.

The truth, however, is that cynicism about the way businesses and managers operate is nothing new. Dilbert is simply an accurate and amusing portrayal of corporate cynicism 1990s-style. From Murphy's Law to Parkinson's Law, from Pudd'nhead Wilson to Stanley Bing, a steady infusion of comic scepticism has been injected into the corporate canon. Perhaps the most enduring, cynical classic is *The Peter Principle*, written by Dr Laurence J Peter with the writer Raymond Hull. First published in 1969, *The Peter Principle* is built around the simple premise that 'In a hierarchy every employee tends to rise to his level of incompetence'. According to Peter, a position of incompetence is the apotheosis of a corporate career – or, indeed, of any career in any profession in which there is a hierarchy. ('There are no exceptions to the Peter Principle'.)

The book explains: 'For each individual, for *you*, for *me*, the final promotion is from a level of competence to a level of incompetence. So, given enough time – and assuming the existence of enough ranks in the hierarchy – each employee rises to, and remains at, his level of incompetence.' The end-result is the corollary to the Peter Principle: 'In time, every post tends to be occupied by an employee who is incompetent to carry out his duties.'

The Peter Principle carries many echoes of that other humorous classic of the sixties, *Catch-22*. Laughter and despair are interspersed. The madness of it all is disturbingly real. The book is laced with wittily cynical advice – 'If at first you don't succeed, you may be at your level of incompetence', it warns – and covers areas of concern to all managers whether it be vision – 'If you don't know where you are going, you will probably end up somewhere else' – or economists – 'An economist is an expert who will know tomorrow why the things he predicted yesterday didn't happen'. For anyone who has worked in an organization, Peter's observations are likely to ring true – or set off alarm bells. There may even be a feeling of guilt that you have engaged in 'cachinnatory inertia' – telling jokes instead of working – or exhibit 'hypercaninophobia complex' ('fear caused in superiors when an inferior demonstrates strong leadership potential'). All corporate life is there.

At the time of the book's creation, the business world was undoubtedly burdened by excessive hierarchies. Corporations creaked under their weight. Executives crowded into office blocks. It was reputed that a depiction of the complex hierarchies at British Steel took up an entire office wall. Such labyrinths were commonplace. However, that does not mean that the Peter Principle is a dusty historical joke. The beauty of the Peter Principle – if it can be called beauty – is that it is timeless. Human inadequacy is universal – as is the human capacity to build vacuous power structures. In our supposedly leaner and fitter times there are still hierarchies aplenty. The difference is, perhaps, that we have simply become more adept at disguising them.

But, apart from pure amusement, *The Peter Principle* continues to have a worthwhile role in the canon of management classics because it is a celebration of failure. Glorious inadequacy is its theme. In the book's glossary the entry for failure simply reads 'see Success' – success, of course, is 'final placement at the level of incompetence'. 'There are two kinds of failures: those who thought and never did, and those who did and never thought', it reflects, later adding 'Fortune knocks once, but misfortune has much more patience' and 'There are two sorts of losers – the good loser, and the other one who can't act.'

The Peter Principle remains a poignant antidote to the blind optimism and sugary reality of most business books. It is a reminder that corporate reality is not usually about grand designs and great decisions. It is more mundane and frustrating ... too mundane and too frustrating to be taken seriously. *The Peter Principle* cuts managers and management down to size. We cannot all be indomitable leaders who get it right every time so why aspire to be so?

The Peter Principle lives on. Dilbert creator, Scott Adams, has noted that: 'Now, apparently, the incompetent workers are promoted directly to management without ever passing through the temporary competence stage. When I entered the workforce in 1979, the Peter Principle described management pretty well. Now I think we'd all like to return to those Golden Years when you had a boss who was once good at something.'

It is striking how relevant to today *The Peter Principle* remains. When Peter refers to 'codophilia' (defined as 'speaking in letters and numbers instead of words') he could be talking of today's consultants. Demonstrating the timeless and universal quality of the Principle, there is also mention of 'computerized incompetence: incompetent application of computer techniques or the inherent incompetence of a computer'. Microsoft's Bill Gates would probably disagree but he may well be a fan. After all, Gates has proposed one of the most brilliant solutions to the Peter Principle: 'The art of management is to promote people without making them managers.'

TOM PETERS & ROBERT WATERMAN

In Search of Excellence

1982

The authors

Tom Peters and Robert Waterman were McKinsey consultants when *In Search of Excellence* was being written. Peters left the company prior to publication and Waterman two years later.

Since that time, the two have taken wildly different paths. Peters (born 1942) has become a high-profile guru, travelling the world, writing books which have been described as 'charismatic shockers'. His books include *A Passion for Excellence* (with Nancy Austin, 1985); *Thriving on Chaos* (1987); *Liberation Management* (1992); and the more recent collections, *The Tom Peters Seminar* (1994) and *The Pursuit of Wow!* (1994). Peters has his own Palo Alto-based company, the Tom Peters Group, but now spends the majority of his time on his Vermont farm.

Waterman (born 1936) has a far lower profile, occasionally producing thoughtful books, but preferring to spend his time painting rather than on the seminar circuit. He has a consultancy company based in California. Since *In Search of Excellence*, Waterman has written *The Renewal Factor* (1987) and *The Frontiers of Excellence* (1994).

The classic

The 1970s was a miserable decade for the Western corporate world. Oil and inflation crises were followed by even deeper crises of business confidence. As Europe and the US lurched from one economic disaster to the next, the Japanese juggernaut was accelerating in the distance. In the decade's twilight, Thomas J Peters, then a young associate at McKinsey & Co. was given an intriguing assignment. His job was to travel the world and seek out best managerial practices wherever he could find them.

'It must have been the late 1970s', recalls Harvard Business School's John Kotter. 'Tom Peters showed up in my office just after he got his PhD from Stanford. He was talking to people about what the key issues were.'

Professor Kotter wasn't alone in receiving a visit from Peters. Undaunted by the magnitude of his task, the energetic and inquisitive young man assiduously cultivated business and academic contacts, visiting business schools, corporate offices, and factories in the US and abroad. Along the way, his search for best practices became a book project and a McKinsey colleague, Robert H Waterman, was enlisted to help.

While Peters was intellectually and physically hyperactive, Waterman was older, quieter, and more considered. Combining energy and experience, in 1981 the duo produced a 1300 page manuscript called *The Secrets of Excellence* that distilled their lengthy research into common characteristics of 'excellent' companies.

Unfortunately, 'The first manuscript was terrible. We'd agreed to do two books, but we had no idea how hard it would be to write a book', recalls Waterman. Meanwhile, the eager first-time authors had distributed 15,000 copies of their draft to interested parties. This, their publishers reckoned, was likely to be substantially more copies than were actually sold.

Then, in December 1981, Peters left McKinsey, and, sidelined by a car accident, set to work revising the manuscript. 'We went through twenty-five different drafts so we couldn't tell whose stuff was where. It was a tough process, but it got better and better,' remembers Peters. In the spring of 1982, they delivered a final manuscript. In the fall of that year it was published by Harper & Row, its name by then – *In Search of Excellence: Lessons from America's Best-Run Companies.*

To everyone's surprise *In Search of Excellence* became a huge international bestseller, and the pre-publication distribution of thousands of copies inspired viral marketing. Corporate America was hungry for encouragement, and Peters and Waterman offered an upbeat spin on grim business conditions. 'We codified lots of loose streams, ideas, and discussions, and put it together in one place. Change was needed, and the marketplace was ready for our ideas said in that way. It turned out to be an important watershed but that had as much to do with the environment as with our own brilliance. Ten years later, it wouldn't have had the impact,' reflects Waterman.

Indeed, the book's timing was impeccable. It provided light at the end of a dark economic tunnel, not something executives necessarily expected from consultants. 'Consultants work with problems. That's what they get paid for. So we were always working with broken things – *In*

Search of Excellence was the first book written about things that work,' says Peters.

Since 1982, *In Search of Excellence* has sold over 5 million copies worldwide and sales are still robust. But the book's significance is not just about its extraordinary sales. In 2002, twenty years after its publication, its legacy has become clear.

First, *In Search of Excellence* marked a fundamental change in management emphasis, from the rationalistic and mechanistic style that had dominated the post-World War II years to a human and humane approach. Despite their rationalist pedigrees – Messrs Peters and Waterman were both engineers by training – *In Search of Excellence* is resolutely people-centred, and its themes reflect the beginnings of a movement in management studies that looks beyond rational analysis to explore social complexity.

Second, it nearly single-handedly invented the business book market. Prior to *In Search of Excellence*, business books had sold in reasonable but unexceptional quantities. In the years to come they became mainstays of publisher's lists. As an adjunct to this, *In Search of Excellence* ignited the business guru market. Although Bob Waterman remained a consultant and eschewed the hyperbole of guru status, the book's success transported Peters to the heady heights of celebrity recognition. He created the management speaker as rock star phenomenon and is still on tour, currently racking up 80 to 90 seminars a year.

Finally, the book established the cult of excellence, and a simple comparative methodology for examining the performance of the best companies. Hardly intellectually inspiring, this focus on best practices nonetheless helped fuel enthusiasm in the 1980s for benchmarking. A host of books have since developed from this formula of comparing companies, most notably James Collins and Jerry Porras' *Built to Last* (1994). Their book took longevity as a performance measure, and featured many of the same companies included in *In Search of Excellence*.

The intellectual cornerstones of *In Search of Excellence* are eight principles identified by Peters and Waterman as characteristics of excellent companies. These are: a bias for action; being close to the customer; autonomy and entrepreneurship; productivity through people; being hands-on and values driven; sticking to the knitting; simple form, lean staff; and what they ingloriously labelled simultaneous loose-tight properties. Peters and Waterman examined 62 companies against these principles, and divided them into three categories.

Among the 18 companies identified as 'excellent but did not meet all the criteria', GE and Exxon have been consistent profit leaders over the past twenty years. Others were sold, stumbled but remained independent, or died. Arco was bought by British Petroleum; NCR was bought by AT&T; Western Electric evolved into Lucent Technologies; and Westinghouse slowly disintegrated and disappeared. Polaroid, Xerox, and American Airlines have had rocky records but still stand on their own.

The 30 companies ranked as 'excellent and met the criteria' had similar histories to the above group. Allen-Bradley was purchased by Rockwell in 1985; Chesebrough-Ponds was bought by Unilever in 1987; Data General was bought by EMC in 1999; Hughes Aircraft merged with Raytheon; Raychem was bought by Tyco; Standard Oil (Indiana)/Amoco was bought by BP. Wang Labs filed for bankruptcy in 1992 before being resurrected and sold to Gerontics. Atari, which the authors say mistakenly made the list ('we were swept in the frenzy', says Waterman), was bought by Hasbro in 1998, and is now part of Warner Communications.

Then there are the 14 'exemplars of excellence'. This select group, given the highest rating and chosen from companies in a range of industries (including computers, consumer products, pharmaceuticals, aerospace, construction, and engineering), have undergone significant challenges and changes. But with one exception, the Digital Equipment Corporation, they have survived with their names intact and remain among the most respected companies in the world.

Looking back, the ideas in the book seem scruffily packaged. The overlap between the characteristics of excellent companies was untidy: they attempted, in themselves, to be both loose and tight.

The concepts seem pretty basic as well: today to say that an organization needs a propensity to action, be closer to its customers, exercise control and be entrepreneurial, and motivate people is accepted wisdom.

But the 1980s was a less sophisticated time. The audience – not that Peters or Waterman imagined an audience – did not expect slogans and carefully crafted phraseology. But the ideas struck a chord, because they effectively re-stated universal truths about human nature and what makes people perform that had been forgotten or obscured by the heavy influence of command-and-control ideology.

The world circa 1982 retained its faith in planning, market research, large-scale organization, numbers, hefty hierarchies, rules and policy manuals. Being driven by behavioural values, for example, was largely out of fashion; mainstream discussion of emotional intelligence and management effectiveness had not even begun. Western companies were mesmerized and bewildered by the visions and missions of their emergent Japanese competitors. In 1982 companies in the West did not have visions or missions. Stating one's organizational values was suspect. Now, of course, it's expected.

Yet, the ideas in the book were not revolutionary either. Peters and Waterman didn't suggest that the corporate manual be torn up. They merely proposed that it needed editing to incorporate the enlightened best practice encountered on Peters' travels. They suggested the corporation need to reacquaint itself with the progressive human relations literature of Elton Mayo, Abraham Maslow, Douglas McGregor, Warren Bennis, and other management gurus. Indeed, today *In Search of Excellence* appears quite timid, almost gentlemanly in its questioning of the way things are done.

The message was clear, however: the quality of people matters as much as the quality of the numbers, although executives inevitably struggle with this shift in their thinking and behaviour. 'Old management ideas going back to Frederick Taylor and before – central control and a lack of trust in people – still have a powerful grip on managers in countries throughout the world. What we were really talking about was a different paradigm in which you don't need so many layers, or so much control,' Waterman says.

Ten years after the publication of *Excellence*, Waterman elaborated on his writings about the effects of hierarchy in *Adhocracy* (1993), a book that he says is 'one of the most useful things I've published'. In another thoughtful book, *What America Does Right: Learning from Companies that Put People First* (1994), Waterman profiled senior executives at companies known for their social views and people-centred management such as Levi Strauss Corporation and the AES Corporation, then a small independent power producer. Waterman was one of the first to write about AES, which has since become a worldwide leader in its industry, and among the most financially consistent rising stars in business, generally.

Peters, whose books now total ten, has been more prolific than his partner. The book he wrote that linked organizations to people most usefully and profoundly was *Liberation Management* (1992), a sprawling epic in need of an editor, but his timing was as precise as his first foray into publishing.

While the intellectual arguments rumble on over the merits of *In Search of Excellence*, its commercial impact is indisputable. *In Search of Excellence* effectively created the business book market. 'It was a watershed event in business publishing. It put business publishing on the map and established it as a big enough niche,' says Cedric Crocker, vice president and publisher for business publishing at Jossey-Bass. 'In any business bestseller, success is a matter of timing – responding to a market need; ideas which are creative and unique; and conveyed with simplicity and clarity.'

The British social commentator Charles Handy was among the book's earliest readers. 'I think it was significant not so much for what it said but how it said it', he says. 'It was the first business book that businesspeople read. I remember when I first saw it being really excited and hugging it to myself. I got hold of a copy in the US before it was published in the UK. I thought I'd got this treasure trove, but then everyone started reading it. What it said wasn't that original, but the way it was written – the style – was new. It created the guru phenomenon. Before Tom Peters there weren't any business gurus.'

The book was bought by a new audience, one that has continued to expand. Between 1995 and 1999 sales of business-related books grew by nearly 40 per cent in the United States, making business books an $862 million market according to the Book Publishing Report, a weekly newsletter covering the industry. 'We had no idea just how big it would be', recounts Robert Waterman. 'We looked at other books and what they'd sold. William Ouchi's *Theory Z* had sold around 200,000 copies, so we thought that if we sold something close we'd be in heaven.'

Linked to the book's success was a panoply of other commercial activities. At the height of the world's enthusiasm for *In Search of Excellence*, an American business magazine wrote an article in which people were asked who they would like to speak to for management advice. Tom Peters was first choice; Jesus Christ second. Emboldened by such recognition, Peters spread his wings. 'The book gave me licence', he says. And the rolling ball of fame carried him breathlessly along. Management was suddenly important and American management was seen as reborn.

In Search of Excellence is not without blemishes, and the authors are the first to say so. 'It has holes in it – not quite as big as black holes but near!' quips Peters.

The most striking is the book's American bias. Despite Peters' globetrotting and Waterman's extensive experience working outside the United States, they took a resolutely American view. International examples are thin – despite some of the research being supported by the German company, Siemens.

The other blemish is the one most commonly cited: the performance of the excellent companies after 1982. The theory, was simple, perhaps too simple for those looking to criticize it. The authors looked for common characteristics among the exemplary companies so that others might try to improve their performance. The duo had seen the same simple idea applied repeatedly to the world of sports. The arrival of Jean-Claude Killy led to people skiing differently; Chris Evert's rise led to the world adopting the two-handed backhand and so on.

Messrs. Peters and Waterman never imagined the extent to which the fortunes of the book's chosen companies, especially the exemplars, would become a matter of debate and media interest. It started with the November 1984, *BusinessWeek*'s lead story entitled 'Ooops', which chronicled the waning fortunes of the 14 exemplars of excellence. Ever since, the performances of these companies have been picked over again and again. One piece of research by financial analyst Michelle Clayman found that the companies featured in *In Search of Excellence* beat the stock market by around one per cent over the five years following the book's publication. Meanwhile, the mass of 'unexcellent' companies beat the stock market by around 12 per cent.[1]

Charles Handy now refers to Tom Peters syndrome in which as soon as a book hits the bookshelves the exemplar companies it features fall flat on their faces. No-one is immune. Gary Hamel has fallen foul of the Tom Peters syndrome – his latest book includes a long case study of Enron.

Still Peters and Waterman stand resolutely by the book's core ideas. 'Anything that successful will have a backlash. Of course people remember the magazine cover and I'd rather that wasn't the case,' says Robert Waterman. But he hastens to add: 'There was great confusion about the book. People say we were wrong. But we never predicted enduring greatness. We just looked at companies that had done well over a decent period. The generalizations in the book are rock solid. I wouldn't change much, just to say ... terrific examples [can] go soft on you.'

Tom Peters gives his characteristically robust riposte as well: 'Of the 62 companies reviewed for *In Search of Excellence*, 46 are in at least pretty good shape. Six suck and ten are unknown to me.'

In many respects the vicissitudes of the excellent companies are an unnecessary distraction. The Peters and Waterman team created the notion that whatever your business you could learn from the best, as long as you recognize that the 'best' is a moving target. Once again this appears commonsensical but, prior to 1982, business literature was largely theorizing from the higher planes of strategy rather than commentary on business realities.

In Search of Excellence taught us to look for cutting edge practices and learn from management practitioners who were doing the work. 'If you want to find solutions to seemingly intractable problems, go to the front lines and find smart people actually solving the problems. There you will find innovative answers,' says the consultant and author Bruce Tulgan of Rainmaker Thinking, the New Haven, Connecticut-based think tank.

Tulgan adds that we can also thank *In Search of Excellence* for popularizing and legitimizing the art and technique of business. 'Getting these insights out of the business schools and onto popular bookshelves has done more than enlighten the broader public and make management thinking into sound-bites and "info-tainment" material. It has put pressure on management thinkers to push learning and discourse, and encouraged business leaders and managers to practise the most up-to-date techniques – or else be able to explain why they don't.'

Note

1 'In Search of Excellence: The Investor's Viewpoint', by Michelle Clayman, *Financial Analyst's Journal*, May–June 1987.

TOM PETERS
Liberation Management
1992

The classic

L arge, rambling, and gushingly anecdotal, *Liberation Management*[1] is a sprawling compendium of Tom Peters' thinking on management in the 'nanosecond nineties'.

The original manuscript was 1900 pages long and was only reduced to a manageable size after a third of the material was cut. It is, observed Karl Weick, written in 'hyper-text'. The language is colourful – 'middle managers, as we have known them, are cooked geese'; 'the definition of every product and service is hanging. Going soft, softer, softest. Going fickle, ephemeral, fashion' – and, at times, impenetrable as Peters' passion overwhelms his prose. *Liberation Management* received the best and worst reviews of Peters' books.

Liberation Management marks an important development in Peters' career. It emerged from an intensive period of reading Chandler and Hayek and is the first of his books since *In Search of Excellence* to feature in-depth examinations of individual companies.

Liberation Management's central message reflects a substantial change of emphasis from that of Peters' earlier works (*In Search of Excellence*, *A Passion for Excellence* and *Thriving on Chaos*). Ten years on from *In Search of Excellence*, Peters contends that his previous work was marred by paying too little attention to the perennially vexed question of organizational structure.

Peters does not mean structure in the traditional hierarchical and functional sense. Indeed, his exemplars of the new organizational structure are notable for their apparent lack of structure. And herein lies Peters' point. Companies such as CNN, ABB and Body Shop thrive through having highly flexible structures able to change to meet the business needs of the moment. Freeflowing, impossible to pin down, unchartable, simple yet complex, these are the paradoxical structures of

Gary Hamel on *Liberation Management*

'Though one might accuse Tom Peters of being more journalist than management scholar, *Liberation Management* previewed many of the themes that would come to occupy management thinkers in the 1990s. One might wish, though, that the ration of insight to data were a bit higher, and that there were a few less case studies and a bit more conceptual structure. Nevertheless, the book remains a good, though overlong, introduction to new age management philosophy.'

the future. 'Tomorrow's effective 'organization' will be conjured up anew each day', says Peters.

Only with such vibrant structures will companies be able to deliver the customer service championed by Peters in his previous books, and it is only through such dynamic organizational forms that companies will be able to survive. Not that Peters forgets customer service. 'How customers perceive their relationship with your company determines whether or not you'll have a customer for life. That's almost obvious, if almost always ignored.'

Key to the new corporate structures envisaged by Peters are networks with customers, with suppliers and, indeed, anyone else who can help the business deliver. 'Old ideas about size must be scuttled. "New big", which can be very big indeed, is "network big". That is, size measured by market power, say, is a function of the firm's extended family of fleeting and semi-permanent cohorts, not so much a matter of what it owns and directly controls,' he writes.

And, networks must move quickly. The book's central refrain is that of fashion – 'We're all in Milan's haute couture business and Hollywood's movie business,' writes Peters. 'This book is animated by a single word: fashion. Life cycles of computers and microprocessors have shrunk from years to months.' The new model organization moves fast and continually does so, seeking out new areas which make it unique in its markets.

Clearly, this requires quite different managerial skills than those traditionally needed by managers. Indeed, Peters says that the new organizational forms he depicts are 'troublesome to conceive – and a downright pain to manage'. The new skills are now familiar. Peters bids farewell to command and control, ushering in a new era characterized by 'curiosity, initiative, and the exercise of imagination'. It is, he argues, a step into the unknown for most organizations but also a return to first principles: 'For the last 100 years or so ... we've assumed that there is one place where expertise should reside: with "expert" staffs at division, group, sector, or corporate. And another, very different, place where the (mere) work gets done. The new organization regimen puts expertise back, close to the action – as it was in craft-oriented, pre-industrial revolution days ... We are not, then, ignoring "expertise" at all. We are simply shifting its locus, expanding its reach, giving it new respect – and acknowledging that everyone must be an expert in a fast-paced, fashionized world.'

In his two subsequent books – *The Tom Peters Seminar* and *The Pursuit of Wow!* – Peters has developed the ideas in *Liberation Management* still further, advocating complete commitment to vibrant, freewheeling organizational structures. Peters identifies *Liberation Management* as the best of his books. Its merits – and drawbacks – lie in its relentless energy and endless examples. Interestingly, many of the companies featured by Peters have been used as examples in a wide variety of later books.

Peters explains:

'I've moved from the hyper-organized *In Search of Excellence* with its McKinsey logic to the very scatter-shot *A Passion for Excellence* to the hyper-organized *Thriving on Chaos* then the mightily disorganized *Liberation Management*. Think of an accordion. It tightened up with *In Search of Excellence*, loosened up and then became anal-retentive with *Thriving on Chaos* and then completely loosened with *Liberation Management*.

'Now, I say, beware of the champions of order, the people who offer "rules" for tidy and righteous living. It doesn't work that way. Seeing complex issues in black and white is stupid. Life is messy, very messy. In the real world, you have to enjoy the mess. This is particularly true in a downturn. You need to see flux as an opportunity, a chance to launch the bold initiatives you have always meant to launch.'

Note

1 Peters, Tom, *Liberation Management*, Alfred P Knopf, New York, 1992.

MICHAEL PORTER

Competitive Strategy

1980

The author

ichael Porter took a doctorate in business economics and an MBA. Precociously talented, he also has a degree in aeronautical engineering from Princeton, joined the Harvard faculty at the age of 26, and could have been a professional golfer (he now settles for rounds with the President). Born in 1947, Michael Porter is now a professor at Harvard Business School and the world's leading authority on competitive strategy. He is the author of 12 books and many articles. His most influential books have been *Competitive Strategy: Techniques for analyzing industries and competitors* (1980); *Competitive Advantage: creating and sustaining superior performance* (1985); *Competition in Global Industries* (1986); and *The Competitive Advantage of Nations* (1990). 'If anyone is capable of turning management theory into a respectable scholarly discipline, it is Michael Porter', noted *The Economist*.[1]

Porter has served as a counsellor on competitive strategy to many leading US and international companies and plays an active role in economic policy with the US Congress, business groups, and as an adviser to foreign governments. He serves on the executive committee of the Council on Competitiveness, a private sector group of business, labour, and academic leaders, formed in 1986.

The classic

Michael Porter's *Competitive Strategy: Techniques for analyzing industries and competitors*[2] is a rationalist's solution to a long-running strategic dilemma. As with many other managerial dilemmas, this involves two opposite ends of a spectrum. At one end are the pragmatists who contend that companies have to respond to their own specific situation. To them,

Gary Hamel on Competitive Strategy

'Strategy is, above all else, the search for above average returns. In *Competitive Strategy,* Michael Porter did a masterful job of synthesizing all that economists know about what determines industry and firm profitability. While *Competitive Strategy* isn't much help in discovering profitable strategies, it is an unfailing guide to whether some particular strategy, once articulated, can be counted on to produce worthwhile profits. What distinguishes *Competitive Strategy* from many other contemporary business books is its strong conceptual foundation. Every MBA graduate in the world can remember Porter's 'five forces'. How many can recall the eight rules of excellence?'

competitive advantage emerges from immediate, fast-thinking responsiveness. As every situation is unique there is no pat formula by which sustainable competitive advantage can be achieved.

At the other end of the spectrum is the line taken by, among others, the Boston Consulting Group. They suggest that market knowledge is all-important. Any company which masters the intricacies of a particular market will be well placed to reduce prices and increase market share.

Porter proposes a logical compromise, arguing that there are three 'generic strategies', 'viable approaches to dealing with … competitive forces'. Strategy, in Porter's eyes, is distilled down to a choice on *how* to compete. (Interestingly, Porter has said that the idea of generic strategies was a late addition to the book.)

The first generic strategy is differentiation, competing on the basis of value added to customers (quality, service, differentiation) so that customers will pay a premium to cover higher costs. The second is cost-based leadership, offering products or services at the lowest cost. Quality and service are not unimportant, but cost reduction provides focus to the organization. Focus is the third generic strategy identified by Porter. Companies with a clear strategy outperform those whose strategy is unclear or those which attempt to achieve both differentiation and cost leadership. 'Sometimes the firm can successfully pursue more than one approach as its primary target, though this is rarely possible', says Porter. 'Effectively implementing any of these generic strategies usually requires total commitment, and organizational arrangements are diluted if there's more than one primary target.'

If a company fails to focus on any of the three generic strategies it is liable to encounter problems. 'The firm failing to develop its strategy in at least one of the three directions – a firm that is "stuck in the middle" – is in an extremely poor strategic situation', Porter writes. 'The firm lacks the market share, capital investment, and resolve to play the low-cost game, the industry-wide differentiation necessary to obviate the need for a low-cost position, or the focus to create differentiation or low cost in a more limited sphere. The firm stuck in the middle is almost guaranteed low profitability. It either loses the high-volume customers who demand low prices or must bid away its profits to get this business away from low-cost firms. Yet it also loses high-margin businesses – the cream – to the firms who are focused on high-margin targets or have achieved differentiation overall. The firm stuck in the middle also probably suffers from a blurred corporate culture and a conflicting set of organizational arrangements and motivation system.'

When *Competitive Strategy* was published in 1980, Porter's generic strategies offered a rational and straightforward method for companies to extricate themselves from strategic confusion. The reassurance proved short-lived. Less than a decade later, companies were having to compete on all fronts. They had to be differentiated, through improved service or speedier development, and be cost leaders, cheaper than their competitors.

Porter's other contribution in *Competitive Strategy* has proved more robust.

'In any industry, whether it is domestic or international, or produces a product or a service, the rules of competition are embodied in five competitive forces', he writes. These five competitive forces are:

- The entry of new competitors. New competitors necessitate some competitive response which will inevitably use some of your resources, thus reducing profits.
- The threat of substitutes. If there are viable alternatives to your product or service in the marketplace, the prices you can charge will be limited.
- The bargaining power of buyers. If customers have bargaining power they will use it. This will reduce profit margins and, as a result, affect profitability.
- The bargaining power of suppliers. Given power over you, suppliers will increase their prices and adversely affect your profitability.
- The rivalry among the existing competitors. Competition leads to the need to invest in marketing, R&D, or price reductions which will reduce your profits.

'The collective strength of these five competitive forces determines the ability of firms in an industry to earn, on average, rates of return on investment in excess of the cost of capital. The strength of the five forces varies from industry to industry, and can change as an industry evolves', Porter observes.

'Porter's Five Forces is a wonderful way to analyze industries but it has nothing to do with making strategy because there's no creativity in it. It's just an input for a process, not the process itself', suggests Henry Mintzberg.

The five forces outlined in *Competitive Strategy* are a means by which a company can begin to understand its particular industry. Initially, they were passively interpreted as valid statements of the facts of competitive life. Now, however, they are more regularly interpreted as the rules of the game, which have to be changed and challenged if an organization is to achieve any impact in a particular market.

Notes

1 'Professor Porter PhD', *The Economist*, 8 October 1994.
2 Porter, Michael, *Competitive Strategy*, Free Press, New York, 1980.

MICHAEL PORTER

The Competitive Advantage of Nations

1990

The classic

ichael Porter's *The Competitive Advantage of Nations*[1] is one of the most ambitious books of our times. Tom Peters, an unlikely bedfellow for the ultra-rational Porter, called it 'magisterial'. At its heart is a radical new perspective of the role and *raison d'être* of nations. From being military powerhouses they are now economic units whose competitiveness is the key to power.

The book emerged from Porter's work on Ronald Reagan's Commission on Industrial Competitiveness. 'The book that projected Porter into the stratosphere, read by aspiring intellectuals and despairing politicians everywhere, was *The Competitive Advantage of Nations*', said *The Economist*. 'This work can be read on three levels: as a general inquiry into what makes national economies successful, as a detailed study of eight of the world's main modern economies, and as a series of prescriptions about what governments should do to improve their country's competitiveness.'[2]

Porter's research, in fact, encompasses ten countries: the UK, Denmark, Italy, Japan, Korea, Singapore, Sweden, Switzerland, the US and Germany (then West Germany). Porter seeks to build on the ideas of his previous books to examine what makes a nation's firms and industries competitive in global markets and what propels a whole nation's economy to advance. 'Why are firms based in a particular nation able to create and sustain competitive advantage against the world's best competitors in a particular field? And why is one nation often the home for so many of an industry's world leaders?' asks Porter. 'Why is tiny Switzerland the home base for international leaders in pharmaceuticals, chocolate and

Gary Hamel on *The Competitive Advantage of Nations*

'While *The Competitive Advantage of Nations* provides a good account of why particular industry "clusters" emerged in some countries and not others, it is essentially backward looking. In a world of open markets, and mobile capital, technology and knowledge, no firm need be the product of its geography. That a German company, SAP, can succeed in the software industry; that a Japanese company, Yamaha, can lead the world in making grand pianos, and a Korean company, Samsung, can become number one in the world in memory semiconductors suggests that geography is having less and less to do with firm competitiveness. *The Competitive Advantage of Nations* was a wonderful historical study and was certainly useful to governments to construct policy that promoted the competitiveness of indigenous firms, but it told us almost nothing about the future of competitiveness – a future in which companies from one part of the world can access and internalize the competitive advantage of far distant geographies.'

trading? Why are leaders in heavy trucks and mining equipment based in Sweden?'

Porter returns to first principles, an ambitious move in itself given the nature of the nationalistic minefield he ventures into. 'The principal economic goal of a nation is to produce a high and rising standard of living for its citizens. The ability to do so depends not on the amorphous notion of "competitiveness" but on the productivity with which a nation's resources (labor and capital) are employed,' he writes. 'Productivity is the prime determinant in the long run of a nation's standard of living.'

Unlike Kenichi Ohmae who champions the 'end of the nation state', Porter's research leads to different conclusions. He identifies a central paradox. Companies and industries have become globalized and more international in their scope and aspirations than ever before. This, on the surface at least, would appear to suggest that the nation has lost its role in the international success of its firms. 'Companies, at first glance, seem to have transcended countries. Yet what I have learned in this study contradicts this conclusion,' says Porter. 'While globalization of competition might appear to make the nation less important, instead it seems to make it more so. With fewer impediments to trade to shelter uncompetitive domestic firms and industries, the home nation takes on growing significance because it is the source of the skills and technology that underpin competitive advantage.'

Porter also lays down a challenge, perhaps to himself, to solve another perennial mystery: 'Much is known about what competitive advantage is and how particular actions create or destroy it. Much less is known about why a company makes good choices instead of bad choices in seeking bases for competitive advantage, and why some firms are more aggressive in pursuing them.'

Porter's conclusion is that it is the intensity of domestic competition which often fuels success on a global stage.

To make sense of the dynamics behind national or regional strength in a particular industry, Porter develops the national 'diamond'. This is made up of four forces:

- Factor conditions – these once would have included natural resources and plentiful supplies of labour; now they embrace data communications, university research and the availability of scientists, engineers or experts in a particular field.
- Demand conditions – if there is strong national demand for a product or service this can give the industry a head start in global competition. The US, for example, is ahead in health services due to heavy national demand.
- Related and supporting industries – industries which are strong in particular countries are often surrounded by successful related industries.
- Firm strategy, structure and rivalry – domestic competition fuels growth and competitive strength.

Notes

1 Porter, Michael, *The Competitive Advantage of Nations*, Macmillan, London, 1990.
2 'Professor Porter PhD', *The Economist*, 8 October 1994.

FREDERICK REICHHELD

The Loyalty Effect

1996

The author

 rederick Reichheld is a director emeritus at the consulting firm Bain & Company and a leading authority on the subject of loyalty. He is also the author of *Loyalty Rules!* (2001).

The classic

In most areas of human endeavour, loyalty is regarded as a virtue. Yet, in business it is often sacrificed for short-term expediency. Hard times tend to accentuate the worst aspects of corporate life. Companies that have spent years assiduously wooing staff are inclined to cut jobs at the first sign of trouble. But Reichheld suggests that companies that stand by their people in hard times may fare better in the long run.

Reichheld argues that companies should consider the longer-term impact of redundancies on staff morale. A more humane approach, Reichheld suggests, can actually be better for business. 'By fostering loyalty, particularly during a downturn, companies can boost productivity, customer retention and referrals, and attract talented staff', he says.

Reichheld has elevated loyalty from the softest of corporate issues into something approaching a science. His approach emphasizes the economic value of long-term relationships.

The roots of Reichheld's work lie in *The Loyalty Effect*,[1] which examines the issue of customer retention. By analysing costs and revenues accruing from serving customers throughout their entire purchasing life cycle he uncovered an important link between customer retention and profits. In many industries, he found, the high cost of acquiring customers made the relationship unprofitable in the early years. Only in later years, when the costs of serving loyal customers fell and purchases increased, did companies generate big returns. His research found that increasing customer retention rates by 5 per cent boosted profits by 25 to 95 per cent.

Later, in *Loyalty Rules!*, Reichheld considers the impact of staff loyalty on the long-term performance of companies. Many business leaders, he says, don't grasp the relevance of employee loyalty to the economic success of their companies. In many cases their actions have alienated employees, who in turn alienate customers – which has a negative impact on profits and growth.

A Bain & Co study examined 288 Fortune 500 companies that weathered the last recession. It found that the share prices of companies that laid off more than 3 per cent of their employees performed no better over a three-year period than those of companies that made smaller cuts or none at all. Companies that announced job losses greater than 15 per cent of their workforce – such as Pan Am in 1991 and Lucent Technologies in the current downturn – actually performed significantly below average. Companies that announced repeated rounds of layoffs, such as Digital Equipment in the early 1990s, fared even worse.

Reichheld's findings add weight to the argument that relationships play a crucial role in business success. Today, in their haste to staunch financial losses, many senior managers seem to have forgotten how fragile loyalty is in the post-downsizing world. Employees have long memories, but corporate memories tend to be short.

Reichheld has also examined the effects of staff retention on performance. Analysis of nearly 100 companies in a dozen industries indicates that staff defections have a clearly defined impact on profits. One of his studies, from 1996, indicated 5 per cent swings in employee retention rates resulting in 25 per cent to 100 per cent swings in earnings – in both directions.

Reichheld advocates a more measured corporate response than knee-jerk downsizing. Leaders should recognise the importance of loyalty, he says. Leadership based on principles and relationships will stand a company in better stead in the long run. 'Loyalty remains the hallmark of great leadership. It provides a far more exacting standard than the profits demanded today by impatient shareholders. The long-term rewards of loyalty ultimately outstrip even the most spectacular short-term profits,' he says.

Over the long run, then, Reichheld does not see a trade-off between loyalty and profits. He asserts that the two go hand in hand. But in the short run, financial performance and loyalty can appear to be in conflict. The essence of loyalty, he suggests, is self-sacrifice – putting principles and relationships ahead of immediate personal financial gain. This jars with traditional short-term thinking, and gives rise to what he describes as the 'paradox of business loyalty', an issue that has traditionally gone unreconciled.

By choosing short-term expediency above staff, too many business leaders, he says, confuse profits with purpose. 'Whether they know it or not, they have abandoned what I'd call the high road of business practice. A single-minded focus on financial results will not create the conditions for loyalty or long-term success, and it may well lead an organization down a slippery slope to the low road. On the low road, where money matters more than people, it becomes standard practice to take advantage of customers, employees, vendors, and a host of other business associates whenever they are vulnerable.'

Low road strategies, he says, may generate impressive financial results for a time. The buoyant earnings and stock price they engender provide the necessary bribes required to buy commitment. Eventually, though, the low road leads to trouble. When hard times hit, the company can no longer fund the bribes. And then, he says, the true value of loyalty will become apparent.

In his most recent research, Reichheld and his Bain colleague Phil Schefter found that the Internet accentuates the loyalty effect. 'Acquiring customers on the Internet is enormously expensive, and unless those customers stick around and make lots of repeat purchases over the years, then profits will remain elusive', Reichheld and Schefter conclude.

Note

1 Reichheld, Frederick, *The Loyalty Effect*, Harvard Business School Press, 1996.

REG REVANS

Action Learning

1979

The author

 eg Revans (born 1907) is a British academic, and sometime Olympic athlete.

The classic

Unsung and unheralded, Reg Revans is a man with a mission. Now in his late eighties, the creator and champion of 'action learning' retains a messianic zeal few younger men could match. 'Unless your ideas are ridiculed by experts they are worth nothing', he says. 'I've been talking about action learning for sixty years but it's not me you should be talking to, talk to the people putting it into practice.'

Interest in Revans' ideas continues to pour in from all corners of the globe. The Pentagon is enthusiastic; the ANC has taken up action learning; Revans fields queries from Australia, Sweden and many more. But he remains an outsider in his homeland.

Part of the reason for Revans' isolation is cultural. While others seize upon action learning as a dynamic, commonsense way forward, the British appear particularly uncomfortable with the idea and its implications. As theories go, action learning is simple, deceptively so. It is concerned with learning to learn by doing, a process for which Revans created a simple equation – $L = P + Q$ – learning occurs through a combination of programmed knowledge (P) and the ability to ask insightful questions (Q). 'The essence of action learning is to become better acquainted with the self by trying to observe what one may actually do, to trace the reasons for attempting it and the consequences of what one seemed to be doing', says Revans.

While programmed knowledge is one dimensional and rigid, the ability to ask questions opens up other dimensions and is free flowing. Revans argues that educational institutions remain fixated with programmed knowledge instead of encouraging students to ask questions and roam widely around a subject.

The structure linking the two elements is the small team or set. 'The central idea of this approach to human development, at all levels, in all cultures and for all purposes, is today that of the set, or small group of comrades in adversity, striving to learn with and from each other as they confess failures and expand on victories', writes Revans in *Action Learning*.

Action learning is the antithesis of the traditional approach to developing managers. Indeed, Revans' contempt is at its most withering when he considers business schools – 'There are too many people concealing their ignorance under a veneer of knowledge. Instead of hiding our ignorance we should be bartering it.' 'Flatulent self-deception' is how Revans colourfully describes the neatly defined case studies which are the cornerstone of business school courses.

'We keep solving the same problems because we do not learn from them. We bring in consultants to provide solutions or send managers on courses where they are taught a lot but learn little. In contrast, action learning is about teaching little and learning a lot,' says David Botham, director of the recently opened Revans Centre for Action Learning and Research at Salford University.

Though it runs against conventional educational wisdom, action learning's ancestry is ancient. Reg Revans peppers his papers and conversation with an array of inspirations – from Buddhism to the Bible. He can trace his personal advocacy of action learning back to the sinking of the Titanic when he was nearing his fifth birthday. His father was a naval architect who was on the inquiry into the disaster. 'He said to me years later that what the inquiry proved was that we must train people in such a way that they understand the difference between cleverness and wisdom. The education system – then and now – encourages cleverness.'

The seed of a lifetime's fascination was sown and began to flourish in the 1920s when Revans worked at Cambridge's Cavendish Laboratories alongside five Nobel Prize winners. In the quest to split the atom, the eminent scientists tended to champion their own particular field. To break the log-jam, physicist Lord Rutherford decided that the team should hold a meeting every week to discuss their difficulties and ask fresh questions. 'Even though they had won Nobel Prizes, they were willing to acknowledge that things could be going on elsewhere. They asked questions,' Revans remembers.

If leading thinkers could introduce humility and the sharing of knowledge into their working practices why couldn't others? After the war, Revans moved on to become the first director of education and training at the National Coal Board and set about applying his ideas. He concluded that colliery managers and miners themselves needed to acknowledge the problems they faced and then attempt to solve them. 'When doctors listen to nurses, patients recover more quickly; if mining engineers pay more attention to their men than to their machinery, the pits are more efficient. As in athletics and nuclear research, it is neither books nor seminars from which managers learn much, but from here-and-now exchanges about the operational job in hand.'

With characteristic frankness, Revans announced that he saw no need to employ a team of specialist tutors: 'The ultimate power of a successful general staff lies not in the brilliance of its individual members, but in the cross-fertilisation of its collective abilities.' Revans spent two years underground to examine the real problems facing miners. This reinforced his idea that learning comes when problems are aired and shared in small groups of 'comrades in adversity'. (In the 1990s Nelson Mandela calls it 'grassroots collaboration'.) The pits which tried Revans' methods recorded a 30 per cent increase in productivity

At the Coal Board Revans worked with E F Schumacher, author of *Small is Beautiful* – 'Small is dutiful', is Revans' retort. 'You must seek to understand each other's problems and develop a sense of responsibility for each other through working in small groups.' Revans' approach was not well received by management and he eventually resigned.

In the sixties, Revans was apparently set on an academic career. The UK's first professor of industrial administration at Manchester University, he was involved in the debate about the nature of the city's soon-to-be-established business school. Again, action learning ruffled establishment feathers and Revans departed for Belgium to lead an experiment launched by the Fondation Industrie–Université with the support of the country's leading business people and five universities.

Here he found more fertile ground. 'Brussels had been selected as capital of the Common Market much to everyone's surprise. They decided if they were to be the administrative centre of Europe they needed to develop international understanding.' The Belgians responded to the idea of action learning with enthusiasm. Top managers were exchanged between organizations to work on each other's problems. 'I wasn't there to teach anyone anything. We got people talking to each other, asking questions. People from the airline business talked to people from chemical companies. People shared knowledge and experience,' Revans explains. With minimal attention from the rest of the world, the

Belgian economy enjoyed a spectacular renaissance – during the 1970s Belgian industrial productivity rose by 102 per cent, compared with 28 per cent in the UK.

Yet again, Revans' success failed to cross the Channel. When his huge book, *Action Learning*, was published he ended up buying most of the copies. (Indeed, it is probably the least successful and the least known book in this collection.) Simple though it may seem, action learning provides a challenge which organizations have found too sizeable even to contemplate. If learning revolves around questioning, there can be no assumption that the manager knows best purely because of their status. When the world was top down, Revans looked from the bottom up and saw a new world of possibilities.

Revans' ideas have been applied to rice-growing in Bihar, among the isolated villages of Nigeria, in London hospitals and in many other situations and organizations. The wide-ranging scope of action learning and the eclectic mind of Revans make it clear that action learning is no quick fix. It requires a fundamental change in thinking. 'People learn in unfamiliar settings faced with unfamiliar problems. While it is relatively easy to achieve the latter, placing people in unfamiliar settings is difficult,' says David Botham of Salford's Centre for Action Learning. He partly attributes scepticism about action learning to the constant urge to measure the outputs of training activity – 'Critics have always wanted to measure and evaluate action learning. In fact, action learning should be evaluating itself.'

Many contemporary management ideas – teamworking, re-engineering, the learning organization – contain elements of action learning. Revans is encouraged, but remains unconvinced: 'What we need now is not a saviour or a guru, but an active movement so that, no matter what their culture, people work together to understand local difficulties. I'm not saying this is the final answer. There is no final answer for anything.'

EDGAR H SCHEIN

Organizational Culture and Leadership

1985

The author

E dgar H Schein (born 1928) studied social psychology at Stanford and then at Harvard. He is now professor of management at Massachusetts Institute of Technology. The roots of his thinking can be traced back to early influences on his career including Douglas McGregor, Warren Bennis and Chris Argyris. Schein taught and profoundly influenced, among others, Charles Handy.

More recently, his work on the 'psychological contract' and his concept of 'career anchors' has attracted attention. Schein believes we have a single 'career anchor', the underlying career value which we are unwilling to surrender.

The classic

Edgar Schein's 1985 book *Organizational Culture and Leadership*[1] paved the way for a plethora of studies of corporate culture. Indeed, Schein is sometimes seen as the inventor of the term 'corporate culture'- and, at the very least, one of its originators.

Schein describes culture as 'a pattern of basic assumptions – invented, discovered, or developed by a given group as it learns to cope with its problems of external adaptation and internal integration – that has worked well enough to be considered valid and, therefore, to be taught to new members as the correct way to perceive, think, and feel in relation to those problems'. Instead of regarding everything an organization does as part of its culture, Schein takes a more psychological view. Schein's 'basic assumptions' are re-phrased and re-interpreted

Gary Hamel on *Organizational Culture and Leadership*

'It is impossible to change a large organization without first understanding that organization's culture. Ed Schein gave us an ability to look deeply into what makes an organization what it is, thus providing the foundation of any successful effort at "transformation" or "change". *Organizational Culture and Leadership* remains essential reading for all aspiring "change agents".'

elsewhere in a variety of ways – perhaps the nearest is Chris Argyris' term 'theories-in-use'.

These basic assumptions, says Schein, can be categorized into five dimensions:

- **Humanity's relationship to nature** – while some companies regard themselves as masters of their own destiny, others are submissive, willing to accept the domination of their external environment.
- **The nature of reality and truth** – organizations and managers adopt a wide variety of methods to reach what becomes accepted as the organizational 'truth' – through debate, dictatorship, or through simple acceptance that if something achieves the objective it is right.
- **The nature of human nature** – organizations differ in their views of human nature. Some follow McGregor's Theory X and work on the principle that people will not do the job if they can avoid it. Others regard people in a more positive light and attempt to enable them to fulfil their potential for the benefit of both sides.
- **The nature of human activity** – the West has traditionally emphasized tasks and their completion rather than the more philosophical side of work. Achievement is all. Schein suggests an alternative approach – 'being-in-becoming' – emphasizing self-fulfilment and development.
- **The nature of human relationships** – organizations make a variety of assumptions about how people interact with each other. Some facilitate social interaction, while others regard it as an unnecessary distraction.

These five categories are not mutually exclusive, but are in a constant state of development and flux. Culture does not stand still.

Key to the creation and development of corporate culture are the values embraced by the organization. Schein acknowledges that a single person can shape these values and, as a result, an entire corporate culture. (This spawned a wave of interest in the heroic creators of corporate cultures from Henry Ford to IBM's Thomas Watson.) Schein identifies three stages in the development of a corporate culture.

In the first, 'birth and early growth', the culture may be dominated by the business founder. The culture is regarded as a source of the company's identity, a bonding agent protecting it against outside forces.

In the next stage, 'organizational mid-life', the original culture is likely to be diluted and undermined as new cultures emerge and there is a loss of the original sense of identity. At this stage, there is an opportunity for the fundamental culture to be realigned and changed.

If this fails to happen the culture moves to the final stage, 'organizational maturity', where it is a burden. Culture, at this stage, is regarded sentimentally. People are hopelessly addicted to how things used to be done and unwilling to contemplate change. Here the organization is at its weakest, as the culture has been transformed from a source of competitive advantage and distinctiveness to a hindrance in the marketplace. Only through aggressive measures will it survive.

Importantly, each stage of the culture's growth requires a different method of change. If culture is to work in support of a company's strategy, Schein believes there has to be a level of consensus covering five areas:

- the core mission or primary task
- goals
- the means to accomplish the goals
- how to measure progress
- remedial or repair strategies.

Schein regards achieving cultural change as a formidable challenge, one that well-established executives in strong cultures often find beyond them. The exceptional executives who achieve cultural change from within a culture they are closely identified with (such as GE's Jack Welch) are rarities, and are labelled by Schein as cultural 'hybrids'.

Organizational Culture and Leadership clarified the entire area of corporate culture in a way no-one previously had achieved. Its perspectives on culture as a constantly changing force in corporate life remain valuable though disconcerting – it begins to feel as if culture has a life of its own and only exceptional people or extraordinary actions can disturb its momentum.

Note

1 Schein, Edgar H, *Organizational Culture and Leadership,* Jossey-Bass, San Francisco, 1985.

RICARDO SEMLER

Maverick!

1993

The author

In 1990 and again in 1992, Ricardo Semler – majority owner of a Sao Paulo manufacturing company, Semco S/A, which specializes in marine and food-service equipment – was elected business leader of the year by a poll of 52,000 Brazilian executives. His book *Maverick!* became an international bestseller. In Brazil it was on the bestseller list for 200 weeks.

Semler has studied at Harvard Business School and has written articles for the *Harvard Business Review*. He was Vice-President of the Federation of Industries of Brazil and is a member of the board of SOS Atlantic Forest, Brazil's foremost environmental organization.

The classic

Ricardo Semler's *Maverick!*[1] is one of the most surprising business bestsellers of recent times. Prior to its publication the thought of learning managerial lessons from a Brazilian corporation was risible. Today, with *Maverick!* having sold one million copies, Semler's unique managerial style has been consumed by managers throughout the world.

In 1980 Semler took over his family's company, Semco, from his father. The company was unexceptional in performance and management. Given two to three weeks to change things, Semler set about restructuring it in a dramatic and revolutionary fashion. In a single day he fired 60 per cent of the company's top management. He based his revolution on three values: employee participation, profit-sharing, and open information systems. 'In these days of the new world order, almost everyone believes people have a right to vote for those who lead them, at least in the public sector', writes Semler. 'But democracy has yet to pen-

---

Gary Hamel on *Maverick!*

'Almost none of the great management books that populate this volume were written by practicing managers. Why is this? Perhaps it is because managers seldom have the time, or the perspective, to generalize from their own experiences. Books by Lee Iacocca, Harold Geneen, and other management icons are typically as idiosyncratic as they are entertaining. While the managerial "solutions" espoused by Ricardo Semler may not be universally applicable, the set of beliefs that animate his particular approach are clearly laid out and can be debated on their own merits.'

---

etrate the workplace. Dictators and despots are alive and well in offices and factories all over the world.'

Take Semco's reaction to a dramatic situation. In 1990 the Brazilian minister of finance effectively seized 80 per cent of the nation's cash. The economy entered a state of chaotic paralysis. At Semco, sales were reduced to zero. The company had $4 million of products which its customers simply couldn't pay for. Costs were slashed in an attempt to stay afloat. Then, gathering the company's employees together, possible solutions were discussed. The employees agreed to a 30 per cent wage cut so long as their profit-sharing was increased from 24 per cent to 39 per cent and providing managers took a 40 per cent pay cut. The final element of the agreement was that a member of the union committee signed every cheque issued by the company.

It is difficult to imagine such an agreement being considered in any other organization, let alone accepted. Semler used it as a means of accelerating the pace of change – if Semco's 850 employees were so committed and so willing to seek out imaginative solutions to the company's problems in a crisis, why couldn't their ingenuity be harnessed all the time?

Semco now has just four grades of staff. The job of chief executive is handled by six senior managers for six months at a time (Semler is one of them). Managers set their own salaries and bonuses and are evaluated by those who work for them. Employees decide their own working hours, set quotas and improve products and processes. 'The company is organized – well, maybe that's not quite the right word for us – not to depend too much on any individual, especially me', writes Semler. 'I take it as a point of pride that twice on my return from long trips my office had been moved – and each time it got smaller. My role is that of a catalyst.

I try to create an environment in which others make decisions. Success means not making them myself.'

Though Semler's message has been granted massive media attention, few have been brave enough to follow Semco's lead. Former BTR chief, Sir Owen Green, is typical of the dismissive reaction from mainstream business leaders, claiming that Semler's 'not maverick; he is an eccentric'. Charles Handy is more positive: 'The way that Ricardo Semler runs his company is impossible; except that it works, and works splendidly for everyone.'

Maverick! is an exception to the general run of books by successful executives. There is none of the usual corporate heroism but, instead, an acceptance that management is concerned with enabling others rather than controlling them.

Note

1 Semler, Ricardo, *Maverick!*, Century, London, 1993.

PETER SENGE

The Fifth Discipline

1990

The author

eter Senge (born 1947) is director of the Center for Organizational Learning at the Massachusetts Institute of Technology and
is chairperson of the Society for Organizational Learning (SOL).
He graduated in engineering from Stanford before doing a Ph.D.
on social systems modelling at MIT.

Senge studies how firms and other organizations can develop adaptive capabilities in a world of increasing complexity and rapid change.
In his book *The Fifth Discipline* he gives managers tools and conceptual
archetypes to help them understand the structures and dynamics underlying their organizations' problems.

Senge also collaborated on two related books. He co-authored
*The Fifth Discipline Fieldbook: Strategies and Tools for Building a Learn-
ing Organization* and *The Dance of Change: The Challenges to Sustaining
Momentum in Learning*.

The classic

Peter Senge's *The Fifth Discipline: The Art and Practice of the Learning
Organization*[1] popularized the concept of the learning organization.

'As the world becomes more interconnected and business becomes
more complex and dynamic, work must become more *learningful*",
writes Senge. 'It is no longer sufficient to have one person learning for
the organization, a Ford or a Sloan or a Watson. It's just not possible any
longer to "figure it out" from the top, and have everybody else following
the orders of the "grand strategist". The organizations that will truly excel
in the future will be the organizations that discover how to tap people's
commitment and capacity to learn at all levels in an organization.'

Gary Hamel on *The Fifth Discipline*

'Like Michael Porter, Peter Senge is a master of synthesis. Like Chris Argyris and Ed Schein, he tackles the deep structure of problems, not their superficial manifestations. While Professor Argyris put organizational learning on the management agenda, Peter Senge married it with system thinking and created a language and approach that makes the whole set of ideas accessible to managers. Peter is no mere theorist, his Organizational Learning Center at MIT has helped launch thousands of in-company learning experiments. *The Fifth Discipline* would certainly be on my short list of the half dozen best business books of the last 25 years.'

Senge argues that managers should encourage employees to be open to new ideas, communicate frankly with each other, understand thoroughly how their companies operate, form a collective vision and work together to achieve their goal. In the learning organization managers will become researchers and designers rather than controllers and overseers.

'In the simplest sense, a learning organization is a group of people who are continually enhancing their capability to create their own future', says Senge by way of definition. 'The traditional meaning of the word learning is much deeper than just taking information in. It is about changing individuals so that they produce results they care about – accomplish things that are important to them.'

Though Senge's book was a bestseller and the idea of the learning organization became fashionable, *The Fifth Discipline* emerged from extensive research. Senge and his team at the Center for Organizational Learning at MIT's Sloan School of Management have been working on the theme for some time. 'For the past 15 years or longer, many of us have been struggling to understand what "learning organizations" are all about, and how to make progress in moving organizations along this path. Out of these efforts, I believe some insights are emerging,' says Senge in the multi-authored sequel, *The Fifth Discipline Fieldbook*.

In *The Fifth Discipline*, Senge suggests that there are five components to a learning organization:

- **Systems thinking** – Senge introduces the idea of systems archetypes. In practical terms this can help managers spot repetitive patterns, such as the way certain kinds of problems persist, or the way systems have their own in-built limits to growth. Senge champions systems thinking, recognizing that things are interconnected. He regards corporations as complex systems. This has pushed managerial thinking towards contemplating complexity theory, which has spawned numerous books though few go beyond the basic metaphor. (Ralph Stacey's *Complexity and Creativity in Organizations* is one of the few to develop from Senge's ideas. Stacey argues that creativity 'is inevitably messy' and 'to remove that mess by inspiring us to follow some common vision, share the same culture and pull together, is to remove … the raw material of creative activity'.[2])

- **Personal mastery** – Senge grounds this idea in the familiar competencies and skills associated with management, but also includes spiritual growth – opening oneself up to a progressively deeper reality – and living life from a creative rather than a reactive viewpoint. This discipline involves two underlying movements – continually learning how to see current reality more clearly – and the ensuing gap between vision and reality produces the creative tension from which learning arises. 'In the simplest sense, a learning organization is a group of people who are continually enhancing their capability to create their future', says Senge. 'The traditional meaning of the word *learning* is much deeper than just *taking information in*. It is about changing individuals so that they produce results they care about, accomplish things that are important to them.'[3]

- **Mental models** – this essentially deals with the organization's driving and fundamental values and principles. Senge alerts managers to the power of patterns of thinking at the organizational level and the importance of non-defensive inquiry into the nature of these patterns.

- **Shared vision** – here Senge stresses the importance of co-creation and argues that shared vision can only be built on personal vision. He claims that shared vision is present when the task that follows from the vision is no longer seen by the team members as separate from the self.

- **Team learning** – the discipline of team learning involves two practices: dialogue and discussion. The former is characterized by its exploratory nature, the latter by the opposite process of narrowing down the field to the best alternative for the decisions that need to be made. The two are complementary, but the benefits of combining them only come from having previously separated them. Most teams lack the ability to distinguish between the two and to move consciously between them.

In practice, corporate habits are hard to break. Says Senge: 'For the traditional organization, the learning organization poses huge challenges. In the learning organization managers are researchers and designers rather than controllers and overseers. Managers should encourage employees to be open to new ideas, communicate frankly with each other, understand thoroughly how their companies operate, form a collective vision, and work together to achieve their goal. This is hard to do and certainly is not the way most managers were taught to do things. I know people who have lost their jobs supporting these theories.'[4]

Transforming companies into learning organizations has proved highly problematical. The principal reason for this is that it involves managers surrendering their traditional spheres of power and control. They have to hand over power to the people who are learning and, if people are to learn, they must be allowed to experiment and fail. In a blame-oriented culture, this requires a major change in attitude.

Senge's concept of the learning organization demands trust and involvement. Again, this is usually notable by its absence. 'Real commitment is rare in today's organizations. It is our experience that 90 per cent of the time what passes for commitment is compliance,' writes Senge

'Perhaps the problem is that although the learning organization sounds as if it is a product, it is actually a process. Processes are not suddenly unveiled for all to see', says Phil Hodgson of the UK's Ashridge Management College. 'Academic definitions, no matter how precise, cannot be instantly applied in the real world. Managers need to promote learning so that it gradually emerges as a key part of an organization's culture. Being convinced of the merits of the learning organization is not usually a matter of dramatic conversion.'

Even so, *The Fifth Discipline* has proved highly influential. Though the learning organization has rarely been converted into reality, the idea has fuelled the debate on self-managed development and employability, and has affected the rewards and remuneration strategies of many organizations.

Notes

1 Senge, Peter, *The Fifth Discipline,* Doubleday, New York, 1990.
2 Stacey, Ralph, *Complexity and Creativity in Organizations,* Berrett Koehler, San Francisco, 1996.
3 Napuk, K, 'Live and learn', *Scottish Business Insider,* January 1994.
4 Brown, Tom, Crainer, Stuart, Dearlove, Des & Rodrigues, J N, *Business Minds,* FT Prentice Hall, 2001.

PATRICIA SEYBOLD

Customers.com

1998

The author

P atty Seybold is CEO of the Boston-based consulting firm the Patricia Seybold Group, a worldwide consulting/research firm, which she founded in 1978.

Seybold has written two books. *Customers.com (1998)*, written with colleague Ronnie Marshak, examined how leading companies design and implement e-business strategies to build customer relationships. It sold more than 300,000 copies.

In her follow-up book, *The Customer Revolution: How to Thrive When Your Customers are in Control (2001)*, Seybold argues that successful companies in the future will be those that use customer lifetime value as a strategic management tool, rather than a marketing discipline.

The classic

Today, change then change again is the commercial mantra. Driving all this upheaval are the usual suspects – new technology, mergers and acquisitions, truculent shareholders, and all the rest. But amid all the noise, one voice often receives scant attention: customers.

Despite its ability to foster two-way communication, the Internet in particular has made companies hard of hearing. Online, the customer is king, queen, and dictator. Yet during the rise of the new economy this was largely ignored. Without customers there is no business.

On the online battlefield customers were seen as little more than prisoners. The onus was on capturing them, rather than delighting them. Or the company regarded itself as the spider, creating sticky websites to ensnare the flies. In the process customers were reduced from individuals to numbers, characterized as little more than human traffic. Even the recent vogue for CRM (customer relationship management) has tended to focus on technological capability – building databases – rather than genuine customer satisfaction.

One exception is Dell Computers. What has made Dell the force that it is today? Not its computers, but its customers. The company does not build a single PC until it's actually ordered and paid for. When customers click, Dell jumps.

Dell has created a direct line to the customer which the company has proved highly adept at maximizing. Dell has a strong rapport with its customers – in a way that Microsoft, for example, has manifestly failed to achieve 'To all our nit-picky – over-demanding – ask-awkward-questions customers ... Thank you, and keep up the good work', read one Dell advertisement.

Patricia Seybold's 1998 bestseller *Customers.com is* a 'how to' guide aimed at executives and technology managers. 'What's the formula for success?' Seybold asks. 'Make it easy for customers to do business with you!' Elementary, you might think, but the book coincided with a time when many companies were mesmerized by the technology – to the exclusion of common business sense.

At a time when many companies were struggling to get their heads around the whole idea of e-commerce, the message was simple. 'It's the customer, stupid', was the much-needed wake up call, and Seybold delivered it with aplomb.

'I noticed that nobody understood what was going on in this so-called "new economy"', she says. 'I believe that the current economy isn't a high tech economy, nor an Internet economy, nor an m-commerce economy, but, instead, is a customer economy. Customers, armed with information and access, are much more demanding than ever before. They are demanding fair, global pricing. They are demanding that companies deal with them using all the distribution channels.'

Today, she says, whether buying direct from manufacturers, or through dealers and retailers, it is customers who are shaping industries. She points to the impact of Napster on the music industry, where customers are demanding the ability to download digital music, to mix and match their own compilations, and to be able to share them with friends and other interested listeners around the world.

Most important, she says, customer relationships now count in a way that they have never counted before. Companies' values will increasingly be based on the value of their customer franchise – the lifetime customer value of their present and future customers. Companies, she says, should reorganize their performance criteria around customer value. This goes well beyond current CRM.

The importance of customer retention may seem self-evident, but is often overlooked by shareholders. 'The companies that will win in the customer economy are already managing their companies by and for customer value', says Seybold. 'The intellectual capital I'm interested in is customer capital. That will be embedded in the minds of employees and in the organization but it will also be embedded in the company's relationships with its customers.'[1]

Successful companies, says Seybold, use customer lifetime value as a strategic management tool, not just a marketing discipline. And they measure what matters to customers in real time. These companies focus on the branded customer experience – on the feelings that customers have when they interact with a company's products and brand across interaction touchpoints (Web, email, phone, face-to-face) and across distribution channels (retail, dealers, agents, brokers, etc.).

'To win in the customer economy you need to build and sustain an exquisite branded experience and to measure and monitor what matters to customers. That's new,' she says.

Companies need a high level executive who is responsible for the total customer experience across product lines and distribution channels, says Seybold. Hewlett-Packard, for example, now has two large customer enterprises – one for consumers and one for business customers. Each one has a president. And reporting directly to that president is a vice president of Total Customer Experience. 'This person is responsible for setting the customer experience measurement for the entire enterprise, on measuring and constantly improving the customer experience, and has the purview and the power to make policy and pricing decisions', she says.

The VP of Total Customer Experience also sets the goals against which all of H-P's executives are compensated. 'In the customer economy, your executives and employees' performance-based pay is based on customer metrics – how you're doing in meeting customer satisfaction and customer loyalty goals', says Seybold.

She predicts that the successful companies of the future will be 'highly adaptive and customer-centric. They will be what I call "sense-and-pro-act" organizations. They will recognize new patterns very quickly – especially in terms of customer behavior. To do so they will require real-time information about that customer behavior. Being able to identify and act on these new patterns and trends more quickly than their competitors will be vital to their success. It will provide competitive advantage.

'The way that companies are organized will also change. Federated and networked organizations – extended enterprises – will be the norm.

In the past, companies have either been highly centralized, with command and control structures, or highly distributed, with autonomous business units. In the past companies have tended to swing from one extreme to the other, but they are now beginning to figure out how they can combine the best attributes of these two models to create federal organizations.'

Note

1 Interview with Des Dearlove, June 2002.

HERBERT SIMON

Administrative Behavior

1947

The author

erbert Simon was Richard King Mellon University Professor of Computer Science and Psychology. His books include *Models of Bounded Rationality* (1997); *The Sciences of the Artificial* (3rd edition, 1996); *Reason in Human Affairs* (1983); *The New Science of Management Decision* (revised edition, 1977); and *Human Problem Solving* (with Newell, 1972). As well as numerous academic awards, Simon won the Nobel Prize in Economics in 1978.

The classic

Herbert Simon's brilliant mind has led the way into the complex world of artificial intelligence and the computer simulation of human thinking. His more recent work focuses on comparing problem solving by experts and novices in the fields of physics and economics; the creation of computer programs able to extract scientific laws from data; and learning processes in humans and computers. These areas of research have led Simon to examine the effectiveness and efficiency of teaching and learning techniques and processes.

These subject areas represent the culmination of a lengthy intellectual career studying the human mind and problem solving and decision-making. The groundwork for Simon's later work was laid in *Administrative Theory*, sub-titled 'A study of decision-making processes in administrative organization'. (Simon later observed that he must have had a 'prophetic gift' for including the words behaviour, decision-making and organization in the book's title as they quickly became the fashionable phrases of social science.)

'Administrative description suffers ... from superficiality, over-sim-plification, lack of realism', Simon laments. 'It has refused to undertake the tiresome task of studying the actual allocations of decision-making functions. It has been satisfied to speak of "authority", "centralization", "span of control", "function", without seeking operational definitions of these terms.'

Organizational theory, says Simon, is in need of realistic theory. At the time, he was largely right. 'We talk about organization in terms not unlike those used by a Ubangi medicine man to discuss disease. At best we live by homely proverbs ... At worst we live by pompous inanities.' Organizational theory remained deeply bedded in vagueness (and is, even today, no stranger to homely proverbs and inanities). Its clearest propo-nent up to that time had been Chester Barnard. Barnard contributes the foreword to Simon's book.[1]

In response, Simon developed 'a theory of human choice or deci-sion-making that aims to be sufficiently broad and realistic to accom-modate both those rational aspects of choice that have been the principal concern of the economist, and those properties and limitations of the human decision-making mechanisms that have attracted the attention of psychologists and practical decision-makers'.

Simon forms a bridge between the humanists and engineers of man-agement thinking. Says Simon: 'Organization is important, first, because in our society, where men spend most of their waking adult lives in organizations, this environment provides much of the force that molds and develops personal qualities and habits. Organization is important, second, because it provides to those in responsible positions the means for exercising authority and influence over others.'

Instead of regarding organizational behaviour as a matter of under-standing people or measuring the performance of people more effectively, he proposes that each act in an organization exists in a complex inter-action with the organizational system as a whole. 'A complex decision is like a great river, drawing from its many tributaries the innumerable component premises of which it is constituted', writes Simon. 'Many individuals and organization units contribute to every large decision, and the problem of centralization and decentralization is a problem of arranging the complex system into an effective scheme.'

To Simon, organization is not an organizational chart, but 'a com-plex pattern of communications and other relations in a group of human beings. This pattern provides to each member of the group much of the information, assumptions, goals, and attitudes that enter into his deci-sions, and provides him also with a set of stable and comprehensible expectations as to what the other members of the group are doing and how they will react to what he says and does.'

Simon's views were ahead of their time. For the next forty years, organizations – in the West, at least – continued to be seen as an act of ordering, simplifying and categorizing rather than as a powerful dynamic and ever-changing force. Only in the early 1990s, partly through the success of Senge's *The Fifth Discipline,* did systems thinking make the leap from academic obscurity to the executive agenda.

Note

1 Most of Simon's book was written in 1942.

ALFRED P SLOAN

My Years with General Motors

1963

The author

Alfred P Sloan (1875–1966), the legendary chief of General Motors, was one of the first managers to write an important theoretical book.

Sloan was General Manager of the Hyatt Roller Bearing Company at the age of 24 and became President when it merged with United Motors which, in turn, became part of General Motors in 1917. Initially a director and Vice-President, Sloan became GM's Chief Executive in 1946 and honorary Chairman from 1956 until his death.

The classic

My Years With General Motors[1] is Alfred P Sloan's account of his remarkable career. It is, however, an often turgid testimony to Sloan's achievements. 'His book is one thing, what he did at GM is quite another', says London Business School's Sumantra Ghoshal. 'Sloan created a new organizational form – the multi-divisional form – which became a doctrine of management. Today, it is not ascribed to him, but Sloan was its instigator.'

When Alfred P Sloan took over General Motors the fledgling automobile market was dominated by Ford. Under Henry Ford the company had become a pioneer of mass production techniques. In 1920 Ford was making a car a minute and the famously black Model T accounted for 60 per cent of the market. General Motors managed to scrimp and scrape its way to around 12 per cent.

With Ford cornering the mass market, the accepted wisdom was that the only alternative for competitors lay in the negligibly sized luxury market. Sloan thought otherwise and concentrated GM's attentions on the, as yet non-existent, middle market. His aim was a car for 'every purse and every purpose'.

Sloan came at things from a completely different angle from Ford. Early in his career with a Ford supplier, Ford had put his company under pressure to reduce the costs of their parts. Sloan came back with a lower selling price but was proud that it did not necessitate lowering wages – 'One thing we did not do was to reduce wages; that was done too often in such cases in those days. But I had learned that increased productivity would support higher wages.'[2]

At the time, GM was an unwieldy combination of companies with eight models which basically competed against each other as well as against Ford. Sloan cut the eight models down to five and decided that, rather than competing with each other, each model would be targeted at a particular segment of the market. The five GM ranges – the Chevrolet, Oldsmobile, Pontiac, Buick and Cadillac – were to be updated and changed regularly and came in more than one colour. Ford continued to offer functional, reliable cars; GM offered choice.

While all this made commercial sense, Sloan inherited an organization which was ill-suited to deliver his aspirations. GM had been built up through the regular and apparently random acquisition of small companies. Any thought of providing some sort of overall corporate culture, structure, or direction had apparently been overlooked – though this was principally because it had never been done before.

Sloan set about creating a coherent organization from his motley collection. Central to this was his 'organization study' which, said one observer, appeared to 'have sprung entirely from his own head in 1919 and 1920'. In the early 1920s Sloan organized the company into eight divisions – five car divisions and three component divisions. In the jargon (invented 50 years later) they were strategic business units.

Each was made responsible for all their commercial operations with their own engineering, production and sales departments, but was supervised by a central staff responsible for overall policy and finance. The operating units were semi-autonomous, charged with maintaining market share and sustaining profitability in their particular area. Alfred Chandler describes the system in *Strategy and Structure*: 'The responsibility attached to the chief executive of each operation shall in no way be limited. Each such organization headed by its chief executive shall be complete in every necessary function and enabled to exercise its full initiative and logical development.'[3] In a particularly innovative move, the components divisions sold products not only to other GM companies, but also to external companies.

This policy of what Sloan labelled 'federal decentralization' marked the invention of the decentralized, divisionalized organization. (While this was its first sustained practical usage, Sloan's ideas can be traced back to Henri Fayol's functional approach.) 'Alfred Sloan did for the upper layers of management what Henry Ford did for the shop-floor: he turned it into a reliable, efficient, machine-like process', recently observed *The Economist*.[4]

The multi-divisional form enabled Sloan to utilize the company's size without making it cumbersome. Executives had more time to concentrate on strategic issues, and operational decisions were made by people in the front line rather than at a distant headquarters. It required a continuous balancing act. 'In practically all our activities we seem to suffer from the inertia resulting from our great size', commented Sloan in the 1930s. 'There are so many people involved and it requires such a tremendous effort to put something new into effect that a new idea is likely to be considered insignificant in comparison with the effort that it take to put it across ... Sometimes I am almost forced to the conclusion that General Motors is so large and its inertia so great that it is impossible for us to be leaders.'

By 1925, with its new organization and commitment to annual changes in its models, GM had overtaken Ford which continued to persist with its faithful old Model T. Sloan's segmentation of the market changed the structure of the car industry – and provided a model for how firms could do the same in other industries.

Human interest in *My Years with General Motors* is limited. The then powerful unions are ignored. So, too, are key figures such as Charles Kettering (who invented the self-starter) and William Olds (of Oldsmobile).

At first glance such omissions are not altogether surprising. Sloan's system aimed to eliminate, as far as was possible, the deficiencies and eccentricities of managerial behaviour. 'It is perhaps the most impersonal book of memoirs ever written', observed Peter Drucker. 'And this was clearly intentional. Sloan's book ... knows only one dimension: that of managing a business so that it can produce effectively, provide jobs, create markets and sales, and generate profits.'[5]

And yet Sloan was committed to what at the time would have been regarded as progressive human resource management. In 1947 Sloan established GM's employee-research section to look at employee attitudes and he invested a large amount of his own time in selecting the right people for the job – Sloan personally selected every GM executive from managers to master mechanics and, though he was prepared to miss policy meetings, he always attended personnel meetings.

Gary Hamel on *My Years with General Motors*

'Can you be big and nimble? The question is as timely today as it was when Sloan took over General Motors. Despite divisionalization and decentralization, Sloan's organizational inventions, GM still fell victim to its size. Though, perhaps, size was simply a metaphor for success. Was it bigness that made GM vulnerable, or the arrogance and sense of invincibility that came with years of success? One thing is certain: the corporate superstructure that emerged to manage GM's independent divisions was more successful in creating bureaucracy that in exploiting cross-divisional synergies. The challenge of achieving divisional autonomy and flexibility on the one hand, while reaping the benefits of scale and coordination on the other, is one that has eluded not only GM, but many other large companies as well.'

Sloan established GM as a benchmark of corporate might, a symbol of American strength and success – 'What's good for GM is good for America', ran the popular mythology. Peter Drucker and Alfred Chandler celebrated Sloan's approach. His legacy was unquestionably long-lasting – within GM at least. Researching her case study of GM for *The Change Masters*, Rosabeth Moss Kanter was told by then GM chairman Roger Smith that his aim was to 'return this company to the way Sloan intended it to be managed'.

Such nostalgia was self-defeating. The deficiencies of Sloan's model have gradually become apparent since the publication of his book. This was most obviously manifested in the decline of GM. The decentralized structure built up by Sloan revolved around a reporting and committee infrastructure which eventually became unwieldy. As time went by, more and more committees were set up. Stringent targets and narrow measures of success stultified initiative.

Sumantra Ghoshal and Christopher Bartlett have pointed to the inward-looking nature of Sloan's approach as one of its major drawbacks. 'Sloan's organization was designed to overcome the limitations of the functional structure in managing large, established businesses. While it did this quite well, at least for a while, it proved incapable of creating and developing new businesses internally. This inability to manage organic expansion into new areas was caused by many factors. With primarily operating responsibilities and guided by a measurement system that focused on profit and market share performance in served markets, the front-line business unit managers in the divisionalized corporation were neither expected to nor could scout for new opportunities breaking around the boxes in the organization chart that defined their product or geographic scope. Besides, small new ventures, as organic developments tended to be at the start of their lives, could not absorb the large central overheads and yet return the profits needed to justify the financial and human investments.'

By the end of the 1960s the delicate balance, which Sloan had brilliantly maintained, between centralization and decentralization, was lost – finance emerged as the dominant function – and GM became paralysed by what had once made it great.

Alfred P Sloan is one of the very few figures who undoubtedly changed the world of management. Henry Ford regarded managers as mere supervisors. In contrast, at decentralized GM, senior executives were charged with three key roles. They had responsibility for the company's strategy; they designed its structure and selected its control systems. This relied on a steady, evenly paced supply of information from below. It is a model which has spawned a host of imitators.

Notes

1 Sloan, Alfred P, *My Years with General Motors*, Doubleday, New York, 1963.
2 Sloan, Alfred P, *Adventures of a White-Collar Man*, Doubleday, Doran & Co, New York,1941, p. 76.
3 Chandler, A D, *Strategy and Structure*, Doubleday, New York, 1966.
4 'The changing nature of leadership', *The Economist*, 10 June 1995.
5 Drucker, Peter F, *Concept of the Corporation*, John Day, New York, 1972.

ADAM SMITH

The Wealth of Nations

1776

The author

Born in Kirkcaldy, Scotland, Adam Smith (1723–90) entered the University of Glasgow at the age of 14. Strongly influenced by the university's professor of moral philosophy, Smith went to Balliol College, Oxford in 1740 and began to concentrate on moral philosophy. He returned to Scotland in 1746 and later joined Glasgow University as a Professor of Logic and then of moral philosophy.

Smith's writing career began in the 1750s and in 1759 he published his *Theory of Moral Sentiments*. After leaving the university in 1763, Smith spent time in France where he met leading thinkers including Voltaire. There is some evidence to suggest that Smith's *Inquiry into the Nature and Causes of the Wealth of Nations* was begun in Toulouse. The bulk, however, was written on Smith's return to Scotland. In 1773 he took his manuscript to London, where he began to live. When it was published in 1776, *The Wealth of Nations* was instantly successful and influential. Lord North's budgets in 1777 and 1778 were influenced by Smith.

Smith returned to Scotland where he worked as a tax collector and oversaw the destruction of most of his papers before his death in 1790 after a long illness.

The classic

For a book that is over two hundred years old, there is a surprisingly modern-sounding ring to a great deal of Adam Smith's *The Wealth of Nations*. Take Smith on customer service: 'The pretense that corporations are necessary for the better government of the trade is without any foundation. The real and effectual discipline which is exercised over a workman is not that of his corporation, but that of his customers.'

> ### Gary Hamel on *The Wealth of Nations*
>
> 'Revisionists be damned. Citizens from Prague to Santiago to Guangzhou to Jakarta owe much of their new-found prosperity to the triumph of Adam Smith's economic ideals. Adam Smith laid the philosophical foundations for the modern industrial economy. Enough said.'

W Edwards Deming never put it better. Alternatively, there is Smith's eighteenth-century version of achieving a focused workforce: 'Men are much more likely to discover easier and readier methods of attaining any object when the whole attention of their minds is directed towards that single object than when it is dissipated among a great variety of things.' Cut through some of the archaic and dense prose and timeless advice can be found.

The trouble is that Smith has been hijacked for political purposes. His best-known book has been picked clean. As a result, *The Wealth of Nations* is usually viewed as a right-wing manifesto, a gloriously logical exposition of the beauty of market forces. Inevitably, this is only partly true. There is more to *The Wealth of Nations* than free market *über alles*. Exploration should not be mistaken for advocacy. Published in 1776, *The Wealth of Nations* is a broad-ranging exploration of commercial and economic first principles. Indeed, Smith is often given credit for the founding of economics as a coherent discipline.

The book had an immediate impact when it was published. It was a bestseller and strongly influenced politicians. 'We are all your scholars', Prime Minister Pitt told Smith. Lord North's budgets of 1777 and 1778 were reputed to be strongly influenced by Smith's thinking. (A modern equivalent would be Will Hutton's *The State We're In* influencing Gordon Brown's budgets.)

For those unversed in the basics of economics, *The Wealth of Nations* remains a useful starting point. Smith lays out the basics with precision. For example, supply and demand: 'The quantity of every commodity which human industry can either purchase or produce naturally regulates itself in every country according to the effectual demand.' Or the rudiments of career management: 'Every individual is continually exerting himself to find out the most advantageous employment for whatever capital he can command.'

Key to the text is Smith's argument that the value of a particular good or service is determined by the costs of production. If something is expensive to produce, then its value is similarly high. 'What is bought with money or with goods is purchased by labour, as much as what we acquire by the toil of our own body … They contain the value of a certain quantity of labour which we exchange for what is supposed at the time to contain the value of an equal quantity,' writes Smith.

Smith's logic is remorseless – 'The real price of everything, what everything really costs to the man who wants to acquire it, is the toil and trouble of acquiring it. What everything is really worth to the man who has acquired it, and who wants to dispose of it or exchange it for something else, is the toil and trouble of which it can save himself, and which it can impose on other people'.

The sceptic will find that, at times, Smith's conclusions are distinctly humanitarian. 'The liberal reward of labour, therefore, as it is the necessary effect, so it is the natural symptom of increasing national wealth', he says. 'The scanty maintenance of the labouring poor, on the other hand, is the natural symptom that things are at a standstill, and their starving condition that they are going fast backwards.'

Indeed, Smith talks less about markets than about labour. Among Smith's sizeable intellectual legacy was the concept of the division of labour. 'The division of labour … occasions in every art, a proportionable increase of the productive powers of labour', Smith wrote. 'The separation of different trades and employments from one another seems to have taken place in consequence of this advantage.' This system of demarcation and functional separation provided the basis for the management theorists of the early twentieth century, such as scientific management champion, Frederick Taylor, and practitioners such as Henry Ford. They translated the economic rigour of Smith's thinking to practices in the workplace. They did so in ways and to a scale which Smith could never have imagined.

It is possible to put a spin on many of Smith's ideas. Agendas can be constructed around them. This is to do them a disservice. *The Wealth of Nations* was the first comprehensive exploration of the foundations, workings and machinations of a free market economy. It was an intellectual triumph, not a manifesto.

Clearly, history puts its own limitations on Smith's theorizing. Physical labour is no longer so important. The twentieth century has seen the emergence of management as a profession – it is barely acknowledged by Smith. Similarly, Smith wrote without knowledge of the power and scope of modern corporations – let alone the power of brand names and customer loyalty. He also wrote in harder times where self-interest was not a choice but a necessity.

Market forces are still at work on Adam Smith – the first edition of this historic work has kept pace with inflation and then some – expect to pay some $85,000 for a decent copy.

THOMAS STEWART

Intellectual Capital

1997

The author

 homas Stewart is a senior editor at *Fortune*. He is also the author of *The Wealth of Knowledge* (2001).

The classic

Intellectual capital can be crudely described as the collective brainpower of an organization. The switch from physical assets to intellectual assets – brawn to brain – as the source of wealth creation has been underway in the developed economies for some time. As an advertisement for Deutsche Bank put it: 'Ideas are capital. The rest is just money.'

Stewart claims that the changes taking place are as significant as the Industrial Revolution. 'Knowledge has become the most important factor in economic life. It is the chief ingredient of what we buy and sell, the raw material with which we work. Intellectual capital – not natural resources, machinery or even financial capital – has become the one indispensable asset of corporations,' he says.

Intellectual capital is irrevocably bound up with the notion of the knowledge worker and knowledge management. Peter Drucker's 1969 book *The Age of Discontinuity* introduced the term knowledge worker to describe the highly trained, intelligent managerial professional who realizes his or her own worth and contribution to the organization. The knowledge worker was the antidote to the previous model – corporate man and woman.

Drucker recognized this new breed, but key to his contribution was the realization that knowledge is both power *and* ownership. Intellectual capital is power. If knowledge, rather than labour, is the new measure of economic society, then the fabric of capitalist society must change.

Converting knowledge into intellectual capital is a new and elusive form of corporate alchemy.

'Intelligence becomes an asset when some useful order is created out of free-floating brainpower', notes Stewart. 'Organizational intellect becomes intellectual capital only when it can be deployed to do something that could not be done if it remained scattered around like so many coins in a gutter.'

'Intellectual capital is useful knowledge that is packaged for others. In this way, a mailing list, a database or a process can be turned into intellectual capital if someone inside the organization decides to describe, share and exploit what's unique and powerful about the way the company operates.'

Intellectual capital is often divided into human capital, customer capital, and structural capital. *Human capital* is implicit knowledge – what's inside employees' heads. *Customer capital* involves recognising the value of relationships that exist between the company and its customers. *Structural capital* is knowledge that is retained within the organization and can be passed on to new employees. According to Stewart: 'Structural capital is knowledge that doesn't go home at night.'

Stewart also argues that the knowledge economy augurs the end of management as we know it. Today's knowledge workers carry the tools of their trade with them between their ears. It is they and not their managers who are the experts and must decide how best to deploy their know-how. As a result, what they do has more in common with work carried out by people in the professions and must be assessed, not by the tasks performed, but by the results achieved.

From this, he says, it follows that the professional model of organizational design should supersede the bureaucratic. So where does this leave managers? The answer, Stewart suggests, is that the only legitimate role for managers is around the task of leadership – although they don't yet have a proper understanding of what's involved.

He says: 'If *values* and *vision* and *empowerment* and *teamwork* and *facilitating* and *coaching* sometimes sound like so much mush-mouthed mish-mash – which they sometimes are – that's a reflection of the fact that managers are groping towards a language and a means for managing knowledge, knowledge work and knowledge-intensive companies.'

While intellectual capital was the height of managerial fashion in the late 1990s, the start of the new century has brought more intense questioning of what it means and how it may best be implemented. 'Intellectual capital is being implemented effectively by some companies. The Scandinavian countries, led by Denmark, are leading the way in terms of reporting intellectual capital,' counters Stewart. 'But knowledge management is being implemented inefficiently in a larger number of companies. To some extent the intellectual capital agenda has been captured by knowledge management to the detriment of both.'

Indeed, separating knowledge management from intellectual capital has proved beyond most executive minds. Stewart offers an explanation:

> 'The difference between knowledge management and intellectual capital is basically the same as the difference between management and capital. Management is something you do to get more out of capital. Knowledge management has become the domain of the technologists, which is useful but not the be-all and end-all.
>
> 'More money has been wasted than made in knowledge management so far. When things go wrong it's usually because it has been introduced for faddish reasons. But increasingly I see companies looking first to discover their knowledge business, their knowledge value proposition – what they know they can sell and how to sell it profitably – and then figuring out how to manage knowledge. That approach works.'

DON TAPSCOTT

Growing Up Digital

1998

The author

Don Tapscott (born 1947) has been described by Al Gore as 'one of the world's leading cyber-gurus'. The Canadian Tapscott is chairman of the Alliance for Converging Technologies, a think-tank conducting research into the impact of the Internet and other forms of new media on business.

Tapscott's books also include *Paradigm Shift: The New Promise of Information Technology* (1992) and *Digital Capital: Harnessing the Power of Business Webs* (2000).

The classic

For better or worse, Don Tapscott can lay claim to bringing the world much of the language associated with the rise of the new economy – he coined 'prosumers' as a combination of production and consumption, was the first to use the term 'the digital economy' and was the originator of 'e-business communities'. His growing influence clearly outweighs his commitment to linguistic purity.

Tapscott's first book, *Paradigm Shift: The New Promise of Information Technology*, was the first to describe the fundamental change in computing from host-based systems for controlling costs to networks for transforming business models and strategy.

In *Growing Up Digital: The Rise of the Net Generation*, Tapscott goes on to look at the societal implications of the rise of a generation of people raised on technology, a generation which takes technology and the Internet for granted. Says Tapscott: 'The kids get on that computer and create those communities, share information, expect to be heard and understood. In return, they listen to others as information comes in and others share what they understand. For kids, computers are for normal people, not for closed communities of technological people or computer addicts.

'When that generation comes to adulthood, it will become a very powerful tool for change in organizations, markets and society. In a certain sense, it has already begun to happen. Children and youngsters lucky enough to have grown up "digitally" are innovators, well taught in the new media, strongly independent, and globally oriented. They're already changing schools, universities, and consumer markets. When they come into the companies, they will bring a new working culture.'

One of Tapscott's more optimistic cultural predictions is the rebirth of community spirit. 'The days of children sitting passively in front of the television are rapidly dying', he explains. 'The TV is dead and that's it. It is being eaten by the Web. The TV sets in the future won't be more than an additional Web site. Same with the personal computer as a site for singular, passive play. Personal computing is more and more "interpersonal" – people use the computers to relate to others online. The PC became a means of communication.'

Tapscott has moved on to study the implications of the net generation on organizations. In *Digital Capital* (written with David Ticoll and Alex Lowy, 2000), he celebrates the arrival of 'a new business form' which is made up of 'fluid congregations of businesses – sometimes highly structured, sometimes amorphous – that come together on the Internet to create value for customers and wealth for their shareholders'. This new organizational form is labelled a 'business web' or 'b-web'. Business webs, as described by Tapscott, are a 'universal business platform' made up of 'a distinct system of suppliers, distributors, commerce services providers, infrastructure providers and customers'.

'The last thing in the world a company needs is a great Web site. You need a great business web. The site, the technology, is the easy part. It is harder to cut a deal with a partner than to get a new piece of software running,' Tapscott says.

Tapscott's work has been influenced by the Nobel laureate, Ronald Coase, whose work he was introduced to in 1993. Coase wrote: 'A firm will tend to expand until the costs of organizing an extra transaction within the firm become equal to the costs of carrying out the same transaction on the open market.' And this is the basis for Tapscott's recent theorizing – 'Coase defined transaction costs broadly including the cost of co-ordination, collaboration, of finding the right people. We have been systematically extending his ideas to the new economy,' he explains. And, in the new economy, the Internet provides low cost markets outside the firm for an array of services.

'The big thing about the Internet is not that it's ubiquitous or high bandwidth, moving from a garden path to a highway to a mile wide, but that it is growing in function', says Don Tapscott. 'All the things Coase wrote about are being built right into the Net whether it is auction tools, payment systems or collaboration tools like Lotus Notes. As the Internet is a public infrastructure, you can deconstruct the firm and then reconstruct it on the web as a business web.'

The business web is regarded by Tapscott as the first significant challenge to the traditional hierarchically and functionally based organization. The corporation is dead; long live the b-web. 'While management fads have been regarded as good medicine, the corporation largely remained sacrosanct and unchanged. The business web provides a new model for the corporation,' he says. It is not simply another take on the virtual organization, which he regards as a transactional system rather than a true business system. Initiatives such as outsourcing, virtual organizations, eco-nets, and keiretsu are regarded by Tapscott as interpretations of business webs. Variations on a theme, but lacking a grasp of the bigger organizational picture.

FREDERICK W TAYLOR

The Principles of Scientific Management

1911

The author

A Philadelphia Quaker, Frederick Taylor (1856–1917) was the quintessentially brilliant Victorian. His interests were wide ranging and in virtually all he was highly successful. He was a tennis champion, changed the rules of baseball so that pitchers threw overarm rather than underarm and took out over 100 patents for his many and varied ideas. His inventiveness and his life's work was driven by a fundamental, sometimes blinding, belief in efficiency and measurement.

Taylor came from an affluent family and was educated in France and Germany. He worked as an apprentice at the Enterprise Hydraulic Works in Philadelphia in the 1870s and than at the Midvale Steel Company. At Midvale he became chief engineer and later general manager of the Manufacturing Investment Company's paper mills in Maine. In 1893 he moved to New York and began business as a consulting engineer.

The classic

Over a century after Frederick Taylor's work began, his influence on how we work and how we perceive work remains undeniably significant. Robert Waterman, co-author of *In Search of Excellence*, believes that most managers remain Taylorists at heart.

Taylor was the instigator of what became known as 'Scientific Management' – and *The Principles of Scientific Management*[1] is its bible. Scientific management emerged from Taylor's work at the Midvale Steel Works, where he was chief engineer. Taylor's 'science' came from the minute examination of individual tasks. Having identified every single movement and action involved in doing something, Taylor could determine the optimum time required to complete a task. Armed with this information, the manager could determine whether a person was doing the job well. 'In its essence, scientific management involves a complete mental revolution on the part of the working man engaged in any particular establishment or industry – a complete mental revolution on the part of these men as to their duties toward their work, toward their fellow men, and toward their employees', Taylor writes.

'At the time Taylor began his work, business management as a discrete and identifiable activity had attracted little attention', observed the British champion of scientific management, Lyndall Urwick. 'It was usually regarded as incidental to, and flowing from knowledge or acquaintance with a particular branch of manufacturing, the technical know-how of making sausages or steel or shirts ... The idea that a man needed any training or formal instruction to become a competent manager had not occurred to anyone.'[2]

Scientific management had an effect throughout the world. A Japanese engineer translated *The Principles of Scientific Management* (in Japan it became *Secrets for Eliminating Futile Work and Increasing Production*). In Japan it was a bestseller – a foretaste of the Japanese willingness to embrace the latest Western thinking. Taylor even numbered Lenin among his admirers – 'We should try out every scientific and progressive suggestion in the Taylor system', noted the Communist leader.

The legacy of Taylor's work remains in companies with a predilection to emphasize quantity over quality and was enthusiastically taken up by Henry Ford in the development of mass production techniques.

While Taylor's concepts are now usually regarded in a negative light, the originality of his insights and their importance are in little doubt. 'Few people had ever looked at human work systematically until Frederick W Taylor started to do so around 1885. Work was taken for granted and it is an axiom that one never sees what one takes for granted. *Scientific Management* was thus one of the great liberating, pioneering insights,' observes Peter Drucker in *The Practice of Management*.[3]

Drucker goes on to identify two fundamental flaws in scientific management. First, it denies integration – 'The first of these blind spots is the belief that because we must analyze work into its simplest constituent motions we must also organize it as a series of individual motions, each if possible carried out by an individual worker' – and, second, that it divorces planning from doing.

The most obvious consequence of scientific management is a dehumanizing reliance on measurement. Taylor confidently predicts:

Gary Hamel on *The Principles of Scientific Management*

'The development of modern management theory is the story of two quests: to make management more scientific, and to make it more humane. It is wrong to look at the latter quest as somehow much more enlightened than the former. Indeed, they are the yin and yang of business. The unprecedented capacity of twentieth-century industry to create wealth rests squarely on the work of Frederick Winslow Taylor. While some may disavow Taylor, his rational, deterministic impulses live on. Indeed, reengineering is simply late twentieth century Taylorism. Though the focus of reengineering is on the process, rather than the individual task, the motivation is the same: to simplify, to remove unnecessary effort, and to do more with less.'

'The determination of the best method of performing all of our daily acts will, in the future, be the work of experts who first analyze and then accurately time while they watch the various ways of doing each piece of work and who finally know from exact knowledge – and not from anyone's opinion – which method will accomplish the results with the least effort and in the quickest time. The exact facts will have in this way been developed and they will constitute a series of laws which are destined to control the vast multitude of our daily personal acts which, at present, are the subjects of individual opinion.'

Taylor envisaged no room for individual initiative or imagination. People were labour, mechanically accomplishing a particular task. They did what they were told – 'You know just as well as I do that a high-priced man has to do exactly as he is told from morning till night', writes Taylor. 'And what's more no back-talk. A high-priced man does just what he's told to do and no back-talk. Do you understand that? When this man tells you to walk, you walk; when he tells you to sit down, you sit down, and you don't talk back at him.'

Robert McNamara has reflected on the end result: 'The system disenfranchised those who were so important in the early stages of American manufacturing, the foremen and plant managers. Instead of being creators and innovators, as in an earlier era, now they depended on meeting production quotas. They lost any stake in stopping the line and fixing problems as they occurred; they lost any stake in innovation or change.'[4]

The plus side of Taylor's work has been outlined by Tom Peters, an unlikely ally. 'In his own fashion, time-and-motion man Frederick Taylor increased human freedom. His schemes for objectively determining "best practices" for every imaginable job helped free front-line workers from the capricious discipline of unscientific, turn-of-the-century foremen.'[5] Indeed, the fact that Taylor's anticipated revolution was two-sided can be forgotten. 'It involves the equally complete mental revolution on the part of those on the management's side – the foremen, the superintendent, the owner of the business, the board of directors – a complete mental revolution on their part as to their duties toward their fellow workers in the management, toward their workmen, and toward all of their daily problems. And without this complete mental revolution on both sides scientific management does not exist.'

The Principles of Scientific Management stands now as a historical artifact. The ideas contained in it, however, live on.

Notes

1 Taylor, Frederick W, *The Principles of Scientific Management*, Harper & Row, New York, 1913.
2 Urwick, Lyndall (editor, *The Golden Book of Management*, Newman Neame, London, 1956 .
3 Drucker, Peter F, *The Practice of Management*, Harper & Row, New York, 1954.
4 Shapley, Deborah, *Promise and Power: The Life and Times of Robert McNamara*, Little, Brown, Boston, 1993.
5 Peters, Tom, 'In praise of the secular corporation', syndicated column, 26 March 1993.

ALVIN TOFFLER

The Third Wave

1980

The author

A lvin Toffler is a bestselling futurologist. His most significant books are *Future Shock*, *The Third Wave*, and *Power Shift*. Toffler was a Washington correspondent and an Associate Editor of *Fortune* before spending time as a Visiting Professor at Cornell University, a Visiting Scholar at the Russell Sage Foundation and teaching at the New School for Social Research.

The classic

Alvin Toffler's *The Third Wave*[1] ushers in the new technological era and bids farewell to the Second Wave of industrialization. 'Old ways of thinking, old formulas, dogmas, and ideologies, no matter how cherished or how useful in the past, no longer fit the facts', Toffler writes. 'The world that is fast emerging from the clash of new values and technologies, new geopolitical relationships, new lifestyles and modes of communication, demands wholly new ideas and analogies, classifications and concepts.'

The Third Wave is the super-industrial society – 'the death of industrialism and the rise of a new civilization' – which was preceded by industrialization and the First Wave, the agricultural phase of civilization's development.

The Third Wave is characterized by mass customization rather than mass production. 'The essence of Second Wave manufacture was the long "run" of millions of identical standardized products. By contrast, the essence of Third Wave manufacture is the short run of partially or completely customized products,' writes Toffler. This notion of mass customization has since been picked up by a wide variety of thinkers and, in some areas, is already in existence.

Whereas the Second Wave strictly separated consumer and producer, Toffler predicts the Third Wave will see the two become almost indistinguishable, as the consumer becomes involved in the actual process of production, expressing choices and preferences. 'The customer will become so integrated into the production process that we will find it more and more difficult to tell just who is actually the consumer and who the producer', says Toffler. He goes on to invent a word to describe this new being: the prosumer.

What is startling about *The Third Wave* is that it was written so recently, and yet the technological leaps made since its publication have been so immense. Toffler, for example, has to explain what a word processor is – and mentions its alternative labels, 'the smart typewriter' or 'text editor'. He envisages the office of the future: 'The ultimate beauty of the electronic office lies not merely in the steps saved by a secretary in typing and correcting letters. The automated office can file them in the form of electronic bits on tape or disc. It can (or soon will) pass them through an electronic dictionary that will automatically correct their spelling errors. With the machines hooked up to one another and to the phone lines, the secretary can instantly transmit the letter to its recipient's printer or screen.' In 1980 to the vast majority of Toffler's readers this read like science fiction. By 1996 it was reality to the vast majority of people in the industrialized world (or de-industrialized world, according to Toffler's perspective).

Toffler predicts the demise of the nine to five working day. 'Machine synchronization shackled the human to the machine's capabilities and imprisoned all of social life in a common frame. It did so in capitalist and socialist countries alike. Now, as machine synchronization grows more precise, humans, instead of being imprisoned, are progressively freed,' says Toffler. They are freed into more flexible ways of working whether it is flexitime or working at home.

Toffler is not, however, a hopeless utopian. While the futurists of the early 1970s predicted a leisure age which failed to materialize, Toffler is aware of the broader ramifications of technology: 'The image of the office of the future is too neat, too smooth, too disembodied to be real. Reality is always messy. But it is clear that we are rapidly on our way, and even a partial shift towards the electronic office will be enough to trigger an eruption of social, psychological, and economic consequences. The coming word-quake means more than just new machines. It promises to restructure all the human relationships and roles in the office as well.'

It is this awareness of the broader impact of technological change which marks *The Third Wave*. Other studies of the future of our working lives tend to plunge head first into celebrations of the miracles of

Gary Hamel on *The Third Wave*

'The post-industrial society is here! And Alvin Toffler saw it coming in 1980. I don't think there's any such thing as a futurist, only people who have more finely tuned antennae, or who are better at understanding the medium-term implications of things that are already changing around them. One of the challenges for anyone reading Toffler, or any other seer, is that there is no proprietary data about the future – your competitors read Toffler, Naisbitt and Negroponte too! The real challenge is to build proprietary foresight out of public data!'

technology with little attempt to understand the human implications. To Toffler, the human side of change is all-important. The Third Wave, he anticipates, 'will produce anxiety and conflict as well as reorganization, restructuring, and – for some – rebirth into new careers and opportunities. The new systems will challenge all the old executive turfs, the hierarchies, the sexual role divisions, the departmental barriers of the past.' Through reengineering, downsizing, empowerment and the management of diversity, as well as a host of other trends, the new systems described by Toffler can be seen to be in place today.

Toffler also accurately predicts the growth of regionalism and the profusion of local media. This, in another of Toffler's ungainly phrases, is the 'de-massifying' of our culture.

The immense implications for organizations are explored by Toffler. 'Instead of clinging to a sharply specialized economic function, the corporation, prodded by criticism, legislation, and its own concerned executives, is becoming a multipurpose institution', says Toffler. The organization is being driven to redefinition through five forces:

- changes in the physical environment: companies are having to undertake greater responsibility for the effect of their operations on the environment.
- changes in the 'line-up of social forces'. The actions of companies now have greater impact with those of other organizations such as schools, universities, civil groups and political lobbies.
- changes in the role of information. 'As information becomes central to production, as "information managers" proliferate in industry, the corporation, by necessity, impacts on the informational environment exactly as it impacts on the physical and social environment', writes Toffler.

- changes in government organization. The profusion of government bodies means that the business and political worlds interact to a far greater degree than ever before.
- changes in morality. The ethics and values of organizations are becoming more closely linked to those of society. 'Behavior once accepted as normal is suddenly reinterpreted as corrupt, immoral or scandalous', says Toffler. 'The corporation is increasingly seen as a producer of moral effects.'

The organization of the future, he envisages, will be concerned with ecological, moral, political, racial, sexual and social problems, as well as traditional commercial ones. Interestingly, it is here that Toffler's picture of the future has largely failed to become reality. While the ways in which work is structured in organizations and the jobs of individuals have been radically altered, in many cases revolutionized, the organization has moved far more slowly.

The Third Wave is far reaching and goes well beyond the impact of the emerging civilization on work and organizations. It has proved a highly accurate picture of a future which has largely arrived. Its ideas, such as the rise of homeworking, have since been developed by others, most notably by Charles Handy.

Note

1 Toffler, Alvin, *The Third Wave*, William Collins & Sons, London, 1980.

ROBERT TOWNSEND

Up the Organization

1970

The author

obert Townsend (1920–98) was President of Avis until it was absorbed into the ITT empire. He was the author of *Up the Organization* and its sequel *Further Up the Organization*.

The classic

The canon of management literature is not noted for its humour. Academic rigour is more highly prized than witty one-liners. And yet, every generation has produced a humorous bestseller debunking managerial mythology and the high-minded seriousness of the theorists. In the fifties there was *Parkinson's Law* and at the end of the sixties, Robert Townsend's *Up the Organization*[1] (sub-titled 'How to stop the corporation from stifling people and strangling profits'). Robert Heller called the book 'the first pop bestseller on business management' which 'owed much of its success to Townsend's derisive title'.

The tone of *Up the Organization* is set from the start, in a memorandum on how to use the book. 'In the average company the boys in the mailroom, the president, the vice-presidents, and the girls in the steno pool have three things in common: they are docile, they are bored, and they are dull', observes Townsend. 'Trapped in the pigeonholes of organization charts, they've been made slaves to the rules of private and public hierarchies that run mindlessly on and on because nobody can change them.'

Townsend then travels through the modern organization from A to Z. Townsend is, by turn, playful, indignant, critical and practical. His greatest vehemence is reserved for Harvard Business School – 'Don't hire Harvard Business School graduates', he advises. 'This elite, in my

Gary Hamel on *Up the Organization*

'Irreverence, impiety, and non-conformity are essential to organizational vitality. They were also the ingredients that made *Up the Organization* essential reading for corporate iconoclasts of the 1970s. This is *Liberation Management* two and a half decades before people knew they needed to be liberated. The real question is, why do these books come along once every twenty or so years? We really are taking ourselves too seriously!'

opinion, is missing some pretty fundamental requirements for success: humility; respect for people on the firing line; deep understanding of the nature of the business and the kind of people who can enjoy themselves making it prosper; respect from way down the line; a demonstrated record of guts, industry, loyalty down, judgment, fairness, and honesty under pressure.'

More useful, if still obtuse, is Townsend's observation that 'top management (the board of directors) is supposed to be a tree full of owls – hooting when management heads into the wrong part of the forest. I'm still unpersuaded they even know where the forest is.'

There is a great deal of good sense buried in *Up the Organization*. Townsend has, for example, no time for the adornments of executive office and his list of 'no-no's' includes: reserved parking spaces; special-quality stationery for the boss and his elite; muzak; bells and buzzers; company shrinks; outside directorships and trusteeships for the chief executive ('Give up all those non-jobs. You can't even run your own company, dummy'); and the company plane. He is, in fact, preaching a brand of empowerment and participation which was 20 years ahead of its time.

'There's nothing fundamentally wrong with our country except that the leaders of all our major organizations are operating on the wrong assumptions', Townsend writes. 'We're in this mess because for the last two hundred years we've been using the Catholic Church and Caesar's legions as our patterns for creating organizations. And until the last forty or fifty years it made sense. The average churchgoer, soldier, and factory worker was uneducated and dependent on orders from above. And authority carried considerable weight because disobedience brought the death penalty or its equivalent.'

Up the Organization is a child of its times – irreverent and humorous, questioning the accepted behaviour of corporate society. Given that

nearly 30 years have passed since its publication, it still retains its fresh-
ness and originality, and its insights into the blind deficiencies of too
many organizations remain sadly apt.

Note

1 Townsend, Robert, *Up the Organization*, Michael Joseph, London,
   1970.

FONS TROMPENAARS

Riding the Waves of Culture

1993

The author

Born in 1952, Fons Trompenaars is also co-author (with Charles Hampden-Turner) of *The Seven Cultures of Capitalism* (1994); *Building Cross-Cultural Competence: How to Create Wealth from Conflicting Values* (2000); and *21 Leaders for the 21st Century: How Innovative Leaders Manage in the Digital Age* (2001).

Trompenaars' reputation is built on his work on the cultural aspects of modern management. The roots of this interest he attributes to being brought up by a French mother and a Dutch father. He studied at Wharton in the US and is now managing director of the Centre for International Business Studies in Amstelveen in the Netherlands.

The classic

'Management in a global environment is increasingly affected by cultural differences', says Fons Trompenaars and his *Riding the Waves of Culture*[1] is an examination of the cultural imponderables faced by managers in the global village. 'Basic to understanding other cultures is the awareness that culture is a series of rules and methods that a society has evolved to deal with the recurring problems it faces', writes Trompenaars. 'They have become so basic that, like breathing, we no longer think about how we approach or resolve them. Every country and every organization faces dilemmas in relationships with people; dilemmas in relationship to time; and dilemmas in relations between people and the natural environment. Culture is the way in which people resolve dilemmas emerging from universal problems.' *Riding the Waves of Culture* is based on meticulous quantitative research, and over 900 seminars presented in 18 countries.

Gary Hamel on *Riding the Waves of Culture*

'So Americans will never understand "foreign" cultures ... Funny how American companies are out-competing their European competitors in Asia and Latin America. Name any region of the world that looks to Europe for its managerial inspiration. (Oh wait, sorry, I'm not sup-posed to be parochial!) Where I agree with Trompenaars is that the future belongs to the cosmopolitans.'

(Trompenaars' 15 years of research has now covered 15,000 people from 50 countries.)

Trompenaars is dismissive of the American managerial model – 'It is my belief that you can never understand other cultures ... I started won-dering if any of the American management techniques I was brainwashed with in eight years of the best business education money could buy would apply in the Netherlands, where I came from, or indeed in the rest of the world.' The answer he provides is simply that they do not.

'The international manager needs to go beyond awareness of cultural differences', Trompenaars writes. 'He or she needs to respect these differences and take advantage of diversity through reconciling cross-cultural dilemmas. The international manager reconciles cultural dilemmas.' Trompenaars' emphasis is not on the emotionally laden area of diversity but on how culture affects our behaviour and how different cultures interact.

Trompenaars' findings are presented by way of seven chapters exam-ining the basic premises that make up a culture. He presents a number of fundamentally different cultural perspectives while acknowledging that, within a country, attachment to any given cultural trait varies widely.

The first of these is the conflict between what Trompenaars labels the 'universalist' and the 'particularist'. Universalists (including Ameri-cans, Canadians, Australians and the Swiss) advocate 'one best way', a set of rules that applies in any setting. Particularists (South Koreans, Chinese and Malaysians) focus on the peculiar nature of any given situation.

Trompenaars examines the extremes by way of archetypal situa-tions. In the universalist–particularist conflict, he presents the following dilemma: You are in a car with a close friend who has an accident in which a third party is injured. You are the only witness, and he asks you to falsely testify about his driving speed. In such a situation, universalists won't lie for their friend while particularists will. The difference becomes even more pronounced if the injury is severe. The universalist becomes even more adherent to the rules while the particularist's sense of obligation grows. (In this example, 74 per cent of South Koreans would assist their friend and lie, compared to just five per cent of Americans.)

Such results allow Trompenaars to provide advice on how business dealings between the two parties might work. Universalists doing business with particularists should, for example, 'be prepared for meandering or irrelevancies that do not seem to be going anywhere'; moreover, we should not 'take get to know you chatter as small talk'. It is important to particularists. Particularists doing business with universalists should 'be prepared for rational and professional arguments and presentations'.

Then there is the 'collectivist' (group oriented) versus 'individualist' frame of mind. The Unites States again falls into the extremist category as emphasizing the individual before the group. Countries such as Egypt and France are at the other end. Individualists working with collectivists must tolerate 'time taken to ... consult' and negotiators who 'can only agree tentatively and may withdraw an (offer) after consulting with superiors'.

The difference between those who show their feelings (such as Italians) and those who hide them (such as the Japanese) is also profound. Other distinctions include how we accord status (through achievement rather than through ascription – based on family, age, etc.); and how we manage time (past versus future orientation).

The cultural imponderables and wide range of basic differences in how different cultures perceive the world provides a daunting picture of the world ridden with potential pitfalls. 'We need a certain amount of humility and a sense of humour to discover cultures other than our own; a readiness to enter a room in the dark and stumble over unfamiliar furniture until the pain in our shins reminds us of where things are', he writes.

In the end, says Trompenaars, the only positive route forward is through reconciliation. 'Our hypothesis is that those societies that can reconcile better are better at creating wealth', he says.[2] Whether this will be borne out by the future experience of transnational organizations will continue to be discussed. What can be said is that the cultural aspects of managing internationally are likely to gain in importance as the full force of globalization affects industries and individuals.

Notes

1 Trompenaars, Fons, *Riding the Waves of Culture*, Nicholas Brealey, London, 1993.

2 Houlder, Vanessa, 'Interview with Fons Trompenaars', *Financial Times*, 26 July 1996.

SUN TZU

The Art of War

500 BC

The author

T he authorship of *The Art of War* remains, perhaps understandably, clouded in mystery. It may have been written by Sun Wu, a military general who was alive around 500 BC. His book is reputed to have led to a meeting between Sun Wu and King Ho-lü of Wu. Sun Wu, not having a flip chart available, argued his case for military discipline by decapitating two of the king's concubines. The book's actual title is *Sun Tzu Ping Fa*, which can be literally translated as 'The military method of venerable Mr Sun'.

The classic

Military examples and imagery have played an important role in the development of management thinking. Even now, military role models – whether they are Colin Powell or Norman Schwarzkopf – are keenly seized upon by executives. The military, with its elements of strategy and leadership, is alluring, and the link between the military and business worlds has existed since time immemorial. Books as diverse as Carl von Clausewitz's *On War* (1908), B H Liddell-Hart's *Strategy* (1967) and Miyamoto Mushashi's *A Book of Five Rings* (1974) have explored the link. Its starting point, as far as it is possible to discern, is Sun Tzu's *The Art of War*, written 2500 years ago.

Generally, the attraction of the military analogy is that it is clear who your enemy is. When your enemy is clear, the world appears clearer if you are a military general or a managing director. Sun Tzu's *The Art of War* is usually interpreted in such terms, as an aggressive counterpoint to the confusion of mere theory. In fact, *The Art of War* is more sophisticated than that. Why destroy when you can win by stealth and cunning? 'A

Gary Hamel on *The Art of War*

'Strategy didn't start with Igor Ansoff; neither did it start with Machiavelli. It probably didn't even start with Sun Tzu. Strategy is as old as human conflict – and if the stakes are high in business, they're rather higher in the military sphere. In fact, one of the best strategy books I've ever read is *Military Misfortune* by two professors of military strategy at America's naval college.'

sovereign should not start a war out of anger, nor should a general give battle out of rage. For while anger can revert to happiness and rage to delight, a nation that has been destroyed cannot be restored, nor can the dead be brought back to life,' writes Sun Tzu. 'To subdue the enemy's forces without fighting is the summit of skill. The best approach is to attack the other side's strategy; next best is to attack his alliances; next best is to attack his soldiers; the worst is to attack cities.'

Sun Tzu also has sound advice on knowing your markets. 'Advance knowledge cannot be gained from ghosts and spirits ... but must be obtained from people who know the enemy situation.'

Elsewhere, Sun Tzu lapses into Confucian analogies which would appear to be anathema to hard-headed modern executives. Often, however, they appear to find them reassuring. 'For the shape of an army is like that of water', says Sun Tzu. 'The shape of water is to avoid heights and flow towards low places; the shape of the army is to avoid strength and to strike at weakness. Water flows in accordance with the ground; an army achieves victory in accordance with the enemy.'

The Art of War is best known as the origin of the concept of strategy, one that has been through a great many re-interpretations in the intervening 2500 years. Here, there is no room for sentiment or distraction: 'Deploy forces to defend the strategic points; exercise vigilance in preparation, do not be indolent. Deeply investigate the true situation, secretly await their laxity. Wait until they leave their strongholds, then seize what they love.'

THOMAS WATSON JR

A Business and its Beliefs

1963

The author

The son of the legendary founder of IBM, Thomas Watson Sr, Watson (1914–93) attended Brown University and served in the Air Corps during the Second World War. He joined IBM in 1946 and worked as a salesman. He became chief executive in 1956 and retired in 1970. He was then US ambassador in Moscow until 1980.

Though always in the shadow of his father, under Watson IBM was propelled to the forefront of the technological revolution. He invested heavily in the development of System/360, which formed the basis of the company's success in the 1970s and 1980s. As well as *A Business and its Beliefs,* Watson also wrote an autobiography *Father, Son & Co* (1990).

The classic

Thomas Watson's *A Business and Its Beliefs: The ideas that helped build IBM*[1] is a statement of business philosophy, an extended mission statement for the corporate giant. Though it was published in the same year as Alfred P Sloan's *My Years with General Motors,* it could not be more different. While Sloan sidelines people, Watson celebrates their potential; while Sloan espouses systems and structures, Watson talks of values.

Behind *A Business and Its Beliefs* stands the more Sloan-like, sober figure of Thomas Watson Sr (1874–1956). Watson Senior was the creator of IBM – something which his son certainly never forgot. ('The secret I learned early on from my father was to run scared and never think I had made it', he said.)

IBM's origins lay in the Computing-Tabulating-Recording Company, which Watson Sr joined in 1914. Under his leadership, the com-

Gary Hamel on *A Business and its Beliefs*

'Never change your basic beliefs, Watson argued. He may be right. But the dividing line between beliefs and dogmas is a fine one. A deep set of beliefs can be the essential pivot around which the company changes and adapts; or, if endlessly-elaborated, overly-codified, and solemnly worshipped, the manacles that shackle a company to the past.'

pany's revenues doubled from $4.2 million to $8.3 million by 1917. Initially making everything from butcher's scales to meat slicers, its activities gradually concentrated on tabulating machines, which processed information mechanically on punched cards. Watson, however, had grander aspirations. 'Father came home from work, gave mother a hug, and proudly announced that the Computing Tabulating Recording Company henceforth would be known by the grand name International Business Machines', recalled Watson Jr in his autobiography. 'I stood in the doorway of the living room thinking, "That little outfit?" Dad must have had in mind the IBM of the future. The one he actually ran was still full of cigar-chomping guys selling coffee grinders and butcher scales.'

IBM's development was helped by the 1937 Wages–Hours Act which required US companies to record hours worked and wages paid. The existing machines couldn't cope and Watson instigated work on a solution. In 1944 the Mark 1 was launched, followed by the Selective Sequence Electronic Calculator in 1947. By then IBM's revenues were $119 million and it was set to make the great leap forward to become the world's largest computer company.

Thomas Watson Jr took on a hugely successful company with a strong corporate culture built around salesmanship and service. In *Liberation Management* Tom Peters notes that Thomas Watson Sr 'emphasized people and service – obsessively. IBM was a service star in an era of malperforming machines.'

In *A Business and its Beliefs*, Thomas Watson Jr codifies and clarifies what IBM stands for. Central to this are the company's central beliefs (or what would now be called core values). 'I believe the real difference between success and failure in a corporation can very often be traced to the question of how well the organization brings out the great energies and talents of its people. What does it do to help these people find common cause with each other?' writes Watson. 'And how can it sustain this common cause and sense of direction through the many changes which take place from one generation to another?'

The answer, says Watson, comes through 'a sound set of beliefs, on which it premises all its policies and actions. Next, I believe that the most important single factor in corporate success is faithful adherence to those beliefs ... beliefs must always come before policies, practices, and goals. The latter must always be altered if they are seen to violate fundamental beliefs.'

Beliefs, says Watson, never change. Change everything else, but never the basic truths on which the company is based – 'If an organization is to meet the challenges of a changing world, it must be prepared to change everything about itself except beliefs as it moves through corporate life ... The only sacred cow in an organization should be its basic philosophy of doing business.'

In *A Business and Its Beliefs* Watson Jr tellingly observes: 'The beliefs that mold great organizations frequently grow out of the character, the experience and the convictions of a single person.' In IBM's case that person was Thomas Watson Senior. The Watsons created a corporate culture which lasted. IBM – 'Big Blue' – became the archetypal modern corporation and its managers the ultimate stereotype – with their regulation sombre suits, white shirts, plain ties, zeal for selling and company song. Beneath this, however, lay a belief in competing vigorously and providing quality service. Later, competitors complained that IBM's sheer size won it orders. This was only partly true. Its size masked a deeper commitment to managing customer accounts, providing service, building relationships and to the values laid out by Watson in *A Business and Its Beliefs*.

Note

1 Watson, Thomas, Jr, *A Business and its Beliefs*, McGraw Hill, New York, 1963.

MAX WEBER

The Theory of Social and Economic Organization

1924

The author

Max Weber (1864–1920) was a multi-talented German who is ill-served by the notion that he was simply the father of bureaucracy. After studying legal and economic history, Weber was a Professor at the University of Freiburg and later at the University of Heidelberg.

He studied the sociology of religion and in this area he produced his best-known work, *The Protestant Work Ethic and the Spirit of Capitalism*. In political sociology he examined the relationship between social and economic organizations.

Towards the end of his life, Weber developed his political interests and was on the committee which drafted the constitution of the Weimar Republic in 1918.

The classic

The yin and yang of business theorizing are the dehumanizing view of commerce and the more optimistic, humane interpretation. Machines versus people. Science versus art. The dehumanists portray industrialization as the triumph of machine over man. The humanists argue that organizations are created and driven by people; business is unpredictable art not predictable science. The debate rumbles on – and will, no doubt, continue to do so as the machines become smarter and smarter.

The man saddled with the reputation as the founding father of the mechanistic world-view is the German Max Weber (1864–1920). This is only partly deserved. It is a great disservice to Weber's formidable

Gary Hamel on *The Theory of Social and Economic Organization*

'Every organization wrestles with two conflicting needs: the need to optimize in the name of economic efficiency, and the need to experiment in the name of growth and renewal. Authoritarian bureaucracies, of the sort that rebuilt the Japanese economy after the war, serve well the goal of optimization – while there is experimentation here, it is tightly constrained. Anarchical networks, of the sort that predominate in Italy's fashion industry, allow for unfettered experimentation, but are always vulnerable to more disciplined competitors. Weber staked out one side of the argument; Tom Peters the other. As always, what is required is a synthesis.'

intellect, which roamed widely and somewhat erratically through the fields of politics, history, sociology, economics and law. It also rests on a misinterpretation of Weber's thinking, outlined in *The Theory of Social and Economic Organization* (published four years after Weber's death, in 1924).

Weber argued that the depersonalizing effects of industrial growth were inevitable. Large organizations require that the people involved put the cause of the organization before their own aspirations – and it doesn't matter whether the organization is building pyramids, fighting battles or making widgets. While Karl Marx saw industrialization as trampling over the rights to the ownership of labour, Weber offered a more pragmatic view – the subjugation of individuals to organizations was reality, not a stepping-stone to proletarian utopia.

The trouble is that *The Theory of Social and Economic Organization* does not read like pragmatism. The ultimate form of organization in this newly industrialized world was the bureaucratic system. This, as envisaged by Weber, was impersonal. People got on with their work. It was entirely hierarchical – 'The organization of offices follows the principle of hierarchy; that is, each lower office is under the control and supervision of a higher one.' It was remorselessly rational with carefully structured promotions and demarcations. The organization operated as a machine. Each cog in the system – each bureaucrat – fulfilled a clearly defined role.

The machine's aim was to work efficiently. No more; no less. Efficient machines were productive and, therefore, profitable. 'The purely bureaucratic type of administrative organization', wrote Weber, 'is, from a purely technical point of view, capable of attaining the highest degree of efficiency and is in this sense formally the most rational known means of carrying out imperative control over human beings. It is superior to any other form in precision, in stability, in the stringency of its discipline, and in its reliability.'

But this did not mean that Weber advocated the bureaucratic system. He simply described it. Weber was interested in scenarios rather than manifestos. The system was the extreme, the eventual outcome if trends observed by Weber continued. In many ways the bureaucratic world mapped out by Weber is similar to Orwell's 1984: the nightmare scenario rather than a prediction.

Unfortunately, in some respects, the nightmare came to pass. Henry Ford, the first great practitioner of mass production, echoed many of Weber's thoughts in his faith in strict demarcations and a fervently mechanistic approach to business. Ford preferred science to art – 'How come when I want a pair of hands I get a human being as well?' he lamented.

Ford was not alone. Corporations were routinely organized in ways similar to those imagined by Weber. The bureaucratic model became the organizational role model. There arose corporate man, adept at smothering individuality and creativity under a dull suit. Unquestioning loyalty was the route to progression up the carefully mapped-out corporate hierarchy. Subjugation was part of the deal, the psychological contract between employer and employee.

At an organizational level, companies were geared to producing as much as possible as efficiently as possible. The trouble was that they often failed to consider for whom the products were intended or to contemplate doing things differently. More was good and faith in mechanical-style efficiency blind.

The image of the corporation as a great machine has largely lasted throughout the twentieth century. The fashion for reengineering at the beginning of the 1990s was perhaps the most potent proof of the longevity of the machine image. Reengineering proposed that companies could be deconstructed. In mechanical parlance they could be reverse engineered, taken apart and rebuilt in more efficient ways. Companies could take a blank piece of paper and re-create themselves. Many reengineering programs bit the dust as companies discovered that mechanical dreams were no match for human reality.

Only in recent years have new metaphors emerged to describe the organizations of the late twentieth century. These also tend to be scientific. Their root, however, is not engineering but biology and the new sciences of chaos and complexity - areas unknown to Max Weber. Today's organizations are talked of in terms of fractals and amoebas – elusive and ever changing rather than efficient and static. The regularity of the machine age has given way to the tumult, ambiguity and complexity of the information age.

Even so, Max Weber remains important. In his book, *Gods of Management,* Charles Handy chose as one of the gods, Apollo, characterized by a Weber-like faith in rules and systems. Weber's bureaucratic model stands as a constant and potent reminder of what could be. And, lest it be forgotten, aspects of the bureaucratic model remain alive and well in a great many organizations where needless hierarchies, pointless demarcations and exhaustive rules dominate. Weber's world lives on and not only in our nightmares.

WILLIAM WHYTE

The Organization Man

1956

The author

illiam H Whyte (1918–99) was an editor at the magazine *Fortune* at the time he wrote *The Organization Man*. The bulk of his career was spent as an 'urbanologist', studying people's movements and behaviour in a city environment. Among his revealing findings was that a large percentage of companies that moved from New York City ended up in locations less than eight miles from the homes of their chief executives. Whyte also found that the corner outside Bloomingdale's at 59th Street and Lexington Avenue had the most daytime pedestrian traffic. His other books included *The Last Landscape* (1968); *The Social Life of Small Urban Spaces* (1980); and *City* (1989).

The classic

During the more stable times of the 1950s and 1960s, the careers enjoyed by corporate executives were built on solid foundations. This was the era of corporate man (there was no such thing as corporate woman at this time). Grey suited and obedient, corporate man was unstintingly loyal to his employer. He spent his life with a single company and rose slowly, but quietly, up the hierarchy.

The life of corporate man was brilliantly and poignantly described by William Whyte in his 1956 book *Organization Man*. Reviewing the book in the *New York Times*, C Wright Mills wrote that Whyte 'understands that the work-and-thrift ethic of success has grievously declined – except in the rhetoric of top executives; that the entrepreneurial scramble to success has been largely replaced by the organizational crawl'.[1]

Implicit to the organizational crawl was the understanding that loyalty and solid performance brought job security. This was mutually beneficial. The executive gained a respectable income and a high degree of security. The company gained loyal, hard-working executives.

Loyalty was key. 'The most important single contribution required of an executive, certainly the most universal qualification, is loyalty [allowing] domination by the organization personality', noted Chester Barnard in *The Functions of the Executive* (1938). (The word 'domination' suggests which way Barnard saw the balance of power falling.) While loyalty is a positive quality, it can easily become blind. What if the corporate strategy is wrong or the company is engaged in unlawful or immoral acts? Also, there is the question of loyal to what? At the time of *Organization Man*, corporate values were assumed rather than explored.

In the world described by Whyte, the corporation becomes a self-contained and self-perpetuating world supported by a complex array of checks, systems, and hierarchies. The company is right. Customers, who exist in the ethereal world outside the organization, are often regarded as peripheral. In the fifties, sixties and seventies, no executive ever lost their job by delivering poor quality or indifferent service. Indeed, in some organizations, executives only lost their jobs by defrauding their employer or insulting their boss. Jobs for life was the refrain and, to a large extent for executives, the reality.

Clearly, such an environment was hardly conducive to the fostering of dynamic risk-takers. The world of *Organization Man* rewarded the steady foot soldier, the safe pair of hands. It was hardly surprising, therefore, that when she came to examine corporate life for the first time in her 1977 book, *Men and Women of the Corporation*, Rosabeth Moss Kanter found that the central characteristic expected of a manager was 'dependability'. William Whyte may well have chuckled.

'It was *Fortune*'s William H. Whyte Jr who made the 'Organization Man' a household word – and the organization wife too. His was a fine achievement in sociological reporting. In it he related the phenomenon of the business organization to questions of human personality and values. The kind of people who are eager to hear the worst about American society assumed that Mr Whyte was predicting the destruction of individualism by the organization,' *Fortune*-founder Henry Luce later commented. 'Whyte was not a doomsayer. True he was uneasy about corporate life, which seemed to stifle creativity and individualism. He was uneasy about the subtle pressures in the office and at home that called for smooth performance rather than daring creativity. But he did not urge the organization man to leave his secure environment. Rather he urged them to fight the organization when necessary and he was optimistic that the battle could be successful.'[2]

Notes

1 Kaufman, Michael T, William H Whyte Obituary, *New York Times*, January 13, 1999.
2 Luce, Henry R, 'The first 35 years of Fortune', *Fortune*, February 1965.

BIBLIOGRAPHY

Igor Ansoff

Corporate Strategy, McGraw Hill, New York, 1965.
Strategic Management, Macmillan, London, 1979.
Implanting Strategic Management, Prentice Hall, London, 1984.

Chris Argyris & Donald Schon

Personality and Organization (Argyris), Harper & Row, New York, 1957.
Understanding Organizational Behavior (Argryis), Dorsey Press, Homewood, Illinois, 1960.
Organizational Learning: A Theory of Action Perspective (Argyris & Schon), Addison-Wesley, Reading, Mass, 1978.
Beyond the Stable State, (Schon), Random House, New York, 1978.
Overcoming Organizational Defences (Argyris), Allyn & Bacon, Boston, 1990.
On Organizational Learning (Argyris), Blackwell, Cambridge, 1993.
Knowledge for Action (Argyris), Jossey-Bass, San Francisco, 1993.
Flawed Advice and the Management Trap (Argyris), Oxford University Press, Oxford, 2000.

Charles Babbage

On the Economy of Machinery and Manufactures, Frank Cass & Co, London, 1963.

Chester Barnard

The Functions of the Executive, Harvard University Press, Cambridge, Mass, 1938.
Organization and Management, Harvard University Press, Cambridge, Mass, 1948.

Christopher Bartlett & Sumantra Ghoshal

Managing Across Borders, Harvard Business School Press, Boston, 1989.
The Individualized Corporation, Harvard Business School Press, Boston, 1997.

Meredith Belbin

Management Teams:Why They Succeed or Fail, Butterworth Heinemann, Oxford, 1984.
Team Roles at Work, Butterworth Heinemann, Oxford, 1993.
The Coming Shape of Organization, Butterworth Heinemann, Oxford, 1996.

Warren Bennis

The Planning of Change (with Benne, K D & Chin, R, 2nd edition), Holt, Rinehart & Winston 1970.
Leaders: Strategies for Taking Charge (with Burt Nanus), Harper & Row, New York, 1985.
On Becoming a Leader, Addison-Wesley, Reading, 1989.
Why Leaders Can't Lead, Jossey-Bass, San Francisco, 1989.
An Invented Life: Reflections on Leadership and Change, Addison-Wesley, Reading, 1993.
Old Dogs, New Tricks (with Ken Shelton), Executive Excellence, 1999.
Geeks and Geezers (with Robert J Thomas), Harvard Business School Press, 2002.

Marvin Bower

The Will to Manage, McGraw Hill, New York, 1966.
The Will to Lead, Harvard Business School Press, Boston, 1997.

James MacGregor Burns

Leadership, Harper & Row, New York, 1978.

Jan Carlzon

Moments of Truth, Harper, New York, 1987.

Dale Carnegie

How to Win Friends and Influence People, Simon & Schuster, New York, 1937.

James Champy & Michael Hammer

Reengineering the Corporation, HarperBusiness, New York, 1993.
Reengineering Management (Champy), HarperBusiness, New York, 1995.
The Arc of Ambition: Defining the Leadership Journey (Champy and Nitin Nohria), Perseus, 2000.

Alfred Chandler

Strategy and Structure: Chapters in the History of the Industrial Enterprise, MIT Press, Boston, 1962.
The Visible Hand: The Managerial Revolution in American Business, Harvard University Press, Cambridge, 1977.
The Coming of Managerial Capitalism: A Casebook on the History of American Economic Institutions (editor with Richard S Tedlow), Richard D Irwin, 1985.
Scale and Scope: The Dynamics of Industrial Capitalism, Harvard University Press, 1990.
Management: Past and Present: A Casebook on the History of American Business (editor with Richard S Tedlow and Thomas K McGraw), South-Western College Publishing, 1995.
Big Business and the Wealth of Nations (editor with Franco Amatori and Takashi Hikino), Cambridge University Press, 1997.

The Dynamic Firm: The Role of Technology, Strategy, Organization and Regions (editor with Peter Hagstrom and Orjan Solvell), Oxford University Press, 1998.

A Nation Transformed by Information: How Information has shaped the United States from Colonial Times to the Present (editor with James W Cortada), Oxford University Press, 2000.

Inventing the Electronic Century: The Epic Story of the Consumer Electronics and Computer Science Industries, Free Press, 2001.

Karl von Clausewitz

On War, Princeton University Press, Princeton, 1984.

James Collins & Jerry Porras

Built to Last, HarperBusiness, New York, 1994.

Stephen Covey

The Seven Habits of Highly Effective People, Running Press, Miniature edition, 2000.

The Nature of Leadership (with A Roger Merrill and DeWitt Jones), Covey Leadership Center, 1998.

Choice: Choosing the proactive Life You Want to Live, Franklin Covey, 1999.

Richard Cyert & James March

A Behavioral Theory of the Firm, 1963.

W Edwards Deming

Quality, Productivity and Competitive Position, MIT Center for Advanced Engineering Study, MIT, Massachusetts, 1982.

Out of the Crisis, Cambridge University Press, Cambridge, 1988.

Peter F Drucker

Concept of the Corporation, John Day, New York, 1946.
The New Society, Heinemann, London, 1951.
The Practice of Management, Harper & Row, New York, 1954.
Managing for Results, Heinemann, London, 1964.
The Effective Executive, Harper & Row, New York, 1967.
The Age of Discontinuity, Heinemann, London, 1969.
Management: Tasks, Responsibilities, Practices, Harper & Row, New York, 1973.
Managing in Turbulent Times, Harper & Row, New York, 1980.
Innovation and Entrepreneurship, Heinemann, London, 1985.
The New Realities, Heinemann, London, 1989.
Managing the Nonprofit Organization, HarperCollins, 1990.
Managing in Times of Great Change, Butterworth Heinemann, Oxford, 1995.
Peter Drucker on the Profession of Management, Harvard Business School Press, Cambridge, 1998.
Management Challenges for the 21st Century, HarperCollins, new York, 1999.

Henri Fayol

General and Industrial Management, Pitman, London, 1949.

Mary Parker Follett

The New State: Group Organization – The Solution of Popular Government, Longman, London, 1918.
Creative Experience, Longman, London, 1924.
Freedom and Coordination, Pitman, London, 1949.

Henry Ford

My Life and Work, Doubleday, Page & Co, New York, 1923.

Harold Geneen

Managing, Doubleday, New York, 1984.
The Synergy Myth, St Martins Press, London, 1997.

Arie de Geus

The Living Company, Harvard Business School Press, Boston, 1997.

Frank Gilbreth

Motion Study, 1911.

Michael Goold, Marcus Alexander & Andrew Campbell

Corporate-Level Strategy, John Wiley, New York, 1994.
Managing the Multibusiness Company (Goold and Kathleen Sommers Luchs), Routledge, 1995.
Strategic Synergy (Campbell and Luchs), Butterworth Heinemann, 1992.
Strategies and Styles (Goold and Campbell), Blackwell, Oxford, 1987.
Strategic Control (Goold with John J Quinn), FT/Pitman, London, 1990.
Break Up! (Campbell and Richard Koch), Capstone Publishing, Oxford, 1996.

Gary Hamel & C K Prahalad

Competing for the Future, Harvard University Press, Cambridge, MA, 1994.
Competence-Based Competition (editors Hamel and Aimé Heene), John Wiley, New York, 1995.
Leading the Revolution (Hamel), Harvard Business School Press, 2000.

Charles Handy

Understanding Organizations, Penguin Books, London, 1976.
The Future of Work, Basil Blackwell, Oxford, 1984.
Gods of Management, Business Books, London, 1986.
The Making of Managers (with John Constable), Longman, London, 1988.
The Age of Unreason, Business Books, London, 1989.
Inside Organizations: 21 Ideas for Managers, BBC Books, London 1990.
Waiting for the Mountain to Move and other reflections on life, Arrow, London, 1991.
The Empty Raincoat, Hutchinson, London, 1994.
Beyond Certainty: The changing world of organizations, Century, London, 1995.
The New Alchemists: How Visionary People Make Something Out of Nothing, Hutchinson, 1999.
Twenty-One Ideas for Managers: Practical Wisdom for Managing Your Company and Yourself, John Wiley, 2000.
The Elephant and the Flea, Hutchinson, 2002.

Frederick Herzberg

The Motivation to Work (with Mausner, B & Snyderman, B), Wiley, New York, 1959.

Elliot Jaques

The Changing Culture of a Factory, Tavistock, London, 1951.
A General Theory of Bureaucracy, John Wiley, New York, 1976.

Joseph M Juran

Managerial Breakthrough, McGraw Hill, New York, 1964.
Juran on Planning for Quality, Free Press, New York, 1988.

Rosabeth Moss Kanter

Men and Women of the Corporation, Basic Books, New York, 1977.
The Change Masters, Simon & Schuster, New York, 1983.
When Giants Learn to Dance, Simon & Schuster, London, 1989.
The Challenge of Organizational Change (with Stein, B & Jick, T D), Free Press, New York, 1992.
World Class: Thriving locally in the global economy, Simon & Schuster, New York, 1995.
Common Interest, Common Good: Creating Value Through Business and Social Sector Partnerships (with Shirley Sagawa and Eli Segal), Harvard Business School Press, 1999.
E-volve!, Harvard Business School Press, 2001.

Robert Kaplan & David Norton

The Balanced Scorecard.
Cost and effect: Using integrated cost systems to drive profitability and performance (Kaplan and Robin Cooper), Harvard Business School Press, 1998.
The Strategy-Focused Organization: How Balanced Scorecard Companies Thrive in the New Business Environment, 2000.

Philip Kotler

Marketing Management: Analysis, Planning, Implementation and Control, Prentice Hall, New Jersey, 1994 (8th edition).

John Kotter

The General Managers, Free Press, 1982.
Power and Influence: Beyond Formal Authority, Free Press, 1985.
The Leadership Factor, Free Press, 1988.
A Force for Change, Free Press, 1990.
Corporate Culture and Performance (with J L Heskett), Free Press 1992.
The New Rules, Free Press, 1995.
Leading Change, Harvard Business School Press, 1996.

Matsushita Leadership, Free Press, 1996.
What Leaders Really Do, Harvard Business School Press, 1999.

Ted Levitt

Innovation in Marketing, McGraw Hill, New York, 1962.
The Marketing Mode, McGraw Hill, New York, 1969.
The Marketing Imagination, Free Press, New York, 1983.
Thinking About Management, Free Press, New York, 1991.

Rensis Likert

New Patterns of Management, 1961.

Nicoló Machiavelli

The Prince, Penguin, London, 1967.

Douglas McGregor

The Human Side of Enterprise, McGraw Hill, New York, 1960.

Abraham Maslow

Motivation and Personality, Harper & Row, New York, 1954.

Konosuke Matsushita

Quest for Prosperity, 1988.

Elton Mayo

The Human Problems of an Industrial Civilization, Macmillan, New York, 1933.

The Social Problems of an Industrial Civilization, Harvard University Press, Cambridge, 1945.

Henry Mintzberg

The Nature of Managerial Work, Harper & Row, New York, 1973.
The Structuring of Organizations, Prentice-Hall, New Jersey, 1979.
Structures In Fives: Designing Effective Organizations, Prentice-Hall, New Jersey, 1983 (This is an expurgated version of the above.).
Power In and Around Organizations, Prentice Hall, New Jersey, 1983.
Mintzberg on Management: Inside Our Strange World of Organizations, The Free Press, New York, 1989.
The Strategy Process: Concepts, Contexts, Cases (with J B Quinn), 2nd edition, Prentice Hall, New Jersey, 1991.
The Rise and Fall of Strategic Planning, Prentice Hall International, Hemel Hempstead, 1994.
Why I Hate Flying, Texere, 2001.

James Mooney & Alan Reiley

Onward Industry, 1931.

Akio Morita

Made in Japan, Dutton & Co, New York, 1986.

John Naisbitt

Megatrends, Warner Books, New York, 1982.
Global Paradox, William Morrow & Co, New York, 1997.

Kenichi Ohmae

The Mind of the Strategist, McGraw Hill, New York, 1982.
Triad Power: The Coming Shape of Global Competition, Free Press, New York, 1985.
The Borderless World, William Collins, London, 1990.

The Evolving Global Economy (editor), Harvard Business School Press,
   Boston, MA, 1995.
The End of the Nation State, HarperCollins, London, 1995.

Taiichi Ohno

Toyota Production System, 1978.

David Packard

The HP Way, Harper Business, New York, 1995.

C N Parkinson

Parkinson's Law, John Murray, London, 1958.

Richard Pascale & Anthony Athos

The Art of Japanese Management, Penguin Books, London, 1981.
Managing on the Edge (Pascale), Viking, London, 1990.
Surfing the Edge of Chaos: The Laws of Nature and the New Laws of Business, (Pascale, Mark Milleman, & Linda Gioja), Crown, New York,
   2000.

Laurence Peter

The Peter Principle, William Morrow & Co, New York, 1969.

Tom Peters & Robert Waterman

In Search of Excellence, Harper & Row, New York & London, 1982.
A Passion for Excellence (Peters with Nancy Austin), Collins, London,
   1985.
Thriving on Chaos (Peters) Macmillan, London, 1987.
Liberation Management (Peters), Alfred P Knopf, New York, 1992.
The Tom Peters Seminar (Peters), Vintage Books, New York, 1994.

The Pursuit of Wow! (Peters), Vintage Books, New York, 1994.
The Renewal Factor (Waterman), Bantam, New York, 1987.
The Frontiers of Excellence (Waterman), Nicholas Brealey, London, 1994.
The Circle of Innovation (Peters), Macmillan, 1998.
The Brand You 50 (Peters), Alfred A Knopf, 1999.

Michael Porter

Competitive Strategy, Free Press, New York, 1980.
Competitive Advantage, Free Press, New York, 1985.
The Competitive Advantage of Nations, Macmillan, London, 1990.
Can Japan Compete? (with Hirotaka Takeuchi and Mariko Sakakibara), Perseus, 2000.

Frederick Reichheld

The Quest for Loyalty (editor), Harvard Business School Press, 1996.
The Loyalty Effect, Harvard Business School Press, 1996.
Loyalty Rules!, Harvard Business School Press, 2001.

Reg Revans

Action Learning, London, 1979.

Edgar H Schein

Process Consultation, Addison-Wesley, Reading, Mass, 1969.
Organizational Psychology (3rd edition), Prentice Hall, Engelwood Cliffs, New Jersey, 1980.
Organizational Culture and Leadership, Jossey-Bass, San Francisco, 1985.

Ricardo Semler

Maverick!, Century, London, 1993.

Peter Senge

The Fifth Discipline: The Art and Practice of the Learning Organization, Doubleday, New York, 1990.
The Fifth Discipline Fieldbook: Strategies and Tools for Building a Learning Organization (with Roberts, C, Ross, R, Smith, B & Kleiner, A), Nicholas Brealey, London, 1994.
The Dance of Change (Senge, et al), Doubleday, 1999.
Schools That Learn (with Nelda H Cambron-McCabe, Timothy Lucas, Bryan Smith, Janis Dutton and Art Kleiner), Doubleday, 2000.

Patricia Seybold

Customers.com, 1998.
The Customer Revolution, Crown, 2001.

Herbert Simon

Administrative Behavior, 1947.

Alfred P Sloan

My Years with General Motors, Doubleday, New York, 1963.

Adam Smith

The Wealth of Nations, Modern Library, New York, 1937.

Thomas Stewart

Intellectual Capital, Nicholas Brealey, London, 1997.
The Wealth of Knowledge, Nicholas Brealey, London, 2001.

Don Tapscott

Paradigm Shift (with Art Caston), McGraw Hill, 1992.
Growing Up Digital, McGraw Hill, 1998.
Creating Value in the Network Economy, Harvard Business School Press,
   1999.
Digital Capital, Harvard Business School Press, 2000.

Frederick W Taylor

Shop Management, Harper & Row, New York, 1903.
The Principles of Scientific Management, Harper & Row, New York,
   1911.

Alvin Toffler

Future Shock, Bodley Head, London, 1970.
The Third Wave, Bantam, New York, 1980.

Robert Townsend

Up the Organization, Michael Joseph, London, 1970.

Fons Trompenaars

Riding the Waves of Culture, Nicholas Brealey, London, 1993.
The Seven Cultures of Capitalism (with Charles Hampden-Turner),
   Piatkus, London, 1994.
*Building Cross-Cultural Competence: How to Create Wealth from Conflict-
   ing Values* (with Charles Hampden-Turner), Yale University Press,
   2000.
*21 Leaders for the 21st Century: How Innovative Leaders Manage in the
   Digital Age* (with Charles Hampden-Turner), McGraw-Hill, 2001.

Sun Tzu

The Art of War, (transl. Griffith), Oxford University Press, Oxford, 1963.

Thomas Watson Jr

A Business and its Beliefs, McGraw Hill, New York, 1963.

Max Weber

The Theory of Social and Economic Organization, Free Press, New York, 1947.
The Protestant Ethic and the Spirit of Capitalism, Scribner's, New York, 1958.

William Whyte

The Organization Man, Simon & Schuster, New York, 1956.

INDEX

accountancy 101–3, 139–41
acquisition 101–3
Action Learning 238–41
Adams, Scott 214, 216
Administrative Behavior 257–9
The Age of Discontinuity 86–9, 269
The Age of Unreason 121–4
Alexander, Marcus 113–15
Ansoff, Igor 3–6
Ansoff Model of Strategic Planning 4–5
Argyris, Chris 7–11
The Art of Japanese Management 206–9
The Art of War 290–1
Athos, Anthony 206–9
attitudes measurement 154–5

Babbage, Charles 12–14
The Balanced Scorecard 139–41
Barnard, Chester 15–17
Bartlett, Christopher 18–23, 263–4
behaviour 161–4, 165–6, 170–2
A Behavioural Theory of the Firm 69–71
Belbin, Meredith 24–6
beliefs 292–4
Bennis, Warren 27–31
Betamax/VHS 168, 183
bibliography 303–17
Blake, Robert 32–3
Blur 72–4
The Borderless World 194–6

Bower, Marvin 34–7
Built to Last 61–4
bureaucracy 295–8
Burns, James MacGregor 38–40
A Business and Its Beliefs 61–2, 292–4

Campbell, Andrew 113–15, 178
capitalism 124
Carlzon, Jan 41–4
Carnegie, Dale 45–7
Champy, James 48–52
Chandler, Alfred 53–6
change 147–9, 157–8, 210–13, 249–52,
    279–82
The Change Masters 135–8
The Changing Culture of a Factory
    128–30
choice 187
von Clausewitz, Karl 57–60
co-ordinative principle 181
collectivists 288
Collins, James 61–4
communications channels 15–16
communications skills 28
competencies, core 118
Competing for the Future 116–20
The Competitive Advantage of Nations
    232–4
competitive forces 230–1
Competitive Strategy 228–31

conflict 95
conglomeration 101–3, 113–15
connectivity 72–4
consumer focus 75–9, 187–8
    see also marketing
core competencies, defined 118
core ideology 62–3
corporate advantage 5
corporate culture 242–5
Corporate-Level Strategy 113–15, 178
corporate longevity 104–6
Corporate Strategy 3–6
corporate strategy 101–3, 113–15,
    116–20
corporate values 61–4
cost-based leadership 229
Covey, Stephen 65–8
cultural issues 286–9
    see also globalization
culture, corporate 242–5
customer capital 270
customer delivered value 145
customer focus 80–5, 168, 191, 226,
    253–6, 265–8
    see also marketing
customer loyalty 235–7
customer service 42
Customers.com 253–6
customization, mass 279–82
Cyert, Richard 69–71

data collection 12–14
Davis, Stan 72–4
de Geus, Arie 104–6
decision-making 69–71
Dell Computers 254
Deming, W Edwards 75–9
desires, blur of 72–4
deutero-learning 10
differentiation 229
The Dilbert Principle 214, 216
Disney 150
division of labour 13–14
double-loop learning 8, 9
downsizing 119

Drucker, Peter F 80–5, 86–9
Dynamic Administration 93–6

economic organization 295–8
economic principles 265–8
economies of scale 13–14
On the Economy of Machines &
    Manufactures 12–14
efficiency, factories 12–14
Emotional Intelligence 109–12
empowerment 186, 283–5
The Empty Raincoat 123
entrepreneurism 168
environmental impact 281

factories, efficiency 12–14
facts, and theory 12–13
Fayol, Henri 90–2
The Fifth Discipline 249–52
financial measurement 101–3, 139–41
Flawed Advice and the Management Trap
    10
flexible working 279–82
Follett, Mary Parker 93–6
Ford, Henry 97–100
Fortune 500; 188
Freemantle, David 59
fulfilment, blur of 72–4
functional effect 181
functions, industrial 90–2
The Functions of the Executive 15–17

gap analysis 5
Gates, Bill 216
Geneen, Harold 101–3
General and Industrial Management 90–2
The General Theory of Bureaucracy 129
de Geus, Arie 104–6
Ghoshal, Sumantra 18–23, 260, 263–4
Gilbreth, Frank 107–8
globalization 18–23, 186, 194–6,
    232–4, 286–9
Goleman, Daniel 109–12
Good to Great 63
Goold, Michael 113–15

government interaction 282
Growing Up Digital 272–4
growth 119

Hamel, Gary 116–20
Hammer, Michael 48–52
Handy, Charles 121–4
Hawthorne Studies 170–2
heartland businesses 101–3, 113–15
Henley Management College 24–5
Herzberg, Frederick 125–7
Hewlett-Packard 200–2
high touch 186
holistic approach 17
How to Win Friends and Influence People 45–7
The HP Way 200–2
human capital 22–3, 104–6, 270
The Human Problems of an Industrial Civilization 170–2
human relations 93–6
The Human Side of Enterprise 160–4
human touch 186, 187–8, 200–3
hygiene factors 126–7

IBM 292–4
ideology, core 62–3
In Search of Excellence 62, 217–24
incompetence 214–16
individualists 288
The Individualized Corporation 21
industrial functions 90–2
industrialization 97–100
information-based industry 86–9, 185, 281
innovation 135–8
Innovation in Marketing 150–3
Intellectual Capital 269–71
international companies 18–23
Internet 253–6, 272–4
ITT 101–3

Jaques, Elliot 128–30
Japanese influence 75–9, 104–6, 131–4, 148–9, 163, 167–9, 182–4,
189–93, 194–6, 197–9, 206–9
Juran, Joseph M 131–4
just-in-time production 197–9

Kanter, Rosabeth Moss 135–8
Kaplan, Robert S 139–41
key factors for success (KFSs) 192
knowledge-based industry 86–9, 101–3, 269–71
Kotler, Philip 142–6
Kotter, John 147–9

Leaders 27–31
Leadership 38–40
leadership 93–5, 157–9, 168, 242–5, 246–8
  defined 28
  styles 32–3, 111–12
The Leadership Factor 147–8
Leading Change 147–9
Leading the Revolution 119–20
lean production 197–9
Leaning into the Future 50
learning 7–11, 8–10, 238–41
learning organizations 249–52
Levitt, Ted 150–3
Liberation Management 225–7
Likert, Rensis 154–6
The Living Company 104–6
Lockheed Corporation 3, 4
longevity, corporate 104–6
loyalty
  customer 235–7
  staff 235–7, 299–301
The Loyalty Effect 235–7
Luce, Henry 300

McGregor, Douglas 160–4
Machiavelli, Nicoló 157–9
McKinsey & Company 34–7
Made in Japan 182–4
maintenance factors 126–7
Management By Objectives (MBO) 82–5
management principles, general 90–2

Management: Tasks, Responsibilities and Practices 82, 84
Management Teams: Why They Succeed or Fail 24–6
The Managerial Grid 32–3
managerial role 82–5, 86–9, 90–2
managerial styles 32–3, 111–12, 155, 160–4
managerial work 173–5
Managing 101–3
Managing Across Borders 18–23
Managing By Wandering About 201
Managing for the Future 88
Managing on the Edge 55, 210–13
March, James 69–71
marketing 97–100, 181
marketing innovation 150–3, 183–4
Marketing Management 142–6
'marketing myopia' 150–2
Maslow, Abraham 165–6
mass customization 279–82
mass production 97–100
Matsushita, Konosuke 167–9
Maverick! 246–8
Mayo, Elton 170–2
MBO *see* Management By Objectives
measurement 101–3, 139–41, 177, 275–8
Megatrends 185–8
Men and Women of the Corporation 137
mental models 251
Meyer, Christopher 72–4
military influences 57–60, 290–1
The Mind of the Strategist 189–93
Mintzberg, Henry 173–5, 176–9
Mitsui 104
models, organizational 9
Moments of Truth 41–4
Mooney, James 180–1
morale 170–2, 235–7
morality changes 282
   moral codes 17
Morita, Akio 182–4
Motion Study 107–8
motivation 32–3, 109–12, 154–6, 170–2

Motivation and Personality 165–6
The Motivation to Work 125–7
Mouton, Jane 32–3
multibusiness organizations 101–3, 113–15
multinational companies 18–23
My Life and Work 97–100
My Years with General Motors 260–4

Naisbitt, John 185–8
Nanus, Burt 27–31
National Training Laboratories 8
nations, role of 232–4
The Nature of Managerial Work 173–5
networking 187
New Patterns of Management 154–6
non-profit social industry 85
Norton, David P 139–41

Ohmae, Kenichi 189–93, 194–6
Ohno, Taiichi 197–9
On the Economy of Machines & Manufactures 12–14
On War 57–60
The One Minute Manager 66
Onward Industry 180–1
order 227
organization 180–1
The Organization Man 299–301
Organizational Culture and Leadership 242–5
organizational forms 18–23, 122–4
Organizational Learning 7–11
organizational models 9
organizational principles 180–1, 257–9, 260–4, 283–5, 295–8
Out of the Crisis 75–9

Packard, David 200–2
Panasonic 167
parent companies 101–3, 113–15
Parkinson, C N 203–5
Parkinson's Law 203–5
particularists 287–8
Pascale, Richard 55, 206–9, 210–13

people
  influencing 45–7
  quality of 221
  revitalizing 22–3, 104–6, 283–5,
    292–4
personal mastery 251
personality 165–6
Peter, Laurence 214–16
The Peter Principle 214–16
Peters, Tom 62, 217–24, 225–7
planning
  defined 176
  strategic 3–5, 176–9
Planning for Quality 131–4
Porras, Jerry 61–4
Porter, Michael 228–31, 232–4
The Practice of Management 80–5
Prahalad, C K 116–20
price focus 97–100
The Prince 157–9
The Principles of Organization 180–1
The Principles of Scientific Management
  275–8
products, defined 144–5
profit 169
prosumers 272–4, 279–82

quality 75–9, 131–4, 168–9, 183, 197–9
Quest for Prosperity 167–9

RAND Corporation 3
Reengineering the Corporation 48–52
Reichheld, Frederick 235–7
Reiley, Alan 180–1
relationship marketing 144
renewal, company 22
resources, blur of 72–4
responsibility 93–5, 101–3
Revans, Reg 238–41
revitalizing people 22–3, 104–6, 283–5,
  292–4
Riding the Waves of Culture 286–9
The Rise and Fall of Strategic Planning
  176–9
Robbins, Anthony 67

SAS (airline) 41–2
scalar process 181
scale economies 13–14
Scandinavian business culture 41–4
Schein, Edgar H 242–5
Schön, Donald 7–11
scientific management 275–8
In Search of Excellence 62, 217–24
self-actualization 166
self-reliance 186
Semco S/A 246–8
Semler, Richard 246–8
Senge, Peter 249–52
service commitment 292–4
*The Seven Habits of Highly Effective
  People* 65–8
Seven S framework 208–9
Seybold, Patricia 253–6
shared vision 251
Shell corporation 104–6
Simon, Herbert 257–9
single-loop learning 9, 10
Sloan, Alfred P 260–4
small business/companies 187
Smith, Adam 265–8
social industry, non-profit 85, 281
social organization 295–8
Sony 182–4
staff loyalty 235–7, 299–301
Stewart, Thomas 269–71
Stora 104
strategic planning 3–5, 176–9, 211–13
strategy 189–93, 194–6, 228–31, 290–1
  corporate 3–6, 101–3, 113–15,
    116–20
  defined 54
Strategy and Structure 53–6
'stretch and discipline' 22
structural capital 270
Sumitomo 104
synergy, Ansoff's 5
systems thinking 250–1

Tapscott, Don 272–4
Taylor, Frederick W 275–8

team functions 25–6
team learning 251–2
teams, management 24–6
theory, and facts 12–13
The Theory of Social and Economic Organization 295–8
Theory X/Theory Y/Theory Z 161–4
The Third Wave 279–82
time-and-motion 275–8
Toffler, Alvin 279–82
Townsend, Robert 283–5
Toyota Production System 197–9
transaction oriented marketing 144
transactional leadership 39–40
transformational leadership 39–40
transnational companies 18–23
Trompenaars, Fons 60, 286–9
Tzu, Sun 290–1

universalists 287–8
Up the Organization 283–5

value stream 197–9

values, corporate 61–4, 292–4
VHS/Betamax 168, 183
vision 28, 207–9, 251
vitality 119

On War 57–60
war influence 290–1
Waterman, Robert 62, 217–24
Watson Jr, Thomas 61–2, 292–4
The Wealth of Nations 265–8
Weber, Max 295–8
When Giants Learn to Dance 136–7
Whyte, William 299–301
The Will to Manage 34–7
work roles 173–5
working flexibly 279–82
working practices 128–30
World Class 138

X Theory/Y Theory/Z Theory 161–4

Ziglar, Zig 66

RICHLAND COUNTY PUBLIC LIBRARY

3 0080 02331 2156

658 Cra
Crainer, Stuart.
The ultimate business library
: the greatest books that
made management /
30080023312156   19.95   M

RICHLAND COUNTY PUBLIC LIBRARY
COLUMBIA, SOUTH CAROLINA 29201

RCPL   JAN 0 8 2003